EZRA POUND AS LITERARY CRITIC

CRITICS OF THE TWENTIETH CENTURY
General Editor: Christopher Norris,
*University of Wales,
College of Cardiff*

A. J. GREIMAS AND THE NATURE OF MEANING
Ronald Schleifer

CHRISTOPHER CAUDWELL
Robert Sullivan

FIGURING LACAN
CRITICISM AND THE CULTURAL UNCONSCIOUS
Juliet Flower MacCannell

HAROLD BLOOM
TOWARDS HISTORICAL RHETORICS
Peter de Bolla

F. R. LEAVIS
Michael Bell

POSTMODERN BRECHT
A RE-PRESENTATION
Elizabeth Wright

DELEUZE AND GUATTARI
Ronald Bogue

ECSTASIES OF ROLAND BARTHES
Mary Wiseman

JULIA KRISTEVA
John Lechte

GEOFFREY HARTMAN
CRITICISM AS ANSWERABLE STYLE
G. Douglas Atkins

INTRODUCING LYOTARD
Bill Readings

EZRA POUND AS LITERARY CRITIC

K. K. Ruthven

London and New York

First published 1990
by Routledge
2 Park Square, Milton Park, Abingdon, Oxon OX14 4RN
Simultaneously published in the USA and Canada
by Routledge
a division of Routledge, Taylor & Francis
711 Third Avenue, New York, NY 10017
Transferred to Digital Printing 2005

© 1990 K. K. Ruthven

Typeset in 10/12pt Baskerville by
Input Typesetting Ltd, London

All rights reserved. No part of this book may be reprinted or reproduced or utilized in any form or by any electronic, mechanical, or other means, now known or hereafter invented, including photocopying and recording, or in any information storage or retrieval system, without permission in writing from the publishers.

British Library Cataloguing in Publication Data
Ruthven, K. K. (Kenneth Knowles)
Ezra Pound as literary critic. – (Critics of the twentieth century).
1. Literature. Criticism. Pound, Ezra, 1885–1972
I. Title II. Series
801.95092

First issued in paperback 2013

*Library of Congress Cataloging in Publication Data
also available*

ISBN13: 978-0-415-02074-9 (hbk)
ISBN13: 978-0-415-86194-6 (pbk)

To Marion Campbell

Contents

Editor's foreword viii
Preface xii
Acknowledgements xiii
Abbreviations xiv

1 The academic critic   1
2 The metropolitan critic   40
3 The practical critic   81
4 The rhetorical critic   109
5 The vanishing critic   141

Bibliography 171
Index 180

Editor's foreword

The twentieth century has produced a remarkable number of gifted and innovative literary critics. Indeed it could be argued that some of the finest literary minds of the age have turned to criticism as the medium best adapted to their complex and speculative range of interests. This has sometimes given rise to regret among those who insist on a clear demarcation between 'creative' (primary) writing on the one hand, and 'critical' (secondary) texts on the other. Yet this distinction is far from self-evident. It is coming under strain at the moment as novelists and poets grow increasingly aware of the conventions that govern their writing and the challenge of consciously exploiting and subverting those conventions. And the critics for their part – some of them at least – are beginning to question their traditional role as humble servants of the literary text with no further claim upon the reader's interest or attention. Quite simply, there are texts of literary criticism and theory that, for various reasons – stylistic complexity, historical influence, range of intellectual command – cannot be counted a mere appendage to those other 'primary' texts.

Of course, there is a logical puzzle here, since (it will be argued) 'literary criticism' would never have come into being, and could hardly exist as such, were it not for the body of creative writings that provide its *raison d'être*. But this is not quite the kind of knockdown argument that it might appear at first glance. For one thing, it conflates some very different orders of priority, assuming that literature always comes first (in the sense that Greek tragedy had to exist before Aristotle could formulate its rules), so that literary texts are for that very reason possessed of superior value. And this argument would seem to find commonsense support in the difficulty of thinking what 'literary criticism' could *be* if it seriously renounced all sense of the distinction between literary and critical texts. Would it not then find itself in the unfortunate position of a discipline that had willed its own demise by declaring its subject non-existent?

But these objections would only hit their mark if there were indeed a special kind of writing called 'literature' whose difference from other kinds of writing was enough to put criticism firmly in its place. Otherwise there is nothing in the least self-defeating or paradoxical about a discourse, nominally that of literary criticism, that accrues such interest on its own account as to force some fairly drastic rethinking of its proper powers and limits. The act of crossing over from commentary to literature – or of simply denying the difference between them – becomes quite explicit in the writing of a critic like Geoffrey Hartman. But the signs are already there in such classics as William Empson's *Seven Types of Ambiguity* (1928), a text whose transformative influence on our habits of reading must surely be ranked with the great creative moments of literary modernism. Only on the most dogmatic view of the difference between 'literature' and 'criticism' could a work like *Seven Types* be counted generically an inferior, sub-literary species of production. And the same can be said for many of the critics whose writings and influence this series sets out to explore.

Some, like Empson, are conspicuous individuals who belong to no particular school or larger movement. Others, like the Russian Formalists, were part of a communal enterprise and are therefore best understood as representative figures in a complex and evolving dialogue. Then again there are cases of collective identity (like the so-called 'Yale deconstructors') where a mythical group image is invented for largely polemical purposes. (The volumes in this series on Hartman and Bloom should help to dispel the idea that 'Yale deconstruction' is anything more than a handy device for collapsing differences and avoiding serious debate.) So there is no question of a series format or house-style that would seek to reduce these differences to a blandly homogeneous treatment. One consequence of recent critical theory is the realisation that literary texts have no self-sufficient or autonomous meaning, no existence apart from their after-life of changing interpretations and values. And the same applies to those *critical* texts whose meaning and significance are subject to constant shifts and realignments of interest. This is not to say that trends in criticism are just a matter of intellectual fashion or the merry-go-round of rising and falling reputations. But it is important to grasp how complex are the forces – the conjunctions of historical and cultural motive – that affect the first reception and the subsequent fortunes of a critical text. This point has been raised into a systematic programme by critics like Hans-Robert Jauss, practitioners of so-called 'reception theory' as a form of historical hermeneutics. The volumes in this series will therefore be concerned not only to expound what is of lasting significance but also to set these critics in the context of present-day argument and debate. In some cases (as with Walter Benjamin) this debate takes the form of a struggle for interpretative power among disciplines with sharply opposed ideological viewpoints. Such controversies cannot simply be ignored in the interests of achieving a clear and balanced account. They point to unresolved tensions and problems which are there in the critic's work as well as in the rival appropriative readings. In the end there is no way of drawing a neat methodological line between 'intrinsic' questions (what the critic really thought) and those other, supposedly 'extrinsic' concerns that have to do with influence and reception history.

The volumes will vary accordingly in their focus and range of coverage. They will also reflect the ways in which a speculative approach to questions of literary theory has proved to have striking consequences for the human sciences at large. This breaking-down of disciplinary bounds is among the most significant developments in recent critical thinking. As philosophers and historians, among others, come to recognise the rhetorical complexity of the texts they deal with, so literary theory takes on a new dimension of interest and relevance. It is scarcely appropriate to think of a writer like Derrida as practising 'literary criticism' in any conventional sense of the term. For one thing, he is as much concerned with 'philosophical' as with 'literary' texts, and has indeed actively sought to subvert (or deconstruct) such tidy distinctions. A principal object in planning this series was to take full stock of these shifts in the wider intellectual terrain (including the frequent boundary disputes) brought about by critical theory. And, of course, such changes are by no means confined to literary studies, philosophy and the so-called 'sciences of man'. It is equally the case in (say) nuclear physics and molecular biology that advances in the one field have decisive implications for the other, so that specialised research often tends (paradoxically) to break down existing divisions of intellectual labour. Such work is typically many years ahead of the academic disciplines and teaching institutions that have obvious reasons of their own for adopting a business-as-usual attitude. One important aspect of modern critical theory is the challenge it presents to these traditional ideas. And lest it be thought that this is merely a one-sided takeover bid by literary critics, the series will include a number of volumes by authors in those other disciplines, including, for instance, a study of Roland Barthes by an American analytical philosopher.

We shall not, however, cleave to theory as a matter of polemical or principled stance. The series will extend to figures like F. R. Leavis, whose widespread influence went along with an express aversion to literary theory; scholars like Erich Auerbach in the mainstream European tradition; and others who resist assimilation to any clear-cut line of descent. There will also be authoritative volumes on critics such as Northrop Frye and Lionel Trilling, figures who, for various reasons, occupy an ambivalent or essentially contested place in modern critical tradition. Above all the series will strive to resist that current polarisation of attitudes that sees no common ground of interest between 'literary criticism' and 'critical theory'.

CHRISTOPHER NORRIS

Preface

The aim of this book is to historicise representative episodes in Ezra Pound's career as a literary critic. Among those who believe, as Pound did, in the importance of regarding certain types of text as 'literary', Pound is usually thought of not as a critic but as a poet who happened to write criticism. Consequently his critical prose is treated either as a gloss on the poetry or as the site of a dispersed poetics. Even when read ostensibly as literary criticism, it has tended to be examined in idealist terms as an ensemble of assumptions whose origins and influence can be reconstructed, and whose development and inconsistencies analysed. Although my own account of Pound as a rhetorical critic approximates to that type of idealist metacriticism, the approach taken in the remaining chapters is much more materialist in its emphasis on the discursive formations which shaped Pound's literary education, and the social and cultural conditions in which he practised as a literary critic. I read Pound's literary criticism, therefore, not as an aesthetics but as the trace of two decisive interventions in the construction of a 'modernist' literature. First his invention and mobilisation of a discourse of 'modernism' in poetry, which privileged his own writing and inferiorised rival versions of what it might mean to write in a 'modern' manner. And secondly his co-operation in the academic appropriation of a Poundian discourse of modernism, and the reproduction of it in the form of a literary history in which, not surprisingly, Pound emerges as the central figure. How those highly successful manoeuvres were prepared for and accomplished is worth investigating, especially in that post-Pound era in which we now find ourselves, dominated as it is by the hermeneutics of suspicion.

February 1990

Acknowledgements

I am grateful to the Council of the University of Melbourne for relieving me of teaching and administrative responsibilities for one semester in order to write this book; to Ian Reid for accommodating me in the Centre for Studies in Literary Education at Deakin University; and to Pat Biciacci, Sue Bilton and Margaret Last for their skill and patience in helping to prepare the manuscript for publication.

An earlier draft of parts of chapters 2 and 3 was published under the title 'Ezra's appropriations' in *The Times Literary Supplement*, 20–6 November 1987, pp. 1278, 1300–1.

Abbreviations

AA	*Active Anthology*, ed. E. Pound, London: Faber & Faber, 1933.
ABCR	Pound, E., *ABC of Reading*, London: Routledge, 1934.
ALS	Pound, E., *A Lume Spento [1908] and Other Early Poems*, London: Faber & Faber, 1966.
BNM	*Book News Monthly*.
Cantos	*The Cantos of Ezra Pound*, New York: New Directions, 1972.
CC	*Confucius to Cummings: An Anthology of Poetry*, ed. E. Pound and M. Spann, New York: New Directions, 1964.
CEP	*Collected Early Poems of Ezra Pound*, ed. M.J. King, intro. L.L. Martz, London: Faber & Faber, 1977.
CH	*Ezra Pound: The Critical Heritage*, ed. E. Homberger, London: Routledge & Kegan Paul, 1972.
CO/EP	*Charles Olson and Ezra Pound*, ed. C. Seelye, New York: Grossman, 1975.
ELH	*English Literary History*.
EP/DS	*Ezra Pound and Dorothy Shakespear: Their Letters: 1909–1914*, ed. O. Pound and A.W. Litz, London: Faber & Faber, 1985.
EP/FMF	*Pound/Ford: The Story of a Literary Friendship*, ed. B. Lindberg-Seyersted, London: Faber & Faber, 1982.
EP/I	Pound, E., *Letters to Ibbotson, 1935–1952*, ed. V.I. Mondolfo and M. Hurley, intro. W. Pilkington, Orono: University of Maine, 1979.
EP/JJ	*Pound/Joyce: The Letters of Ezra Pound to James Joyce*, ed. F. Read, New York: New Directions, 1967.

Abbreviations

EP/LU	*EP to LU: Nine Letters Written to Louis Untermeyer*, ed. J.A. Robbins, Bloomington, Ind.: Indiana University Press, 1963.
EP/LZ	*Pound/Zukofsky: Selected Letters of Ezra Pound and Louis Zukofsky*, ed. B. Ahearn, London: Faber & Faber, 1987.
EP/M	*Ezra Pound and Music: The Complete Criticism*, ed. R.M. Schafer, London: Faber & Faber, 1978.
EP/MC	*Ezra Pound and Margaret Cravens: A Tragic Friendship 1910–1912*, ed. O. Pound and R. Spoo, Durham, NC: Duke University Press, 1988.
EP/MCA	*Pound/The Little Review: The Letters of Ezra Pound to Margaret Anderson*, ed. T.L. Scott, M.J. Friedman, and J.R. Bryer, New York: New Directions, 1988.
EP/VA	*Ezra Pound and the Visual Arts*, ed. and intro. H. Zinnes, New York: New Directions, 1980.
EP/WL	*Pound/Lewis: The Letters of Ezra Pound and Wyndham Lewis*, ed. T. Materer, London: Faber & Faber, 1985.
EPS	*'Ezra Pound Speaking': Radio Speeches of World War II*, ed. L.W. Doob, Westport, Conn.: Greenwood Press, 1978.
G-B	*Gaudier-Brzeska: A Memoir by Ezra Pound* [1916], New York: New Directions, 1961.
GK	Pound, E., *Guide to Kulchur* [1938], Norfolk, Conn.: New Directions, 1952.
H&H	*Hound & Horn*.
I	Pound, E., *Impact: Essays on Ignorance and the Decline of American Civilization*, ed. and intro. N. Stock, Chicago: Regnery, 1960.
JML	*Journal of Modern Literature*.
L	*The Letters of Ezra Pound 1907–1941*, ed. D.D. Paige, London: Faber & Faber, 1951.
LE	*Literary Essays of Ezra Pound*, ed. and intro. T.S. Eliot, London: Faber & Faber, 1954.
LR	*Little Review*.
MN	*Make It New: Essays by Ezra Pound*, London: Faber & Faber, 1934.
NA	*New Age*.
NEW	*New English Weekly*.
NF	*New Freewoman*.
NPL	*The Natural Philosophy of Love*, by Remy de Gourmont [1922], trans. and intro. E. Pound, London: Spearman, 1957.

Abbreviations

P	*Personae: The Collected Poems of Ezra Pound* [1926], New York: New Directions, 1949.
PD	Pound, E., *Pavannes and Divagations* [1958], London: Owen, 1960.
P&D	*Poetry and Drama*.
PE	Pound, E., *Polite Essays*, London: Faber & Faber, 1937.
PM	Pound, E., *Patria Mia and The Treatise on Harmony*, London: Owen, 1962.
PMLA	*Publications of the Modern Language Association of America*.
PR	*Paris Review*.
SP	Pound, E., *Selected Prose 1909–1965*, ed. and intro. W. Cookson, London: Faber & Faber, 1973.
SeR	*Sewanee Review*.
SoR	*Southern Review*.
SR	Pound, E., *The Spirit of Romance*, London: Dent, 1910.
T	*The Translations of Ezra Pound*, intro. H. Kenner, London: Faber & Faber, 1953.

1

The academic critic

In 1907, as a postgraduate student at the University of Pennsylvania, Ezra Pound managed to fail a course in the history of literary criticism. Almost half a century later, the man who was then the most influential literary critic in the English-speaking world, T.S. Eliot, would observe in his introduction to a substantial selection of Pound's literary criticism that its author had produced 'the *least dispens[a]ble* body of critical writing in our time' (*LE* xiii), comparable to the work of such canonical English poet-critics as John Dryden, Samuel Johnson and Samuel Taylor Coleridge. To anyone interested in Pound's literary criticism, that Penn episode is symptomatic, although of what, exactly, will depend on whether or not you admire academic criticism, and whether you believe Pound was a literary genius or a charlatan.

To fail a postgraduate course is never easy, given the high level of intelligence required to get into it in the first place. Nevertheless, Pound failed that graduate course in literary criticism, and happened to be the only student in his year to do so. He coped with the trauma of failure by rewriting it as an easily overlooked triumph. As 'the only student' (he would recall in 1930) 'who was making any attempt to understand the subject of literary criticism and the only student with any interest in the subject' (Stock 1970: 34) he had had the nous to perceive that the Penn course in the history of it was both ill-conceived and taught by a bore with administrative ambitions. To have passed such a course, and thereby won the approval of such a teacher, would have been to demonstrate that he was lacking in both critical acumen and intellectual integrity. What, then, was wrong with the course? 'One was expected to remember' (he remembered in 1929) 'what some critic (deceased) had said, scarcely to consider whether his views were still valid, or ever had been very intelligent' (*LE* 16). Conceived of as an exercise in scholarly thoroughness, the course manifested only too well a preoccupation with 'multitudinous detail' endemic to that Germanic conception of *Literaturwissenschaft* on which postgraduate study in America was modelled at that time, and taught by 'men whose scholarship [was] merely a pasteurized, Bostonized imitation of Leipzig' (*LE* 223). It was a pedagogic practice which made it more difficult than it need be to locate those 'luminous details' Pound himself was looking for, and which were at the heart of that 'New Method in Scholarship' he was to introduce to readers of the London-based *New Age* on 7 December 1911, using as a specimen his version of an Old English poem, 'The Seafarer' (*P* 64–6). Unlike the method of a currently dominant scholarship which lumped together the durable and the transient indiscriminately in the interests of coverage and completeness, the 'new method' was to focus selectively on those 'luminous details [which] remain unaltered' by the passage of time and the meddlings or negligence of historians. It would yield a new kind of knowledge very different from that produced by American graduate-school procedures which, 'in presenting all detail as if of equal import' (*SP* 23), multitudinously, left students in the unfortunate position of being unable to see the wood for the trees. The principal problem with a *wissenschaftlich* approach to the diachronic study of literary criticism was that it reproduced the past as a comprehensive history of opinions, irrespective of their usefulness or otherwise in 1907. An uncritical history of criticism, in addition to being self-contradictory, was altogether too antiquarian an activity for Pound, whose interests in the past were never those of a tourist in search of mere heterogeneity, but always those of a salvage contractor on the lookout for reusable commodities.

The Penn course on the history of literary criticism was taught by a professor of English, Josiah Penniman, who is perhaps best known as the author of *A Book about the English Bible* (New York, 1919). When Pound encountered him he was a specialist in seventeenth-century English drama who had published a book on *The War of the Theatres* (Boston, 1897), and who knew a great deal about the critical writings of John Dennis, Thomas Rymer and Jeremy Collier (Wallace 1983: 24). Years later when Pound read the chapter on Sidney's *Defence of Poesy* and Renaissance English criticism in T.S. Eliot's *The Use of Poetry and the Use of Criticism* (London, 1933) it stirred memories of those days at Penn when he had been a 'good boy who did the required reading in University courses labelled "The History of English Literary Criticism"', and studied 'Campi[o]n on which what, and Daniel on what which' (Pound 1934: 131), or, more precisely, Thomas Campion's *Observations in the Art of English Poesie* (1602) and the 'answer' to it, Samuel Daniel's *A Defence of Ryme* (1603). Penniman was also Dean of Faculty at the time Pound failed his course, and was to continue moving up the administrative hierarchy of the University until he became Provost in 1923, a position he held until 1939. To Pound he was an academic careerist of the worst type, one of those intellectual nonentities who 'regarded their "subject" as a drill manual' before defecting into administration and rising 'rapidly to positions of executive responsibility' (*LE* 15). Because of Pound's brush with Penniman, the word 'dean' came to have pejorative connotations in his criticism. Within a year of the publication of what was to become an immensely influential volume of critical essays, *The Sacred Wood* (London, 1920), T.S. Eliot was complaining to Richard Aldington that Pound had called him 'the Dean of English Letters' (Eliot 1988: 488). It was an illuminating mistake: what Pound had in fact called Eliot in the *Little Review*, presciently, was 'The Dean of English criticism' (Pound 1921a: 39), and he had done so in response to the onset in Eliot's critical writings of a debilitating academicism, signalled by fatuous statements like 'the greatest of poets have been concerned with moral values' ('The "greatest of poets" (Herr Je! what a phrase) have also eaten food, walked... upon *legs*'). Pound's subsequent inspection of two other critical works by Eliot, *After Strange Gods* (London, 1934) and *The Use of Poetry and the Use of Criticism* (London, 1933), did nothing to modify his verdict that Eliot had turned himself into the Matthew Arnold of the twentieth century, 'the dean of English moral criticism' (Pound 1936a: 510).

Penniman's course no doubt had its *longueurs*, but it probably helped Pound to acquire that sense of the history of English literary criticism from the sixteenth to the twentieth centuries – from Gosson to Gosse – which he alluded to somewhat self-consciously in 1913 when describing his essay on 'The Serious Artist' as a rewriting of Sidney's *Defence of Poesy* (*LE* 41). The Penniman approach is discernible also in Pound's synopsis of the introductory lecture in a series he delivered at the Regent Street Polytechnic in London and published in a revised form as *The Spirit of Romance* (1910). Pound's synopsis indicates that as late as January 1909 he was still so immured in conventionally academic ways of doing things as to assume that the best way of introducing his audience to what he called 'the essential qualities of literature' was by surveying the 'Dicta of the great critics: – Plato, Aristotle, Longinus, Dante, Coleridge, De Quincey, Pater and Yeats' (Stock 1970: 58). The inclusion of Yeats's name in this list of great critics looks like a category mistake, but it was part of Pound's preparations for making himself known to 'the greatest living poet', as he was to describe Yeats to his Penn friend, William Carlos Williams, in May 1909 (*L* 41-2). When Yeats was free enough of Abbey Theatre business in Dublin to return to London, Pound's first meeting with him in April 1909 was arranged by a former lover of Yeats's and future mother-in-law of Pound's, Olivia Shakespear, whom Pound had met late in January that year (Carpenter 1988: 103). But, whereas the tradition of great critics thought suitable for public presentation in London in 1909 culminated in Yeats, the version of it communicated late in 1907 to a former classmate bypassed Yeats altogether for a quite different but no less surprising destination: 'since Longinus', Pound told L. Burtron Hessler, 'you have in the field of literary criticism: Dante, De Quincey and Coleridge, and "your humble servant" ' (Stock 1970: 41).

As a bespectacled and articulate little boy whose speech was freighted with polysyllabic words, Pound had been called 'professor' by his schoolmates from the age of six, and demonstrated his academic precociousness by entering the University of Pennsylvania in the autumn of 1901, when he was still not quite sixteen years old. As an institutional base from which to operate as a scholar and a poet the academy had obvious attractions, which is one of the reasons why Pound decided to undertake postgraduate study: having 'spent four years learning to be a college man', he explained to Viola Baxter, 'it seems to be the only thing I can do' (Tytell 1987: 25). A couple of undergraduate years at Penn from 1901 to 1903 were followed by two more years at Hamilton College in New York state from 1903 to 1905 in order to complete his BA degree. He then returned to Penn to study for the degree of MA, after which he enrolled there as a doctoral student and went to Spain as Harrison Fellow of Romanics for the academic year 1906–7 to research 'a thesis on the Gracioso (Sancho Panzas etc.) in Lope [de Vega]'s plays' (*GK* 219). Increasingly dissatisfied with the nature of postgraduate study and some of the people who designed and taught it, Pound did not re-enrol at Penn in the autumn of 1907. Instead, he accepted a position as Chairman of the Department of Romance Languages at Wabash College in Crawfordsville, Indiana, which was known locally as the 'Athens of America' (Boyd 1974: 43–4). On arriving there Pound discovered that the Department of Romance Languages was a signifier without a signified, there being nobody else in it except himself. He was employed as the sole instructor in French and Spanish in a Presbyterian college from which, in the words of one of its graduates, 'women students were . . . excluded', and ' "manly sports" claimed the attention of most students and professors' (ibid.: 51). By February 1908 he had been paid up to the end of the academic year and dismissed after his unmarried landladies had found a young woman in his room and reported the matter to the President of Wabash, who did not accept Pound's explanation of how she came to be there (she was an actress stranded in Crawfordsville and needed shelter for the night) or what happened as a result (nothing). That was Pound's last formal contact with academic life. He was twenty-two years old.

With his severance pay Pound went first to Venice to be a poet and then to London to gain more publicity for his own writing by becoming a metropolitan man of letters. 'Criticism', of course, was not yet a function of the American academies as it is nowadays, and was not to become so until the 1930s with the emergence of what came to be known in the USA as New Criticism after the publication of John Crowe Ransom's book, *The New Criticism* (Norfolk, Conn., 1941). Instead of attempting, twenty-odd years before it would in fact happen, to campaign in the academy on behalf of 'criticism' as against 'scholarship', Pound decided to put into practice his view of himself as the greatest living literary critic by concentrating on contemporary writing, and to do so as a literary journalist whose critical judgement had been fashioned by a firsthand acquaintance with the canonical writings of several European literatures besides English. For, in the years framed by his entry into Penn in September 1901 and his expulsion from Wabash in February 1908, Pound was given the opportunity to sample a wide range of literary texts in a variety of European languages. According to the narrative he constructed long after the event, he carefully planned and clandestinely executed an investigation into literary evaluation, using as data the literary texts he was required to read by teachers whose principal and sometimes only interest in them appeared to be philological. By subverting what the official education system offered him, he managed to develop concurrently a theory of transhistorical and universal literary value which would enable him, as he was to phrase it in his first book of criticism, to 'weigh Theocritus and Mr Yeats with one balance' (*SR* vi). A typical formulation of this position is to be found in the telegraphese of a letter written in 1930 to Louis Untermeyer: 'Entered U.P. Penn at 15 with intention of studying comparative values in literature (poetry) and began doing so unbeknown to the faculty' (*EP/LU* 15). Whether or not that decision was quite so clearly formulated at the time, Pound enrolled in various university courses in which he was required to study literary texts written in French, Italian, Spanish and German, in addition to English and Latin, his proficiency in which had gained him entry into Penn. He also persuaded one of his Hamilton teachers, William P. Shepard, to teach him a subject not on the syllabus, Provençal.

What the academy offered him as Romance philology Pound tried to reconstitute as comparative literature, which was a radically new type of literary knowledge at the turn of the century, first envisaged by H.M. Posnett in *Comparative Literature* (1886). The first Chair of Comparative Literature in the USA had not been established until 1890, when Harvard University created the position which was to be occupied by Arthur Richmond Marsh, who was to tell members of the Modern Language Association meeting in Boston in 1896 that the new discipline of comparative literature was still 'undeveloped in theory' and 'extremely limited in practice' (Weisstein 1973: 209). Harvard University had no Department of Comparative Literature until 1904; the first American university to inaugurate such a department was Columbia University, which did so in 1899, appointing as its head George E. Woodberry, who is disparaged for his derivativeness in a 1915 poem of Pound's called 'L'Homme Moyen Sensuel' (ibid.: 210; *P* 239). The first *Journal of Comparative Literature* appeared and disappeared after one year in 1903, while Pound progressed from being a sophomore at Penn to becoming a third-year student at Hamilton. Whatever his teachers may have had to say about the fledgling discipline of Comparative Literature, their version of it was associated in Pound's mind with philology: the very first sentence of *The Spirit of Romance* (1910) warns readers that the book is 'not a philological work', and that 'only by courtesy can it be said to be a study in comparative literature' (*SR* v). If, as Pound claimed in

1934, he did indeed begin 'an examination of comparative European literature in or about 1901' (*LE* 77), then he did so in opposition to a discursive formation whose principal function was to enable romance philology to reproduce itself.

Pound was especially fortunate in the teachers of romance languages he encountered at both Penn and Hamilton, whom he was to refer to Byronically as his 'pastors and masters' (*SP* 21). At Hamilton, for instance, he came into contact with William P. Shepard, whose doctoral study at the University of Heidelberg had been printed by the Chemical Publishing Company of Easton in 1897 as *A Contribution to the History of the Unaccented Vowels in French*, and whose current research included a couple of lengthy articles which were soon to appear in *PMLA*, one in 1905 on the syntax of Antoine de la Sale, and the other in 1906 on parataxis in Provençal. The Hamilton courses Pound took in French, Italian, Spanish and Provençal were all taught by Shepard, a committed and productive scholar whose energies went into editing a thirteenth-century troubadour poet (Jausbert de Puycibot), a fourteenth-century mystery play (*La Passion Provençale*) and *The Oxford Provençal Chansonnier* (Princeton, 1928). It was Shepard's versatility which shaped Pound's assumption that the various romance languages were merely different 'ways of speaking Latin . . . corruptly' (*SR* 2), and emanated from a Europe whose constituent countries were so interrelated linguistically as to render national boundaries quite arbitrary. From his trips to Europe Pound knew that before the First World War travellers were able to cross national frontiers without passports. It was a freedom not easily surrendered by a man who crossed disciplinary boundaries with the same inquisitive nonchalance as he crossed linguistic ones, much to the annoyance of those who believe that knowledge should be balkanised and the frontiers of its sovereign states policed against intruders. When passports became obligatory in Europe after the war, false passports were to become increasingly necessary for an eclectic *flâneur* who found himself harassed by disciplinary specialists. Consequently, as a literary journalist in postwar London, Pound slipped into music criticism in the guise of 'William Atheling' and into art criticism alias 'B.H. Dias'.

The model of the humanities which Pound encountered and became disillusioned with in the early years of this century was the product of various nineteenth-century configurations, prominent among which were two sets of assumptions, one about what constitutes knowledge in the humanities, and the other about the most appropriate ways of institutionalising that knowledge. A key term in the first set of assumptions was 'philology', and in the second set, 'professionalism'. As Gerald Graff makes clear in his institutional history of literary studies in the USA, 'philology' was the site of conflicting conceptions of linguistic enquiry in the nineteenth century. 'The history of the word "philology" itself', he writes, 'reflected a conflict between broad, humanistic generality and narrow, positive science' (Graff 1987: 69). In the broad sense, philology was perceived as moving outwards from the study of particular languages to the cultural practices represented in and by those languages, such that to study any one language properly was to acquire a historical understanding of the total culture of its native speakers. This particular construction of philological endeavour was a guarantee of the claim that the humanities are socially indispensable on account of their ability to humanise people by encouraging an informed and sympathetic understanding of cultural heterogeneity. In its diachronic form, a curiosity-driven exposure to alterity sustained the rubric, *autres temps, autres moeurs*.

The nineteenth-century exemplars of humanistic philology included scholars like Friedrich Max Müller and Jacob and Wilhelm Grimm, whose legacy of dazzling erudition continues into the twentieth century in the work of such scholars as Leo Spitzer, Erich Auerbach and Ernst Robert Curtius. But pedagogic practices, unfortunately, tend to be known by their weaknesses rather than their strengths, largely because of the difficulty most run-of-the-mill practitioners experience in achieving those ideals reached from time to time by acknowledged masters of the method. Teachers who seemed merely to waffle on about literature and culture for a living were therefore easy targets for another breed of scholar who believed that the only way for humanities subjects to justify their existence in a modern university was by introducing scientific methods into humanistic enquiry. Twenty years before Pound was to enrol as an undergraduate at Hamilton College, its Professor of German, H.C.G. Brandt (who was to help Pound get appointed to Wabash College), told the first meeting of the Modern Language Association of America in 1883 that too many teachers of modern languages fail to realise 'that their department is a science'. The best way of combating a prevalent and professionally demoralising conviction among the general public that *'any body* can teach French or German or ... English', Brandt argued, is to ensure that every teacher of modern languages is 'specially and . . . scientifically trained for his work' (Graff 1987: 67–8). The tropes used by proponents of the *rigor philologicus* were predictably masculinist when deriding the humanities as a 'soft' option in comparison with the 'hard' sciences, to which philology should aspire in order to stiffen an otherwise effeminate activity, thus easing the guilt of indolent enjoyment among staff and students alike, and demonstrating to hard-nosed colleagues in the Faculty of Science that studying the humanities can make a man of you.

'Scientific method', for Brandt and the scholars he represented, meant importing into modern language study certain techniques developed by German scholars for dealing with ancient Greek and Roman texts. As Graff describes it, the debate between 'generalist' philologists and 'specialist' *Philologen* falsely polarised the issues into 'dilettantes versus investigators: the one all interesting but untrue generalizations, the other all true but sterile particularities, and evidently nothing in between' (ibid.: 95). Shortly before Pound became an undergraduate, resistance to the teutonisation of literary studies was evident in a collection of essays by professors of English edited by William Morton Payne as *English in American Universities* and published in 1895. That was also the year in which a professor of English at Cornell University, Hiram Corson, attacked the Germanic style of philological scholarship as a form of 'piddling analysis which has no end but itself' and constitutes 'a great obstacle to the truest and highest literary culture' (ibid.: 47–8). This was the line of attack taken concurrently in England and with great gusto by John Churton Collins in a series of forays beginning with *The Study of English Literature* (London, 1891) and culminating in *Ephemera Academica* (London, 1902). But these were of doubtful polemical value to American anti-philologists, who were up against an opposition which would see Collins as one of those British amateurs despised by the professionals.

What was displayed in moves to introduce scientific methods into the humanities was a desire to secure for those who taught there the kudos of a high-status profession. That move had been made already on behalf of producers of literature by G.H. Lewes in an essay on 'The Principles of Success in Literature' (1865); and a recognition of the fact that 'creative' writing had lost its amateur standing was signalled when Herbert Spencer, in *The Principles of Sociology* (London, 1896), included 'belles lettres' in his survey of professional institutions. If those who produced literature could be regarded as professionals, those who reproduced it as criticism and scholarship – and in addition had the responsibility for communicating it to the young – might be expected to regard themselves likewise as professionals. Guided by Magali Sarfatti Larson's sociological analysis of *The Rise of Professionalism* (Berkeley and Los Angeles, 1977), Louis Menand describes how in the late nineteenth century 'the vocational values of independence, ingenuity, and entrepreneurship' came to be overlaid or displaced by professional standards of conduct (Menand 1987: 99). He argues that the contradictions of capitalism are replicated systemically in professionalism, which paradoxically seeks to combine free-market enterprise with a protectionist attitude towards its own members, and claims to serve the needs of others best by being accountable only to itself (ibid.: 114). Under capitalism, professionalism appears to guarantee the freedom of professionals to get on with their own work in a politics-free space, but in fact it is a mechanism for ensuring the complicity of professionals in the status quo; for, in extending 'the characteristic capitalistic system of the division of labour to all areas of work, it provides the specialists necessary to serve the legal, financial, and technological needs of a competitive and highly interdependent economy' (ibid.: 113). With the establishment of professional journals in the humanities – the *American Journal of Philology* in 1880, *Modern Language Notes* in 1886, *Modern Philology* (1903) and *PMLA* (1884) – scholarship could be turned into an industry in which professional merit could be measured in terms of the number of pages published in this or that trade journal or in one of those monograph series which came into existence with the establishment of university presses at Chicago in 1892 (the year the University opened) and Columbia in 1893. By the time Pound left the academy in 1908, Yale University Press was about to go into production; but there was to be no Harvard University Press until 1913.

The point of mentioning these matters is to keep in mind the fact that as an undergraduate Pound entered the American academy at one of its more productive moments of crisis, and that some of the misgivings he had about what happened to him there are not unrelated to what were recent and contemporary debates about the nature and aims of the humanities. Pound first articulated these in print in 1906 when, as a twenty-one year old MA student at Penn, he published an essay on Renaissance Italians who wrote in Latin. It provided an occasion for him to ridicule 'the Germanic ideal of scholarship' as an ensemble of such diversionary activities as the study of *Privatleben* trivia (what an 'author wore and ate') and insoluble textual cruxes (trying to decide whether the lection *seca* was preferable to *secat* in an epigram 'not worth reading'). Developed by men whose professional nightmare was to be accused of dilettantism, scholarship of this sort had blinded its practitioners to 'the beauty of the classics' and discouraged students like himself from reading Latin 'widely and for pleasure' (Pound 1906: 31). The study of writers whose medium was 'Raphaelite' Latin needed to be preserved, therefore, against philological practices which interposed between Renaissance texts and twentieth-century readers a barrier more impenetrable than the Latin language. Pound proposed doing research in this area to an assistant professor at Penn whose seminars on Catullus and Martial he had attended, Walton Brooks McDaniel, who had recently completed a Harvard Ph.D. on the Homeric Hymns, and was eventually to publish a book on Pound's *bête noire*, *Roman Private Life and Its Survivals* (New York, 1927). As a centenarian McDaniel would recall being 'challenged by Pound's exuberance and brilliance' (Wallace 1983: 21), although he was clearly not persuaded by it at the time. According to Pound, McDaniel thought it too risky to work on authors whose reputations had not yet been determined by the academy; ' "And besides, Mr Pound, we shd. have to do so much work ourselves to verify your results" ' (*GK* 215). That put-down was recalled in 1925 in Pound's letter to his 'ancient professorial enemy' (*EP/DS* 264) and Head of the English Department at Penn, Felix Schelling, pointing out to him that 'the American parody of German philology is often . . . a conspiracy to prevent the student from learning more than his teacher' (*L* 269). McDaniel's veto on Pound's proposal to do research on Renaissance Latin meant that any hopes he might have had of subverting the Germanic ideal of classical scholarship by writing in a non-philological manner on non-canonical authors of a post-classical period were thwarted. Consequently, Pound moved out of classics and into romance languages to work under the supervision of Hugo Rennert on Lope de Vega. His decision to go to Spain rather than Germany as a research fellow was a minor act of rebellion itself, given the university policy at that time to 'go to Germany for systematized information' (*GK* 219).

By 1913 Pound had moved beyond the aestheticist objection that philology spoils the pleasure of the text, and was complaining at the way in which universities support the wrong sort of enquiries in the humanities. They will subsidise studies of 'the development of ablauts in Middle High German', he wrote, perhaps recalling Shepard's labours on the unaccented vowels of Old French, but they will not support 'literary creation or experiment' (*EP/VA* 2). 'The "Professional" ' was to be blasted in *Blast* (1914), but it was 1917 before Pound developed a conspiracy theory about a hidden political agenda in the teutonisation of American universities by philology. At this time he was living in Britain, which had recently been joined by America in its protracted war against Germany. The first of Ford Madox Ford's literary contributions to the war-effort, *When Blood Is Their Argument*, had been published in March 1915, four months or so before Ford took the precaution of ridding himself of his German surname, Hueffer. Among various 'defects' which he thought had corrupted German universities into mere institutions 'for providing State officials of an orthodox turn of mind', Ford lists 'the gradual deterioration of all learning into philology' (Longenbach 1987: 99–100). Pound was impressed by this analysis which, however compromised it may have been by patriotic opportunism on Ford's part, pointed towards a political genealogy of the epistemic formation in which he had found himself a decade ago at Penn. 'I trust the faculty of my rotten University will read and digest it', he wrote to his mother (*EP/FMF* 28) before recommending the book to Felix Schelling in June 1915 (*L* 106).

By the time Pound published his essay attacking provincialism in July 1917 the main components of the conspiracy were clear to him. 'People see no connection between "philology" and the Junker', he wrote, and are therefore unable to see that 'the "university system" of Germany is evil' (*SP* 161). Why? 'Because it holds up an ideal of "scholarship", not an ideal of humanity.' It decoys intelligent people away from the central issues of their times by offering them the lure of becoming authorities on marginal specialisms such as '*ablauts*, hair-length, foraminifera', and spending the rest of their professional lives in the kind of stultifying 'research' which F.R. Leavis called, in his response to Pound's *How To Read*, 'the higher navvying' (Leavis 1932: 27). Instead of institutionalising *Bildung* ('the humanist belief that a man acquires knowledge in order that he may be a more complete man'), 'the Germano-American "university" ideal' promoted *Wissenschaft*, the arts version of which is '*Kunstwissenschaft*' (*SP* 161, 166). *Wissenschaft* is the fetishisation of knowledge for its own sake: 'you are to acquire knowledge in order that knowledge may be acquired' (*SP* 161). When ' "Philology" laid hold of the arts' (*SP* 166), it produced a redefinition of what counts as knowledge. Its effect on literary criticism was disabling, because people became so preoccupied with 'questions of morphology' that they forgot how important it is 'to know good literature from bad' (*SP* 162). Its effect on social criticism was devastating. One of the things Pound admired about Major C.H. Douglas's exposition of Social Credit in *Economic Democracy* (London, 1920) was its provision of an alternative to that 'German philology' which had sacrificed individual intelligence to 'the Moloch of "Scholarship" ' (Pound 1920: 40).

Pound's conspiracy theory is given fictive embodiment in an imaginary conversation (also published in 1917) between a past master called 'Rabelais' and a Pound-proxy called 'Student', who explains that 'the whole . . . drive of modern philology is to make a man stupid' by smothering him 'with things unessential' (*PD* 90). By 1929 Pound knew the date at which the catastrophe produced by 'philology' (a state apparatus 'designed to inhibit thought') had occurred: it was 'after 1848 . . . in Germany' that 'the thinkists were given a china egg labelled scholarship', manufactured with the express purpose of keeping the minds of the professoriate 'off life in general, and off public life in particular'. The practice had spread to America 'from precedent' as something worth emulating, it being understood there that Germany had 'a "great university tradition" ' (*LE* 20). Specialists accordingly became 'book-fools' (*GK* 277), licensed to spend their time 'obscuring the texts with philology' (Canto 15), and complicit in a *trahison des clercs* which neutralised the humanism Rabelais had stood for (*EPS* 292). 'Take a man's mind off the human value of the poem he is reading,' Pound had written in 1917, 'switch it on to some question of grammar and you begin his dehumanization' (*SP* 167). That was the year in which he told Harriet Monroe how pleased he was to learn that some American professors were advocating 'the unGermanization of universities': it may well have been for patriotic rather than pedagogic reasons, he feared, but it was nevertheless a move in the right direction to expose philology as 'a system of dehumanization' (*L* 183).

For many years Pound's attitude towards the academy was highly ambivalent. On the one hand he wanted to believe that escaping from it was the best thing he ever did; and whenever he was in that mood (which was often) he was virulently anti-academic in his attacks on 'Institutions for the obstruction of learning' (*LE* 15) and the 'subsidized drifters' (*L* 341) employed there. Anti-academic sentiments made him receptive to maverick 'authorities' like Silvio Gesell, who 'was right in thanking his destiny that he had begun his study of money unclogged by university training' (*SP* 243). Like Major Douglas, Gesell was one of those 'free men' we must look to for modes of enlightenment which will never come from 'preconditioned bureaucrats (governmental, universitaire and/or ecclesiastic)' (*GK* 246). Anti-academicism manifested itself also in Pound's admiration for *clerici vagantes* like Ernest Fenollosa, whose life as an amateur orientalist, he wrote in 1916, 'was the romance par excellence of modern scholarship' (*T* 213). Knowing that Fenollosa had spent his life 'scrapping with the academic fatheads' (Bridson 1961: 177), his widow determined to pass on to Pound rather than to a sinologist those rough English cribs of Chinese poems and plays which her husband had assembled with the aid of two Japanese scholars, and which (Pound told Glenn Hughes in 1927) 'Fen. wanted... trasd *as* literature not as philology' (*L* 289). Pound saw it as his duty to treat the Fenollosa manuscripts creatively as a scholar-poet instead of obscuring them with philology. In the literary renascence he was predicting for America from his vantage-point in Georgian London (*PM* 26), he would play the same role in his transmission of Chinese culture as Chrysoloras had played in the transmission of Greek culture to the Italian Renaissance. Fenollosa's 'Essay on the Chinese Written Character as a Medium for Poetry' was to be presented as a contribution to modern poetics and not as a document whose sources were to be traced, arguments historicised, and errors corrected editorially. Pound's versions of Fenollosa's notes on Mori and Ariga's versions of Chinese poems were published as *Cathay* (1915) and established Pound, in Eliot's phrase, as 'the inventor of Chinese poetry for our time' (Eliot 1948: 14). Thus literary texts in one language were to engender literary texts in another by evading the attentions of those morticians of genius, the professors, who are said to 'dislike the existence of new books' (Pound 1939: 281), and who, rather than confront a living Leonardo, prefer to 'codify his results' when he is dead (*G-B* 100).

In other moods Pound continued to seek recognition from a university system he felt had rejected him unjustly. For several years after his dismissal from Wabash he tried to secure an academic position in the USA, especially at times when, as in February 1911, he felt 'the need of a mental rest' (*EP/MC* 64) from that 'damn'd profession of writing, / where one needs one's brains all the time' (*P* 117). As late as November 1920, when he'd had quite enough of London, he sounded out the lawyer and art patron John Quinn about the possibility of teaching at Columbia University or the College of the City of New York, but not 'HAAvud' (Reid 1968: 437). He never lost his respect for university qualifications: his first critical book, *The Spirit of Romance* (1910), declared itself to be the work of 'Ezra Pound, M.A.', and the printed syllabus of the London Polytechnic lectures they were based on added in parentheses, 'Sometime Fellow in the University of Pennsylvania' (Stock 1970: 58). But the MA was not enough: he wanted his Ph.D. If the German army had occupied London, he told Margaret Anderson on 17 July 1917 (with America now in the war), he would 'have gone peaceably to Leipzig' – where 'all classic authors have been authoritatively edited and printed by Teubner' (*LE* 240) – 'to take [his] higher degree, and have ended up as the complete KULTURMENSCH' (*EP/MCA* 92). In February 1920 he told his father that Hugo Rennert had assured him as long ago as 1911 that *The Spirit of Romance* would be acceptable in lieu of a thesis for the degree of Ph.D. (Wilhelm 1985: 154); but when Homer Pound broached the matter with the Penn authorities, Felix Schelling, after canvassing opinion, recommended that the degree be not awarded because Pound had not satisfied all the Ph.D. requirements (Stock 1976: 87–8). Pound then sent a copy of his *Poems 1918–21* (New York, 1921) to Schelling, a specialist in Elizabethan drama, who was not impressed by Pound's academic competence as a translator either of Provençal in the 'Langue d'Oc' sequence or of Latin in *Homage to Sextus Propertius*, although he was not wholly unsympathetic to Pound's 'eccentric and often very clever verse' (Stock 1976: 88). Pound tried again to get the doctoral degree awarded for his palaeographic edition of *Guido Cavalcanti: Rime* (Genoa, 1932), in the preparation of which, he told Lawrence of Arabia a couple of years later, he had gone 'down into the very nadir of philology' (Redman 1987: 341); but Etienne Gilson's faintly patronising review of the book in the October 1932 issue of the *Criterion*, to which Pound responded by saying he had produced a deliberately 'inexact... translation' of the Cavalcanti text to indicate that it was 'IN THE FIRST PLACE A POEM' (Brooks, D. 1984: 31), probably helped convince the Penn authorities that it was not an academically serious piece of work, and they again refused to award him a Ph.D. This second rejection proved to Pound that 'the "university" is dead': 'anyone interested in assessing the value of university degrees is invited to compare that volume with any batch of theses for Ph.D. that he fancies' (*I* 264). He wrote those words in 1938. Within a year, on 12 June 1939, he had accepted the honorary degree of Doctor of Letters offered him not by Penn but by Hamilton College. In possession at last of that long-desired qualification, he broadcast from Radio Rome during the Second World War as 'Dr' Pound, under a dictatorship which treated 'free expression of opinion' as something not granted as of right but available only to 'those who are qualified to hold it' (Stock 1970: 393).

Whatever resentments Pound felt towards the academy, he picked up certain tricks of the trade there which were to prove extremely useful when he worked as a metropolitan critic. He also retained a recognisably academic way of going about things which, in the long run, enabled his own writings to be appropriated by younger generations of academics who continue to work in the Pound industry, producing that paraphernalia of indispensable guides, checklists, indexes, concordances, bibliographies and marginalia which accumulate, 'philologically', around all major authors. In that respect, Pound's vengeance on the academy which rejected him is *The Cantos*, a polyglot masterpiece designed (as Joyce said of *Ulysses*) to keep the professors busy for decades.

As a poet who wanted to be an academic, Pound was no more interested in preserving generic distinctions between poetry and criticism than he assumed Browning had been when presenting his knowledge of the Middle Ages in a poem, *Sordello*, instead of a work of scholarship (*SR* 122). And although Pound conceded that the state of the manuscripts of the Provençal poet Arnaut Daniel was 'an affair scholastic rather than artistic' (Pound 1918c: 5), his translations of Daniel's poems were designed to incorporate scholarship into poetry. The 'New Method in Scholarship' Pound envisaged in 1911 was to break with philological conventions by using poems and translations rather than monographs as a means of exploring hypotheses. 'Near Perigord' (*P* 151–6), for instance, seeks to persuade us that the Provençal poet Bertrans de Born had political motives in mind when writing what reads like a love poem. Whether or not that is a plausible explanation of Bertrans's poem, Pound wrote in a note on 'Near Perigord' for the benefit of its original readers, 'I must leave the philologists and professional tacticians to decide' (Pound 1915: 146). This note presents 'Near Perigord' as a poem based on Pound's first-hand knowledge of the topography of Provence while on location there: 'my own observations of the geography of Perigord and Limoges'. It does not entertain the possibility that the kind of reading it offers has been shaped by the application to a Provençal poem of certain reading practices developed by philologists working in adjacent fields, notably classics, where Homeric scholars like Walter Leaf were arguing concurrently that the Trojan War might not have been about Helen and love after all but about the Hellespont and trade (Roessel 1988: 106–7).

Like those 'creative' translations which Pound pioneered, the 'scholarship-poem' is a tricky genre to assess. In the case of *Homage to Sextus Propertius*, for example, Pound wants us to believe that his poem manages, without aspiring to be a literal translation of the Latin, to reveal more clearly than any other scholar or translator exactly what Propertius was on about. In that respect, he told Schelling in 1922, it had 'scholastic value' (*L* 245), and would constitute a 'service to classical scholarship' if it managed to 'induce a few Latinists really to look at the text of Propertius' instead of finding there only what the textbooks tell them to expect (*CH* 164). And 'Near Perigord' similarly frustrates readers who want to know whether it is making truth-claims in a scholarly way on behalf of an interpretative hypothesis, or merely exercising a traditionally sanctioned poetic licence. In the case of the verse translations in *Sonnets and Ballate of Guido Cavalcanti* (London, 1912), Arundel del Re could see that Pound was 'earnestly striving after a vital idea', but could not understand why he had used such an 'obsolete and untrustworthy' text of Cavalcanti, and why such a manifest labour of love should be spoiled on page after page by unscholarly 'slovenliness and inaccuracy' (*CH* 88, 86). Such problems are magnified enormously, of course, for readers of that vast scholarship-poem, *The Cantos*, which advances the hypothesis that civilisation is perpetually at risk from bankers who make money out of money and arms-manufacturers who promote wars for personal profit.

This move to situate criticism 'inside' poetry was done in the interests of keeping criticism solely in the hands of 'creative' writers, on the grounds that these are the only people with the necessary qualifications for the task. Once criticism is opened up as a separate discursive space, various people move into it who have no right to be there, like 'the present Cambridge school of "critics" ', as Pound noted in 1933 with an eye on the *Scrutiny* group (*SP* 201). Unlike 'literature', which for Pound as for Horace is a *monumentum aere perennius*, outbraving the ravages of time, 'criticism' is regarded as something merely instrumental to a writer's real work, and therefore of secondary importance. 'I consider criticism merely a preliminary excitement,' he wrote in 1923, 'a statement of things a writer has to clear up in his own head sometime or other, probably antecedent to writing' (Pound 1923: 146). Genuine criticism, if Pound were to have his way, would be organised as a wholly in-house affair among accredited writers. Conceived of as merely a prolegomenal activity, it would 'consume itself and disappear' in its author's next piece of creative work, 'as I think it mostly does in my *ABC of Reading*', he told Laurence Binyon in 1934 (*L* 347). To situate that book in a history of literary criticism would be to mistake the instrumental for the autotelic, and to perpetuate the *Scrutiny* group's error of boosting 'the production of writing about writing, not only as autotelic, but as something which ought to receive more attention from the reading victim than the great books themselves' (*SP* 359–60).

For somebody who professed to have such a low opinion of criticism ('one work of art is worth forty prefaces and as many apologiae' (*LE* 41)), Pound produced it in enormous quantities. Much of it relates to his poetry only obliquely, and, therefore cannot be considered a merely prolegomenal activity; and, since he took the trouble of putting it into print, there was no prospect of its disappearing as a self-consuming artefact. He published critical essays, as most people do, as a means of having his say about many subjects, on many of which he could not claim (as he did in the case of literary criticism) to write with the privileges of an insider. To specify who was 'qualified' to write about literature was an authoritarian move designed to silence, among other people, academics who might historicise and challenge his own cultural generalisations.

Pound's experience of the history of literary criticism as represented by Penniman left him with the conviction (which he never bothered to question) that all academics who study criticism are mindless cataloguers of other people's opinions. The possibility that writers and academics might meet on the common ground of literary theory never occurred to him, and so he took no interest in a book published in 1915 called *The Modern Study of Literature*. Its author, Richard Green Moulton, taught at the University of Chicago, where he was Professor of Literary Theory and Interpretation, a title which may surprise those who think of literary theory as something invented in the 1960s. Unlike Pound, who believed in the existence of timeless aesthetic values, Moulton was a relativist who argued that 'progressive arts must have progressive definitions', and who ranked philosophy (defined as 'the attempt to arrive at theory of literature') above the history of criticism, which, like Pound, he thought had 'a place in academic schemes out of proportion to its real value' (Moulton 1915: 314, 329, 330). He argued, as Terry Eagleton was to do some sixty years later, that 'the ignoring of literary theory itself constitutes a theoretic position, and a bad one'; and his typology of critical activities includes 'creative' criticism, in which 'by his act of criticizing the critic becomes an author' (ibid.: 506, 325).

In the period in which Moulton's book appeared, Chicago was constantly in Pound's mind as the site of a literary renascence marked by two journals of avant-garde writing: *Poetry*, edited by Harriet Monroe, and the *Little Review*, edited by Margaret Anderson. If he ever thought at all about the University of Chicago it was only negatively in connection with its Professor of Classics, W.G. Hale, who was to ridicule as the work of someone 'incredibly ignorant of Latin' (*CH* 156) those parts of Pound's *Homage to Sextus Propertius* published in *Poetry*. Much better than Moulton, Hale fitted Pound's stereotype of the academic as philologist, the tenured ignoramus who is hostile to new ways of doing things. Pound's prejudices against the 'professoriality' (*L* 437) were to remain when the academy compensated for its earlier dealings with him by permitting his own writings to become the subject of scholarly enquiry. The first book to be called *The Poetry of Ezra Pound* – a modest account of Pound's career up to the time when he appeared to have given up literature for economics – was written by Alice S. Amdur, published by Harvard University Press in 1936, and sent by William Carlos Williams to Pound, whose impression of it was that he had been carried into Jerusalem on the back of an ass. The second, an equally sympathetic but much smarter performance, was published by Hugh Kenner in 1951, and inaugurated the professionalisation of Pound studies in the academy. While noting that Kenner's book, which quotes generously from Pound's writings, 'gets some of the needed stuff back into print', and 'packs a punch in the tail', Pound nevertheless deplored the way it 'starts with necessary (I spose necessary) professorial wind' (*EP/JDI* 135).

As a graduate student at Penn, Pound read James McNeill Whistler's *The Gentle Art of Making Enemies* (London, 1892), which confirmed his view that you could know as much about aesthetics and art history as the Slade Professor of Fine Arts, John Ruskin, did, and still be hopelessly out of your depth when encountering the work of an original painter like Whistler. Whistler's castigation of Ruskin struck Pound in 1906 as an exemplary instance of a recurrent scandal in the history of the fine arts, namely that of 'the "Great Critics" maundering in the realm of paint' (Berryman 1983: 98). Pound's conviction that they maunder just as badly in the realm of poetry points to the strength of another epistemic formation in which his conception of criticism was shaped: the Romantic mystification of individual genius as the sole and inexplicable origin of literature, and the special authority it confers on criticism written by poets. Anglo-American attitudes to poet-critics continue to be profoundly contradictory. On the one hand a residual Romantic cult of creative genius perpetuates the notion that poets are so involved in the actual making of poetry that they are bound to have an insider's view of it which makes them critically more acute than even the best-read of non-poets. Criticism written by poets can be 'technical and exact', Pound wrote in March 1914 when explaining his impatience with 'any criticism of the arts save that which is made by . . . a painter on painting, a poet on verse, a musician on music' (*EP/VA* 185). And because many editors share this view, poets continue to be hired as reviewers despite the historical evidence that they are no more free of critical blindspots than anybody else, and often complicate matters even further when suffering from the kind of professional jealousy so markedly on display in Robert Graves's attack on other modern poets in *The Crowning Privilege* (London, 1955). But the same forces which ensure that poets are given the opportunity to write on the work of other poets operate also to their detriment by making their criticism appear idiosyncratic. When Pound published *Section: Rock-Drill* in 1957, it may have seemed a good idea in the offices of the *Manchester Guardian* to have those Cantos reviewed by a distinguished anti-modernist poet, Philip Larkin; but the result was much more interesting to admirers of Larkin than to critics of Pound (*CH* 444–5). The whole point of such exercises, it would appear, is to enable poets to write obliquely on their own work while ostensibly reviewing somebody else's, and thus provide another critic with tips on how they themselves are to be read.

Pound's own literary criticism is always in danger of being sidelined in similar ways, its brusqueness and outrageousness treated as reasonable grounds for classifying it as the work of a poet who tried his hand at criticism but lacked the finesse of T.S. Eliot. Reproduced in this way, Pound's collected criticism is perceived as constituting a dispersed poetics of his collected poems. That is how the relationship between a poet's criticism and poetry has tended to be defined since 1798, when Wordsworth and Coleridge published their revolutionary volume of poems, *The Lyrical Ballads*, and kept on attaching prefaces to different editions of it, the point of which was to explain to otherwise mystified readers of those poems exactly what was revolutionary about them. 'Every author,' Coleridge had told Wordsworth, 'as far as he is great and at the same time *original*, has had the task of *creating* the taste by which he is to be enjoyed: so has it been, so will it continue to be' (Wordsworth 1926: 951). The evolution of the literary manifesto as a Romantic genre supports the notion that when poets write about poetry they do so principally with their own poems in mind, and that what they produce as a result can be abridged and reconstituted as poetic theory. Within that particular cultural formation, readers of Pound's criticism can then pursue such matters as the adequacy of the theory as an account of the practice, and try to determine whether Pound was correct in claiming that in most cases 'the work outruns the formulated or at any rate the published equation' (*LE* 75). In these terms, Pound's *How To Read* (1931) is really a book about how to read Pound. To Ford, Pound's criticism constituted 'craftsman's notes' rather than the balanced prose of 'the Born Critic', whatever that might be (*EP/FMF* 53). To Eliot, reviewing *Pavannes and Divisions* (1918) in December that year, Pound's critical writings were 'the comments of a practitioner upon his own and related arts' – what Eliot would later call 'workshop criticism' (Eliot 1957: 107) – and belonged to a genre in which there had been 'very little since Dryden's Prefaces of any permanent value' (Eliot 1918a: 132). 'Intelligent criticism', as Eliot defined it, is produced by 'men who are engaged in creative work'

(Eliot 1918: 69); so much, then, for the criticism of those who are not.

All of this supported Pound's conviction that the academic study of literature had been founded on a massive contradiction. In providing a space in which literature could be canonised and poetry in particular idolised, the universities had conducted themselves admirably; but then they had made the appalling mistake of placing this precious commodity, literature, in the care of philologists who behaved as if they would rather do anything with it than treat it as literature. Intellectually they were the walking dead, a testimony to the truth of Eliot's claim that, on account of its specialised nature, postgraduate study – and he was speaking in 1916 from first-hand experience as a recent drop-out – was 'fatal to the development of intellectual powers' (Eliot 1916: 404). Pound's first critical book, *The Spirit of Romance* (1910), is consequently the scholar's equivalent of D.H. Lawrence's *Look! We Have Come Through!* (1917), the log-book of a survivor from 'the slough of philology' who, having disemburdened himself of 'morphology, epigraphy, [and] *privatleben*' (*SR* v), exercises his freedom to read medieval poetry as poetry, and to judge it by the same standards as he would judge poetry from any other period, ancient or modern. 'The scholars have not known anything about poetry', he declares in the opening chapter of this book (*SR* 14), which was designed to show romance philologists back home how they might go about rehumanising their discipline, if only they would stop behaving like those bald-headed pedants in Yeats's poem 'The Scholars', who cough in ink and wouldn't know what to say, should 'their Catullus walk that way' (Yeats 1950: 158).

You don't have to read very far into *The Spirit of Romance* to realise that Pound's emancipation from turn-of-the-century textual practices was far from complete when he wrote it. Apart from its polemical introduction, which is the *locus classicus* of a number of his critical positions, the book propels itself along by a mixture of historical information, paraphrases, personal observations, and lengthy quotations of whole poems or substantial parts of them, all translated into a form of English which makes their authors sound like minor members of the Pre-Raphaelite Brotherhood. The book begins by wondering where to begin before settling on the second century AD, when Apuleius wrote the 'scurrilous, bejewelled prose' (*SR* 10) of *The Golden Ass*. It then moves chapter by chapter through Arnaut Daniel ('Il Miglior Fabbro'), a few more

Provençal poets, the Spanish *Poema del Cid* and French romances, Tuscan poetry, Dante and Villon. After one chapter on the Spanish dramatist he began studying for his Ph.D., Lope de Vega, and another on the Portuguese epic poet Camoens, Pound ends his book by sampling some of those Latin poets of the Italian Renaissance his classics professor at Penn had advised him not to get involved with academically. He acknowledges the 'refined and sympathetic scholarship' (*SR* viii) of William P. Shepard, who introduced him at Hamilton to so much of this material; but there is no mention of Hugo Rennert, whose Penn seminars Noel Stock says formed the basis of those London Polytechnic lectures which were a dry-run for *The Spirit of Romance* (Stock 1976: 76).

By design, what Pound called 'Tedescan' (i.e. German) philological practices were largely but not wholly expunged from this book. For as an ex-postgraduate student who had resented having to spend time on textual variants like *seca* and *secat*, Pound was proud to present himself in this book as a scholiast, capable of contributing to Provençal scholarship by pointing out that the word *queren* derives 'not from the Latin *quaero*, but from *quaeror*, a deponent with all four participles, habitually used of birds singing or complaining (*vide* Horace, "C.S.," 43; Ovid, "Am.," i. 29)' (*SR* 47). The rhetorical point of this piece of throw-away erudition was to let it be known that if Pound scorned the philological processing of literary texts under a Teutonic régime of scholarship it was not because he was no good at it but because he thought there were other and more important things to do with poems, and that he had earned the right to be a critic after submitting himself to the discipline of philology. This was to be the stand he would take later against any artist who moved straight into an avant-garde style without first having worked through the dominant traditional modes in a recapitulatory fashion. 'The strength of Picasso', he wrote in 1921, 'is largely in his having chewed through and chewed up a great mass of classicism', which is what set his work apart from that of 'flabby cubists' incapable of doing anything else (*EP/VA* 214). Pound saw his own poetic experiments with Provençal forms in English as analogous prentice work, which qualified him to experiment with *vers libre*: 'no one can do good free verse', he told Iris Barry in 1916, 'who hasn't struggled with the regular' (*L* 128; cp. *EP/MCA* 80). Hence his contempt for 'the subsequent easy riders' (*EP/VA* 306) who, never having put themselves through any comparable discipline, would never understand the force of Eliot's aphorism, 'No *vers* is *libre* for the man who wants to do a good job' (*LE* 12).

This notion of traditional practices as the grounds on which innovations must always rest if they are to avoid being meretricious – and the accompanying diachronic doctrine that we cannot possibly know where we are until we see where we have been – testifies to the residual influence on Pound of academic conceptions of scholarship and research, which were to survive his anti-academic moods and continue to manifest themselves in both his poetry and his criticism. His conception of knowledge as something to be advanced by carefully considered gap-filling activities is an example of this. 'Agenda', he called them, defined as 'things to be done'. His study of Provençal poems was academically unusual in that he was far more interested in how they had been put together than in amassing 'extrinsic' data about their provenance, but it nevertheless constituted 'research' as that term might be understood by a poet-critic. As a poet, he determined to do for Provence what Robert Browning had done for the Italian Renaissance in *Men and Women* (1855); as a critic, he would do for it what D.G. Rossetti had done critically for Tuscany, first in *The Early Italian Poets* (1861) and finally in *Dante and His Circle* (1874). Yet, although Pound was quite capable of resisting any academic practice of which he was conscious, he was unable to avoid those practices which are so endemic to the academic enterprise as to appear not worth questioning, such as the assumption that literature is something you can not only learn about but also teach systematically to other people.

Although Pound never taught for a living after his dismissal from Wabash College in 1908, his professed ambition in publishing *The Spirit of Romance* was 'to instruct painlessly' (*SR* vii), and he struck many of his contemporaries as a teacher *manqué*. He was written off by Gertrude Stein, who adopted similar attitudes towards her own *saloniers*, as 'a village explainer, excellent if you were a village, but if you were not, not' (Stein 1946: 166). He held forth to other writers just as he had held forth to his Wabash students: 'he will be the pedagogue, yearning for pupils to instruct', Robert McAlmon observed after a ten-year friendship with the 'instructorial' Pound (McAlmon 1970: 30, 29). To one of his poet-pupils, Iris Barry, he was 'everybody's schoolmaster' (Norman 1969: 199). What disturbed some of the recipients of his didactic attentions was the level at which Pound saw himself as operating, which was rather that of an elementary school-teacher than an academic. He explained to his mother in November 1913, when many poets were wanting to know about *Imagisme*, that he was 'conducting a literary kindergarten for the aspiring' (*L* 63), all of whom were no doubt required to read a now famous essay of his called 'A Few Don'ts by an Imagiste' (*LE* 4–7), described to Dorothy Shakespear as 'a little kindergarten course in Ars Poetica for Chicago' (*EP/DS* 182–3). His reflections on religion, deposited anonymously in the *New Freewoman* in October 1913, were presented catechismally and subtitled, 'The Child's Guide to Knowledge' (*PD* 96–8).

To assume in such ways the speaking-position of teacher when writing is to cast one's readers inevitably in the role of pupils. Most explainers, whether village or college, feel uneasy about this, well aware of the fact that nobody likes being talked down to. One way of problematising the teacher-pupil model of the writer-reader relationship is to foreground it mockingly, as Pound went on to do in *The Treatise on Harmony* (1924). Here the reader is addressed initially as 'mon élève', and presumed unable to reply when the teacher asks what is omitted from all treatises on harmony (answer: 'the time interval that must elapse between one sound and another' (*SP* 77)). In containing imagined objections to his line of argument, however, Pound transforms his passive *élève* into 'mon contradicteur' (*SP* 83), whose existence immediately threatens the authority of his discourse. Consequently, he interposes between teacher and *élève* another and well-informed person called 'the reader', who is reminded that the author of *The Treatise on Harmony* is not nearly so simple-minded as the fictive teacher who occupies the speaking-position in this text, because Pound himself happens to know 'all about superpartient sesqui octaval proportion' and is quite familiar with 'Lemme Rossi's *Sistema Musico overo Musica Speculativa*. [Perugia 1666.]' (*SP* 85). At this point, most readers find themselves relocated discursively to the position of *élève*, and reconstituted as pupils to Pound's mastery by a deployment of erudition designed to make potential objectors feel too ignorant ever to open their mouths. Such was John Gould Fletcher's response when, after mentioning *vers libre* to Pound on one occasion, he received a lecture which cited 'so many critics and theorists whose works [he] had not read, from Gustave Kahn down to the Italian futurists, that [he] decided to keep silence' (Norman 1969: 103). In these power games played with readers and listeners, the omniscience-effect was an indispensable tool of one-upmanship. Anglophone critics could be humbled by references to writers in other European languages, and polyglot Europeans made to feel culturally provincial by references to Chinese. 'What have you read? is still his attack on me', Williams complained in 1947 (Goodwin 1967: 1), although unlike Fletcher he was confident enough about his own writing not to be silenced by Pound, who succeeded in making even well-read people feel they had not read as many of the right books as he had.

Harriet Monroe, who had dealings with him as editor of *Poetry*, wrote that 'Ezra Pound was born to be a great teacher', and thought that American universities, in failing 'to install him as the head of an English department, missed a dynamic influence which would have been felt wherever English writing is taught' (Monroe 1938: 268). Was he a good teacher? Conrad Aiken thought he was, although 'something of a tyrant' (Aiken 1963: 215). His mother might have agreed with that diagnosis after he told her in January 1914 how 'profoundly pained' he was by her confession that she would rather read Marie Corelli than Stendhal. 'I can not help it', he added: ineducable, she joined the ranks of the invincibly ignorant (*L* 68). Equally worrying in a man dismissed by Gertrude Stein as a mere explainer were Pound's evident difficulties in explaining things at an elementary level. For although he believed in the importance of primers, on the grounds that 'the ultimate goal of scholarship is popularisation' (*SP* 168), he lacked the patience of a first-rate expositor. Preferring to engage polemically with whatever he was writing about, he tended to leave his readers feeling rather like Byron felt after reading Coleridge on the subject of metaphysics: 'I wish he would explain his explanation' (*GK* 295). Editors were well aware of Pound's shortcomings as an expositor. 'I asked you to write an article which would explain this subject to people who had never heard of it', Eliot once complained apropos of an essay he had commissioned Pound to write on economics for the *Criterion*; 'yet you write as if your readers knew about it already, but had failed to understand it' (Eliot 1946: 336).

In spite of such rebuffs, Pound continued to put a great deal of energy into what he himself considered to be much-needed popularisations of his literary criticism. An important sequence of his didactic writings begins with three essays contributed to the *New York Herald Tribune Books* in January 1929 and published in book form as *How To Read* (1931). It was followed by *ABC of Reading*

(1934), the Eurocentrism of which he later acknowledged just before publishing his sequel to that book, *Guide to Kulchur* (1938), described to Ford as his 'D/E/F on the orient' (*EP/FMF* 151). Why a poet of Pound's stature would want to waste time writing something like *How To Read* was a puzzle to admirers, who would have preferred him to get on with his *Cantos*, especially since the desire to do precisely that was the principal reason he had given for saying farewell to London and Paris, and settling in Rapallo. 'I expect his next will be How To Dance or How to Vote Republican', commented Archibald MacLeish (MacLeish 1983: 258), perhaps unaware that in the guise of 'B.H. Dias' Pound had contributed in 1918 to A.R. Orage's journal, the *New Age*, a piece headed 'The A.B.C.' which begins, pertly, *'How to look at a house front'* (*EP/VA* 82). Nor, apparently, did MacLeish concede that to write something called *How To Read* is a very American thing to do, a manifestation of that American phenomenon Dwight Macdonald once called 'how-to-ism', the literary career of which Edward Said has sketched whimsically from its positive form in Herman Melville ('what to do if you want to go whaling') to its negative form in Ernest Hemingway ('how not to get gored') (Said 1985: 19).

The essays Pound collected in *Instigations* (1920), he told Lewis, constituted 'a primer for barbarous americans, a substitute for bochized American university course[s]' (*EP/WL* 126); and the didactic tone was recognised by the *Dial* reviewer who called Pound a 'Super Schoolmaster' (*CH* 191). *How To Read* was in one sense an indication that a particular era of his intellectual life was finished with, notably the days when he had taught the aestheticist doctrine that great art is non-didactic. 'It exists as the trees exist', he had written in 1913, but exhibits no purposefulness, for it 'never asks anybody to do anything, or to think anything, or to be anything' (*LE* 46). Such was his Whistlerian credo before encountering in Orage's office Social Credit in the person of its principal exponent, Major C.H. Douglas, who sharpened Pound's awareness of the economic basis of all textual production. By the time he wrote *How To Read* he knew differently, of course; but, nevertheless, he didn't question the educational usefulness of giving the widest possible publicity to what he described in 1928 as his 'conclusions after 25 years of examination of comparative poesy' (Pound 1928: 109). He had not waited so long before putting out a comparable primer (in a well-established genre (Coyle 1988: 21-2)) on economics, a sequel to Orage's *An Alphabet of Economics* (London, 1917), called *ABC of Economics* (London, 1933). In the Social Credit journal edited by Orage, the *New English Weekly*, reviewers treated both of Pound's books as primers in name only: *ABC of Reading* undoubtedly contained a 'mass of invaluable tips', but it would be 'sheer drollery to pretend it is a classbook' (M[airet] 1934: 212). To understand why Pound thought it useful to publish this kind of work we need to think back to his own undergraduate days when, as he saw it, nobody had got around to writing the kind of primers he himself would have been grateful for.

Pound's anti-academicism was the product of disaffection with American academies as currently constituted, but not with academies as such, provided they were staffed by the right kind of people, that is, by people who contributed creatively and significantly to the arts, and who could therefore be trusted to know what they were talking about. He first raised with his patron, Margaret Cravens, in November 1910 the possibility of setting up some such 'college of the Arts' (*EP/MC* 55). As the prospects of transforming the existing academy from within receded with his failure to secure another academic appointment, Pound began to plan a 'super-college' of a hundred artists (*PM* 70), free of academicism, from which a new and vital critique of the arts could emanate. Broadcasting from Fascist Rome in October 1941, Pound said he had always thought of returning to America 'to put some sort of college or university into shape' where the young could be taught something other than the 'god damn saw dust and substitutes for learnin' and literature' handed out to them in existing institutions of higher learning (*EPS* 9–10).

His first attempt to establish such a college coincided opportunistically with the outbreak of the First World War, when it occurred to him that American postgraduate students who normally would be sent to European universities to be teutonised could well be diverted to London to be tutored counter-academically by himself and other friends and acquaintances whose work he admired. A two-page 'Preliminary Announcement of the College of Arts', written by Pound and published in the 2 November 1914 issue of the *Egoist*, indicated that painting and sculpture were to be taught there by 'the most advanced and brilliant men of [the] decade', Wyndham Lewis and Henri Gaudier-Brzeska. The Music faculty would include the American pianist, Katherine Ruth Heyman, whose concert tours Pound had thought of organising when they were both in Venice in 1908, and Arnold Dolmetsch, who tried to recreate the materiality of earlier music by building the instruments on which it had been played, and who had just sold Pound a clavichord. 'Mrs. Dolmetsch' was to be in charge of Dance, and Photography would be taught by an American friend of theirs, Alvin Langdon Coburn, who turned photographs into 'vortographs' with the aid of a 'vortoscope' he and Pound had invented while pioneering a vorticist photography which would free the camera from the tyranny of representation. The Crafts department was still at the planning stage, it appeared, but Letters already had a staff of four. So in addition to learning Dramatic Criticism from a former drama critic of the *New York Tribune*, Cecil Inslee-Dorrian, and hearing (three years before the Revolution) about Russian Contemporary Thought from Zinaida Vangerowa, students could look forward to learning about Russian Novelists from the Russian-born John Cournos, who was to increase his credibility for the task by resurrecting the family name and operating as Ivan Korshune. Those enrolling in Comparative Poetry would be taught by Ezra Pound, 'M.A.', the only member of staff acknowledged to have a degree. Students of Letters were assured that 'a knowledge of morphology is not essential to the appreciation of literature'.

What were to make this College of Arts different from all those other ' "institutions" for the most part academic, sterile, [and] professorial' were the opportunities it would give for study under the direction of 'artists of established position, creative minds, men for the most part who have already suffered in the cause of their art'. This prospectus was read in Oxford by an American postgraduate student at Merton College, T.S. Eliot, who told Pound in April 1915 that it ought to include 'a more crystallised statement of the function of the university' (Eliot 1988: 95). No revised prospectus was ever issued, and the College was quietly forgotten. For the war which was to have brought American students into the College of Arts also took away key members of staff like Gaudier-Brzeska, killed in action at the age of twenty-three on 5 June 1915, and Wyndham Lewis, who enlisted as a gunner in the Royal Artillery in March 1916. It survived, however, as an ideal university in which Pound's various collections of critical essays, from *Instigations* (1920) onwards, were to find their place as textbooks. In these we can still find traces of ideal assignments set for ideal students challenged (for example) to 'find a poem of Byron or Poe without seven serious defects' (*ABCR* 64). 'Instigations WAS the university for people who were getting educated in 1920', Pound wrote in 1934 (*L* 343). The model for that enterprise had been Walter Savage Landor's *Imaginary Conversations* (1824–9), which he and Yeats read in the winter of 1915–16, and which he was to describe in November 1917 as 'the best substitute for a University education that can be offered to any man in a hurry' (*SP* 354–5). Pound was immensely pleased when Yeats accused him of trying 'to provide a "portable substitute for the British Museum" ', adding that he would do so, 'like a shot, were it possible. It isn't' (*LE* 16; cp. *L* 343). But that never stopped him from trying, and nowhere more succinctly than in his long poem designed to be read as a Book of Wisdom, *The Cantos*.

By 1940, with Europe in the process of being devastated by yet another war, Pound turned again to thoughts of an ideal university, only this time as something to be planned rather than actually set up. Its blueprint was to take the form of 'a volume or triptych' (*L* 437) published by Faber & Faber and written in collaboration with T.S. Eliot and George Santayana, who had proved himself ideologically sound in these matters by repeating a remark by Henry Adams subsequently preserved in the amber of Canto 74: 'Teach? at Harvard? . . . It cannot be done'. However different this projected institute of higher learning was to have been from those three Pound had experienced at first hand or the others he read about, it would have manifested such right-wing characteristics as a core curriculum, 'The Proper Curriculum' (*L* 437), defined (with respect to literary studies) as 'the minimum basis for a sound and liberal education in letters', in the absence of which 'the critic has almost no chance of sound judgment' (*LE* 38–9). To propose founding an ideal university on the suppression of heterogeneity and difference was an odd move to make, given Pound's earlier view, as communicated to Lewis in 1931, that what makes British and American universities so 'dead and deadening' is the fact that all their ' "products" have read the same books in same order with same criticism applied' (*EP/WL* 176). Evidently Pound was less interested in liberalising literary studies by abolishing its canonical texts than in setting up a rival and equally inflexible canon of his own. When interviewed in 1959 he recalled Santayana saying, ' "It don't matter what they read so long as they all read the same thing" ', but added the rider that 'that same thing ought to be a body of common knowledge' (Bridson 1961: 180).

The first rumblings of canon formation occur in letters written by Pound in 1916 to a young poet, Iris Barry, advising her what to read; his first published canon of European literature from Homer to Joyce appeared in an essay 'On Criticism in General', contributed to the *Criterion* in 1923 and recycled without acknowledgement in *How To Read* (1931). Those reading lists, he assures us, were produced 'after very considerable search and weeding' (Pound 1923: 154); and although he supplies no comparable 'weeding' lists – as Brigid Brophy and others were to do in *Fifty Works of English Literature We Could Do Without* (New York, 1968) – we know that they would have included such classic English poets as Milton, Wordsworth and Tennyson, on whose writings Pound consistently made dismissive remarks as part of his campaign to destabilise the academic model of English literature in the USA, the British equivalent of which Stephen Potter was to deride in *The Muse in Chains* (London, 1937) as 'Ing. Lit.'.

One of the few to take seriously Pound's attempts at transforming literary criticism into a pedagogy was a man with a similar mission, F.R. Leavis, who was affiliated institutionally (although by no means securely) to a Cambridge in which I.A. Richards had recently conducted an experiment in reading practices and displayed the disturbing results in a now classic text of English literary studies, *Practical Criticism* (London, 1929). Leavis responded to *How To Read* (1931) with *How To Teach Reading* (1932), in which he argues that you cannot turn people into literary critics simply by telling them which authors in your experience are worth reading and which not. 'This "telling about discoveries" ', Leavis complained, 'can clearly have little to do with the training of a critic': critical sensibilities were to be nurtured not by tips of the sort Pound had to offer but by 'responding fully, delicately and with discriminating accuracy to the subtle and precise use of words' (Leavis 1932: 17, 16). To a self-styled 'species of pachyderm' (*SP* 405) like Pound, such thin-skinned sensitivity evoked an etiolated aestheticism characteristic of the Bloomsbury critics he despised, especially Clive Bell, and could have no place in the development of critical certitude. Leavis's own reputation as a critic, of course, was to be jeopardised by lazy Leavisites willing to let him do their critical thinking for them and receive his discoveries as dogma. But Leavis distinguished between saying things deliberately and saying them dogmatically. What he objected to in Pound's criticism was not its anti-academicism, which Leavis conceded was done 'with scornful, but not too scornful, unceremoniousness' (Leavis 1932: 5). Nor was he troubled by Pound's iconoclastic attitude to some famous literary reputations, since he himself was to rejoice in the 'dislodgement' of Milton, and (like Pound) use the adjective 'Tennysonian' as a pejorative. What troubled him was the authoritarian method by which Pound promulgated his revaluations of canonical authors.

The Eliot–Pound–Santayana syllabus for an ideal university never got as far as becoming one book, let alone a triptych, and so what would have been inevitable problems with the project never in fact arose. Being a one-man university was not difficult for Pound to imagine. After all, at Wabash College he had been a one-man Department of Romance Languages, and during his London years had become 'a universal committee for the arts' (Reid 1968: 248), which is how he described himself in March 1916 when writing to the art patron John Quinn, whom he persuaded to invest in the sculpture of Henri Gaudier-Brzeska, the drawings of Wyndham Lewis, the fiction of James Joyce and the poems of T.S. Eliot. That imaginary committee was upgraded to university status with the creation in Rapallo in the 1930s of what James Laughlin (its best-known graduate, class of '35) calls the 'Ezuversity' (Laughlin 1985: 368). In Laughlin's experience, the Ezuversity was 'the best beanery since Bologna' (Carpenter 1988: 528), a claim which would not have surprised one of Pound's intellectual heroes, the German anthropologist and exponent of *Kulturmorphologie*, Leo Frobenius, who is said to have thought Pound worth 'three Oxfords with four Cambridges on top' (*CO/EP* 104). Having no investment in buildings or plant, the Ezuversity could be transferred from Italy to America for little more than the cost of an air fare (paid for in the event by American taxpayers when the American government had Pound flown in from Pisa to Washington to stand trial for treason after the Second World War) and reconstituted in a Washington psychiatric hospital, St Elizabeths, after it had been decided that Pound was not sane enough to face criminal charges. Those who went there to learn about writing often found themselves lectured to instead on the real foundations of writing, economics. What the Ezuversity offered was not debatable knowledge but wisdom to be received gratefully. By telling people things they might otherwise spend years trying to find out for themselves, Pound thought he would save them valuable time in offering them helpful shortcuts: for why else spend '30 years . . . trying to reorganize the study of literature' if not in the hope of making it 'of some use to the student' (*EPS* 64)?

From a relatively early age Pound gave the impression of knowing a great deal about a great many subjects, a phenomenon which evoked widely different responses among those who knew him, and which still troubles those whose only contact with him is through his writings. To some, Pound's knowledgeableness is to be taken at face value as the result of what Eliot called his 'extensive erudition' (Eliot 1928: 6); but according to Witter Bynner, D.H. Lawrence considered Pound to be 'a mountebank' (*CH* 38), and he struck Douglas Goldring likewise as 'a bit of a charlatan' (Goldring 1943: 48). Felix Schelling recalled telling Pound that he was 'either a humbug or a genius' (Wallace 1983: 27), it being 'characteristic of American genius', according to the Canadian Hugh Kenner, 'that the casual eye does not easily distinguish it from charlatanry' (Kenner 1975: 12). Pound's most recent biographer, Humphrey Carpenter, thinks that the education system Pound was put through gave him a taste for 'varied diet rather than the thorough study of one subject', and that in learning how to pass courses like those offered by Hamilton College (which were 'little more than a hasty tour of the various languages and their literatures') Pound learnt how to 'get the "feel" of a subject, picking up its jargon and the kind of questions that would interest real experts, thereby giving an impression of genuine knowledge' (Carpenter 1988: 36, 55). Carpenter's Pound is not really erudite at all, but wears that 'mask of erudition' which unsympathetic observers, like Amy Lowell, recognise as the insignia of a charlatan: what 'give[s] one the feeling of infinite background' is 'all just a trick of that consummate quack, Pound' (Lowell 1955: 432).

Each of these constructions – Pound-as-savant and Pound-as-charlatan – rests on an essentialist theory of human subjectivity and an expressivist theory of language. The one holds that Pound was ('essentially', 'fundamentally', 'in the final analysis', and other fictive states) an immensely learned man, a twentieth-century reincarnation of a Renaissance *doctus poeta*. The other holds ('essentially', etc.) that Pound faked what he didn't know very well, if at all. Both responses are at odds with the more recent speculation that human characteristics are not 'essential' qualities which exist outside of language, waiting to be 'expressed' there, but on the contrary are produced discursively by language itself. As Michel

Foucault has demonstrated, what a text makes available to its readers is not its author but a bundle of 'author-effects' from which different readers produce different author-constructs. In these terms, a text which reproduces the discursive effects of knowledge may well be read as evidence of knowledgeability, irrespective of whether its author is, in essentialist terms, 'really' knowledgeable. Such texts produce 'knowledge-effects', or in Pound's case, 'omni-science-effects'.

Although literary students are never taught how to produce knowledge-effects, they learn to do so very quickly by internalising the sorts of things said about books by their teachers and the critics they are recommended to read. As Northrop Frye observed thirty-odd years ago in his *Anatomy of Criticism* (Princeton, 1957), 'literature' is unteachable, and so what gets taught in the academies is 'criticism', which is the generic term for the various discourses about literature. Consequently, what English-speaking students learn in departments of English language and literature is neither 'language' nor 'literature' but some of the discourses which constitute the study of those phenomena, that is, the metalanguages of linguistic and literary enquiry. Whatever is required, a 'successful' student will soon learn how to reproduce the appropriate discursive effects – the 'personal-response-effect', for instance, if personal responses seem called for, or the 'erudition-effect' if that happens to be the constitutive discourse which dominates the academy, as it was when Pound was a student, and philology was in the process of reproducing itself as an object of desire.

Pound attempted to theorise these matters in the discursive domain of poetry rather than of criticism. Against a Romantic conception of poetry as the expression of a self, he developed a theory of poetry as the deployment of 'masks' or personae, each of which would produce a different subjectivity-effect. And in formulating a vorticist theory of the arts in 1914 he defined the key-term 'vortex' in a non-essentialist way as something 'from which, and through which, and into which, ideas are constantly rushing' (*G-B* 92), but which has no content of its own – no essence – other than traces of what transverses its space. If the modern movement articulates, as it appears to do, a crisis in subjectivity – a moment when writers recognise, in Eliot's words, that they have 'not a "personality" to express, but a particular medium' (Eliot 1928a: 56) – we should at least entertain the possibility that Pound's criticism provides a 'vortex' or discursive space inhabited by sometimes startling configurations of different knowledge-effects. Some readers will find such configurations stimulating, and others not; but their efficacy or otherwise as discursive effects is not going to be dependent on whether, in essentialist terms, Pound 'really' knew as much as the essays attributed to him (and which deploy many knowledge-effects) would have us believe.

'I've read too little and I read very slowly', Pound told Santayana's secretary in 1966 (Cory 1968: 38). Slow reading can be turned to advantage in the domain of philology, which demands of its practitioners a detailed attention to the morphological structures of the words on the page. Pound could also recommend slow reading to other people as a means of appreciating his own intricately allusive and polyglot poems, which (he told Thomas Hardy in 1921) need to be 'read as carefully as . . . a difficult latin or greek text' (Hutchins 1968: 100). But slow reading is a major problem if you desire, as Pound did when he was a student, to take the whole of European literature as your province; for, as Francis Bacon remarked, 'If a Man . . . Reade litle, he had need have much Cunning, to seeme to know that, he doth not' ('Of Studies'). Pound's solution to this problem was to define literature by and large as poetry, thus minimising the importance of time-consuming novels. 'I never did like NOVELS just as such', he told Ford (Carpenter 1988: 111), and when interviewed in 1959 he remembered how glad he had been to come upon 'a short book that saved [him] the trouble of reading Melville' (Bridson 1961: 163). With notable exceptions like his 1918 essay on Henry James (*LE* 295–338), the six months spent on which he slightly resented (*L* 191), the bulk of Pound's literary criticism concerns poetry, and is symptomatic of that nineteenth-century ideology which privileges poetry as the quintessence of literariness (*Imagisme*, as theorised by Pound, was to be the quintessence of that quintessence). After redefining literature as poetry, Pound reduced poetry metonymically to a few poets, each of whom could be represented metonymically by a few poems. While doing this in his native language, he repeated the operation in other languages. Not knowing other languages thoroughly was a problem, of course, but not an insuperable one, given Pound's claim that all you need to know are 'the few hundred words in the few really good poems that any language has in it' (*L* 145; cp. *LE* 37). On the basis of such practices Pound proceeded to draw up his lists of canonical authors in a variety of languages, assuring any reader who might be daunted by the omniscience-effect produced by such lists that one could get away with 'knowing thirty or forty pages of each (in some cases less)', thus activating suspicions that that may have been about the extent of his own knowledge of them too (Pound 1923: 152). Against a current academic conception of literary expertise as the product of years of specialised study, Pound set up the rival claim that the sort of literary knowledge which counts can be obtained relatively swiftly and painlessly. What you need is the right sort of guidance (which his various primers would provide) plus a close acquaintance with a manageable amount of representative material – the literary equivalent, in fact, of 'a picture-gallery containing a few paintings by the greatest masters' (*SP* 298). If you were willing to put in 'an odd half-hour or so with Bion, the troubadours, and French poetry between 1880 and 1910' (ibid.) you could pick up what you needed to know about poetic metre. 'With one day's reading a man may have the key in his hands', we read in Canto 74; and the key may be that single volume of Italian state papers in which, Malcolm Cowley was told in 1923, Pound had discovered 'the lowdown on the Elizabethan drama' (Cowley 1951: 120). Slow reading could be compensated for, in other words, by knowing a few things well.

In *How To Read* Pound is critical of 'flamboyant advertisements telling "how to seem to know it when you don't" ' (*LE* 15), and tries to establish a distance between his own primer and the kind of cribs parodied in the Bluffer's Guide series (Partridge Green: Ravette). *How To Read* is designed for people who 'haven't had time for systematized college courses': it moves from writing as a technique to reading as a technology, ostensibly to enable 'low-brow' readers 'to read fewer [books] with greater result' (*LE* 16). Inherited as a pedagogic practice from medieval times – Pound noted in 1910 that candidates for the degree of Doctor of Laws or Medicine in those days were required to know only 'four to six books' well (*SR* vii) – it replicated the methods of *Imagisme* by substituting the well-read passage for the well-wrought fragment. For, if you adhere to the *Imagiste* doctrine that 'it is better to present one Image in a lifetime than to produce voluminous works' (*LE* 4), then the close reading of a few texts will come to seem preferable to a casual acquaintance with many. For as long as students continue to have too many claims on their time, academic and otherwise, the prospect of reading fewer books than are required is always going to be attractive. So when Pound writes (apropos of a couple of long poems in Renaissance Latin, one on chess and the other on the immortality of the soul) that 'Life is perhaps too short to read either poem in its entirety' (*SR* 249), he is in even less danger of being challenged by his principal readership than F.R. Leavis was when he wrote that 'life isn't long enough to permit of one's giving much time to Fielding or any at all to Mr. [J.B.] Priestley' (Leavis 1948: 3). Close reading, as a critical practice which deals with wholes by focusing on symptomatic parts (on the grounds that once you have learnt to read the part you will go on to read the whole with discrimination), is similarly vulnerable to misappropriation by busy people who are only too glad to take the part as a substitute for the whole. Nevertheless, what *How To Read* teaches is that reading a few good books is better than reading none at all, or 'reading some ignorant or half-educated ape's theories about 'em', which is what he wrongly accused 'Richards, Leavis and Co.' of doing (Pound 1933: 551).

In the domain of literary criticism, slow reading is a problem only to those who are scrupulous enough to believe that they ought to read something in its entirety before passing judgement on it. When Pound left the academy and became a metropolitan critic he found himself among journalists and publishers who were severely constrained by deadlines, and who took whatever shortcuts were available in order to make a living out of writing. The literary editor of the *Westminster Gazette*, Naomi Royde-Smith, astonished Eliot (another self-confessed slow reader) by telling him in 1916 that 'she could read and review *six* novels in an evening', and encouraged him to do likewise (Eliot 1988: 149). By 1918 Eliot had developed the 'knack of acquiring superficial information at short notice', and was regarded by those who attended his adult education lectures as 'a prodigy of information' (ibid.: 219). Omniscience-effects which were successful in the lecture-hall worked equally well, he discovered, on the pages of sophisticated literary journals. The trick was to exercise 'a certain cunning in avoiding direct bluff', he told Aldington in 1921, by which time, incidentally, he had just completed an essay on 'The Metaphysical Poets' which was to dominate English literary studies for the next forty years. He got away with it, he said, by 'dealing chiefly with what I *do* know', and 'only hinting at my pretended knowledge of what I don't know' (ibid.: 469). As an experienced faker of erudition, Eliot was able to write his own scholarly notes on *The Waste Land* before dismissing them eventually as 'bogus scholarship' (Eliot 1957: 109).

In London Pound worked for editors like Orage of the *New Age* and Ford of the *English Review*. Orage declared in 1915 that, 'read properly, fewer books than a hundred would suffice for a liberal education' (Orage 1974: 66); Ford, not to be outdone, claimed to get by with reading hardly anything at all. In 1909 Ford published in his *English Review* a short story called 'Odour of Chrysanthemums' by an unknown writer, D.H. Lawrence, apparently after reading no more than its first paragraph. Years later, Ford produced a sentence-by-sentence analysis of that paragraph, ostensibly to show by close reading just how good it was, but in fact to remind everybody of the inscrutable brilliance of his own literary judgement, which had been mobilised immediately and unerringly on first encountering Lawrence's story without having to go through the pedestrian processes of a detailed justification (Ford 1937: 97–8). Here was evidence of that 'inevitable swiftness and rightness' which Pound later identified as the operation of genius (*GK* 105–6). He had once appalled Williams by saying it was 'not necessary to read everything in a book in order to speak intelligently of it' (Williams, W.C. 1919: 5); but Ford's alleged editorial practice and the indubitably high quality of the *English Review* under his editorship indicated to Pound that his own instinct in this matter was right. He may not have been alert, of course, to the specifically English affectation of gentlemanly effortlessness revealed in Ford's account of how he picked the winners, nor to its pedigree in the *obiter dicta* of wits like Sydney Smith, who said he 'never read a book before reviewing it' because 'it prejudices a man so' (Pearson 1934: 54). But the Ford anecdote was almost certainly in Pound's mind when he told Harriet Monroe that if he himself were an editor he would probably publish D.H. Lawrence's work 'without reading it' (*L* 59).

By the 1930s Pound's confidence was such that he was willing to accept a commission to write on Robert Bridges for the *Criterion* provided he would 'not necessarily [have to] read the ole petrifaction' (Gallup 1970: 78). Why persevere with Leavis's *How To Teach Reading* if you believe it unnecessary 'to eat the whole of a rotten egg to know that it [is] bad'? (Carpenter 1988: 469). Such attitudes left him in no position to complain, therefore, when he himself was written off by people who couldn't be bothered to read him, like Virginia Woolf, who said her 'conviction of his humbug' was 'unalterable', despite the fact that she had not 'read more than 10 words by Ezra Pound' (Raffel 1985: 89). How many words of hers did Pound read, I wonder, before dismissing in 1934 'the weak minded Woolf female' (Carpenter 1988: 244)? But this sort of thing was only part of the rough trade he became expert in when, with a prematurely terminated academic career behind him, he tried to make a living in London as a metropolitan critic.

2

The metropolitan critic

The republication of Pound's most celebrated poem, *Hugh Selwyn Mauberley* (1920), in the first 'collected' edition of his poems to be published in America, *Personae* (1926), is prefaced by an ironical warning directed at unwary natives: 'The sequence is so distinctly a farewell to London that the reader who chooses to regard this as an exclusively American edition may as well omit it' (*P* 185). By means of a couple of *personae*, 'E.P.' and 'Hugh Selwyn Mauberley', the poem represents various aspects of literary life in late Edwardian and early Georgian London as Pound experienced it between his arrival there in 1908 from Venice and his departure for Paris at the end of 1920. It is a fairly bizarre world, which still has vivid memories of 'decadent' excesses in the 1890s, a world of penurious stylists and conspicuously successful bookmen, of Nietzschean hot gospellers and apostate Jews, and titled female culture vultures at whose literary salons British class distinctions are momentarily suspended and sexual opportunities appear to abound. This is the corrupt and cultivated world entered by an American innocent abroad, who is figured on the one hand as 'E.P.', a pragmatic sort of person fully aware of his own historicity and working in unpropitious conditions at nothing less than a literary renascence, and on the other hand as 'Mauberley', who tries to act out some twenty years after the event a sort of parodic version of a nineties aesthete, politically indifferent to what's going on all around him as he cultivates a life of exquisite sensations. The poem chronicles a failure 'to resuscitate the dead art / Of poetry' (*P* 187), and invites speculation as to whether this is to be attributed to some personal failings in a poet who is both 'E.P.' and 'Mauberley', or to the irresistible pressures of historical circumstances which, as the poem appears to claim in a section on the

Pre-Raphaelites, had succeeded in stifling all attempted revivals of the art of poetry since the middle of the nineteenth century.

If 'Near Perigord' is a scholarship-poem, *Hugh Selwyn Mauberley* is a history-poem, or more specifically a literary-history-poem, in so far as it tries to preempt historical reconstructions of its genealogy by thematising and incorporating a version of that history into its own formation. In this way literary history is turned into a myth whose function is to align readers of the poem with its own point of view so that they will read it not as a work of fiction but as literary history. And, seeing that *Hugh Selwyn Mauberley* has many admirers, its own version of what happened is easily read as an account of what in fact went on in the period it talks about, and thus it becomes part of the evidence in a construction of the modern era as the Pound era. For, according to the myth which masquerades as literary history in *Hugh Selwyn Mauberley*, Pound and his associates were dedicated artists who refused to compromise their standards by capitulating to what the age demanded. By holding out against a publishing world corrupted by nepotism, old-boy networks and a profiteering mentality, they were martyred for their artistic integrity, and condemned either to live in poverty or to produce writing of a commercially viable mediocrity. Sources outside the poem, however, demythologise it by representing Pound and his associates as being far from merely passive victims. Careerists themselves and professionally jealous of their own reputations, as is indicated by their intermittent alliances and breaks with one another, they made use of commercial publishers wherever possible, ran alternative presses and magazines, and built up networks of their own which were as ruthlessly self-serving as anything operated by that publishing establishment they saw themselves as up against.

Back home in Philadelphia, where Homer Pound doubled as doting father and unpaid press agent for his *wunderkind*, myths could pass for realities, as they did on 26 March 1914, when the *Philadelphia Press* informed its readers that 'Ezra Pound is a young man who went from Wyncote to England and there wrote poems of so much merit that he gained a special place in the highest literary circles' (Stock 1976: 82). But the meritocratic illusion that the Wyncote boy had made it in literary London by self-evident excellence alone was far removed from the realities of the reputation-mongering which went on there, where the right contacts could work wonders, and those who controlled the literary pages of the principal journals determined what got reviewed and whether it was received favourably or otherwise. 'Merit', it appeared, was not something internal to poetry as opal is to rocks, self-evidently there to anybody who took the trouble to look. On the contrary, merit was in the eye of the beholder: it was the product, in other words, not of literary texts but of the discourse which circulates about them, which is literary criticism. To get hold of the means of production of that discourse – as a reviewer, *faute de mieux*, but preferably as an editor or publisher – was a more urgent task therefore than writing any number of poems whose merits would never be noticed until a revolution in critical discourse had been achieved. For only in that way would it be possible for Pound to create the taste for his own poetry and other writing he approved of.

Pound aimed at occupying as much of the available discursive space as possible for himself and the writers he identified as modernist. Criticism became an enabling activity on a far grander scale than he had imagined in the days when he thought of it as an optional and in any case self-consuming prolegomenon to 'creative' work of one's own. From about 1912 onwards, which was the year in which, he recalled in 1920, he 'abandoned [his] own work for criticism' (Henderson 1984: 281), he not only produced a body of poetry and poetic theory which is of central importance in the history of Anglo-American modernism as it is understood at present, but also invented ways of talking about the modernist movement in literature which are so much part and parcel of our conception of it that it is only within the last decade or so that other discursive possibilities have been explored. What Pound saw in retrospect as a necessary though temporary abandonment of his real work as a 'poet' – which was the 'rank or profession' he declared on his marriage certificate in April 1914 (Ackroyd 1980: 35) – gave him time to develop and implement a style of critical discourse of such originality that René Wellek ranks him with T.E. Hulme and Wyndham Lewis as one of only three innovators in the history of English criticism in the first half of this century (Wellek 1986: 144). The belatedness of that recognition is yet one more testimony to the power of those myths which Pound himself promulgated in determining both literary history and critical history. It is principally because Pound has presented himself as a poet rather than a critic, a poet-critic who (as the designation suggests) is a poet first and only secondly a critic, that he has figured more prominently in histories of modern poetry than in histories of modern criticism. The material circumstances of his operation as a literary critic in London during the decade marked by the First World War are therefore worth investigating.

In the subtitle to *Hugh Selwyn Mauberley* (1920) Pound acknowledged the real foundations of a literary career when he rewrote the formula used by belletristic biographers, 'life and letters', as 'life and contacts'. The point was not taken, however, by the editor of the *New Statesman*, Desmond MacCarthy, when he resigned from that journal to found and edit in 1928 a literary monthly called *Life and Letters*. Pound had discovered the importance of contacts, it appears, long before arriving in London. As a boy in Wyncote, Pennsylvania, he was friendly with Hawley Chester, whose father was the minister at the local Calvary Presbyterian church. Carlos Tracy Chester became co-editor of the Philadelphia *Book News Monthly*, which in September 1906 printed Pound's first published essay (the one on 'Raphaelite Latin', with its side-swipe at Germanic scholarship) and another half-dozen essays and poems between then and August 1909, by which time Pound had gained access to Ford Madox Ford's *English Review* in London. And, although the *Book News Monthly* had reservations about the bookishness of the poems in Pound's *A Lume Spento* (1908), which it reviewed in May 1909 (*CH* 42), it would probably have ignored them altogether (as other journals did) if Pound had not been known already as a contributor. Pound dedicated *Exultations* (1909) to Chester, 'amicitiae longaevitate', and preserved the dedication in selections from that volume reprinted in *Provença* (1910) and *Umbra* (1920). The Presbyterian contact proved valuable also in Venice, where the minister there, Dr Alex Robertson (a friend of the family), recommended him to the man who printed *A Lume Spento* in July 1908.

Pound arrived in London on 27 August 1908 with copies of that book and 'with £3 knowing no one' (Pound 1913a: 707). A family friend and travel agent in Philadelphia had given him a contact at the London Polytechnic, which didn't offer him as he had hoped the position vacated by the death of another crusader for 'literature' as against 'philology', John Churton Collins, or even any lecturing in the Michaelmas term of that year. They agreed, however, to hire him to give half a dozen lectures in the first two months of 1909 on the development of literature in southern

Europe; and those were followed by a full course of lectures on the same topic in September that year, out of which Pound put together his first critical book, *The Spirit of Romance* (1910).

In literary London potential contacts congregated in a variety of places: pubs and restaurants, bookshops, the satellite teashops of the British Museum (Pound got his permanent reader's ticket on 8 October 1908), the private flats and houses of writers, and the more lavishly appointed homes of upper-class people who were interested in the arts for a variety of reasons. Some writers held open-house 'evenings' at which solidarity could be reaffirmed, and opportunities offered to hear shop-talk, gossip and the occasional reading. Yeats, for instance, had his 'Mondays' when he was in London, and Pound followed in 1912 with his 'Tuesdays'; Thursdays seem to have been reserved for meetings of T.E. Hulme's group, which is where Pound met the editor of the *New Age*, A.R. Orage, who offered him a column in his paper and was to become the principal source of Pound's income as a literary journalist during his London years, and again in the 1930s, when Orage edited a Social Credit journal called the *New English Weekly*. Each group of writers would meet at a regular time in a particular restaurant with a modestly priced menu. Pound made his debut with the Hulme group at the Tour Eiffel Restaurant on 22 April 1909, where he read his 'Sestina: Altaforte' so energetically that one of those present, F.S. Flint, remembered how 'the decanters and cutlery vibrated in resonance with his voice' (*CH* 97). Pound and his friends would meet at Bellotti's Ristorante Italiano, that 'moderate chop-house' (discovered by the editor of *Poetry and Drama*, Harold Monro) which is referred to obliquely in Pound's poem 'Amities' and directly in 'Black Slippers: Bellotti' (*P* 101, 111).

As for the female socialites with 'artistic' interests, they had their ritual round of luncheons (prized as occasions when you could 'meet them without meeting their husbands' (*PM* 36)), as well as afternoon teas, dinners and weekends, at which high-ranking civil servants, politicians, members of the aristocracy and people from various professions were likely to be present as well as publishers, editors and other artists. This is the Edwardian and pre-war world evoked in the memoirs of a woman blessed in *Blast* (1914), Mrs Belloc Lowndes. *The Merry Wives of Westminster* (London, 1946) presents 'a world as exotic as that of the Andaman Islanders', in the words of Donald Davie, who first drew attention to its usefulness as a means of reconstructing the social milieu in which Pound tried to establish himself as a London bookman (Davie 1980: 103). A few of the *habitués* of such circles, like Edward Marsh, whom Pound first met at one of Hulme's gatherings in 1912, moved effortlessly between their professional duties and literary pleasures. Marsh was the patron of a whole group of 'Georgian' poets and editor of those volumes of *Georgian Poetry* published between 1911 and 1922 which Eliot called an 'annual scourge' (Eliot 1918: 69); but he was also a first-rate civil servant who occupied such positions as private secretary to Winston Churchill and assistant private secretary to the prime minister in the Asquith government. It was in some ways easier for an exotic like Pound to move in that social sphere than it was for a working-class midlander like D.H. Lawrence: the pair of them met at Violet Hunt's house in November 1909, after which Lawrence told his current girl-friend, Loue Burrows, that Pound knew 'W.B. Yeats & all the Swells' (*CH* 38). At the home of Lord and Lady Glenconner Pound gave three lectures in March 1912 on Cavalcanti, Arnaut Daniel and Anglo-Saxon poetry (*EP/DS* 89); there Pound met the woman who had sold the tickets, Lady Low, for whom he gave a lecture at her Kensington home in March 1913 on the strophe and recent developments in French poetry. For this privilege the swells each paid 7s 6d, the cash value of which can be calculated from the fact that when Ezra and Dorothy Pound honeymooned at Stone Cottage a year later they expected to have to pay no more than 10s 0d per week for a housekeeper who could cook (*EP/DS* 313).

Contacts like Edward Marsh could be even more useful than the swells when it came to cutting red tape. Marsh was a regular visitor at literary gatherings organised by Lady Maud Cunard, whose husband was a shipping magnate. In 1916 she was living in a house owned by the prime minister, Asquith, and was a friend and patron of Yeats, who had a government pension and was convinced by Pound that Joyce ought to have one too. Instead of delaying matters with a formal application, Yeats asked Lady Cunard to persuade Marsh to get Asquith to use his discretionary powers as prime minister to award Joyce £100; which he did to the delight of Joyce, who called Pound 'a wonder worker' (*EP/JJ* 80). Writers apparently not *echt* Britons were similarly grateful that they had high-ranking contacts when war broke out in August 1914. When Ford (whose surname at this time was still Hueffer) received an official request from the Chief Constable of West

Sussex to leave the county, presumably on the grounds that with a name like that he couldn't be relied upon not to collaborate with the Germans in the event of an invasion, he got in touch with a cabinet minister he played golf and holidayed with, Charles Masterman, whose wartime job was to counter German propaganda in the USA, and the relocation order was cancelled (Mizener 1985: 250–1); a grateful Ford wrote a couple of propaganda books in 1915 for Masterman's department, *When Blood Is Their Argument* and *Between St. Dennis and St. George*. A year later Pound was in similar trouble. Indifferent to a war which he thought 'possibly a conflict between two forces almost equally detestable' (*L* 88), Pound had never bothered to register as an alien. Early in 1916 the authorities caught up with him at Coleman's Hatch, and told him to report regularly to the local police-station, since whenever he worked as Yeats's secretary at Stone Cottage he and Dorothy (American now by marriage) were technically unregistered 'aliens in [a] prohibited area' (Canto 83). Yeats appealed to the poet laureate, Robert Bridges, to intervene, but the letter he wrote was apparently useless; so Pound, on Ford's advice, contacted Masterman, and the police harassment ceased (Carpenter 1988: 255; Tytell 1987: 128).

Pound knew nobody in London when he arrived there from Venice 'hungry . . . for "interesting people" ' (Pound 1913a: 707), but by the time he left he had met just about everybody in literary circles except those who were determined to avoid him, like Virginia Woolf, who in 1923 told the most famous literary hostess of this period, Lady Ottoline Morrell, that she'd 'never seen him' (Raffel 1985: 96). Upper-class hostesses were thought to be worth cultivating because of their alleged influence on middle-class editors of the reviewing journals, whose snobbery made them vulnerable to exploitation. When Eliot expressed pleasure that the poems he had contributed to Pound's *Catholic Anthology* (1915) had been well received by the *Nation* reviewer, Bertrand Russell said it was probably because the editor of that journal, H.W. Massingham, had been leaned on by Lady Ottoline Morrell, whose husband was the Liberal MP for South Oxfordshire (Eliot 1988: 149–50). Pound had already advised Eliot in the summer of 1915 that if he wanted to break into London literary journalism he ought 'to secure introductions to editors from people of better social position than themselves' (ibid.: 104). At this stage in their relationship Eliot was not at all impressed by Pound as a poet: 'his verse is well-meaning', he had told Conrad Aiken in September 1914, 'but touchingly incompetent' (ibid.: 59). As a tactician, however, Pound struck Eliot as being 'shrewd', and so he wrote to his brother in July 1915 asking him to get a well-known Boston hostess and admirer of his work, Mrs Isabella Gardner, to persuade the editor of the Boston *Atlantic Monthly*, Ellery Sedgwick, to appoint Eliot as British correspondent to the journal. Sedgwick was likely to agree to this, Eliot had been led by Pound to believe, in order to spite Pound ('whom he hates'), never suspecting that very shortly Eliot would be in cahoots with Pound in their London-based campaign against editors like Sedgwick. The fact that nothing came of this Machiavellian manoeuvre is neither here nor there. What is interesting is that Pound seems to have believed that this was how to infiltrate the corridors of power, and that Eliot was sufficiently persuaded by it all to ask his brother in Boston to set about making the necessary contacts there, one of whom, incidentally, was to have been Amy Lowell (ibid.: 108), who had already clashed with Pound over the ownership of *Imagisme*.

Literary studies as taught to undergraduates at Penn and Hamilton when Pound was a student there fostered the suspicion common in people who are educated outside the old imperial centres that literature is something which was created overseas a long time ago. As a freshman at Penn, Pound made friends with the tubercular William Brooke Smith, to whom *A Lume Spento* (1908) is dedicated *in memoriam*. Brooke Smith had given Pound a copy of Oscar Wilde's *Salomé* (1894) illustrated by Aubrey Beardsley, and stimulated his interest in various British poets of the 1890s whose works he read as a sophomore to the detriment of those studies in which he was formally enrolled. In 1906–7, however, as a postgraduate at Penn, Pound took Cornelius Weygandt's course in contemporary poetry, and was required to read what he would probably have read anyway, including poems by Laurence Binyon, John Davidson, W.E. Henley, both Housmans, Kipling, Newbolt, Arthur Symons, Lionel Johnson and Yeats (Leigh 1986: 144–5). He read them not merely in aestheticist terms as arrangements of words on pages but also as traces of presences he yearned to encounter. And so when he finally got to London in 1908 he made a point of meeting as many of the older poets as he could, and relished anecdotes about the celebrated dead from people who had known them. Some of the anecdotes told about a particular author were comically at odds with that person's most celebrated poems – 'Shelley sliding down his front bannisters', for instance, ' "with almost incredible rapidity" ' (Pound 1913a: 707).

Mere entertainment, however, was not all that Pound was after in his vicarious meetings with 'Victorians and Pre-Raphaelites and men of the nineties through their friends', the purpose of which was to enable him to 'come in touch with the tradition of the dead' (ibid.). With slight embarrassment he explained that 'people whose minds have been enriched by men of genius retain the effects of it' by a 'sort of Apostolic Succession' (ibid.). The aura was discernible in sacred objects, like Rossetti's own copy of *La Vita Nuova*, which Pound had in his possession, or Rossetti's brown velvet coat, which Ford wore at the time when he was editing the *English Review*. It also surrounded sacred places, like Stone Cottage in Sussex, in which Milton had once lived (*L* 66): and in his poem 'Moeurs Contemporaines' Pound records an apostolic meeting with 'a very old lady' who told him, 'Shelley used to live in this house' (*P* 182). But people were more evocative than objects or places, which is why he tried to meet great writers and those close to them. 'Swinburne my only miss', Pound recollected in Canto 82 (Swinburne died in April 1909). 'The conception of poetry as a "pure art" . . . revived with Swinburne', Pound wrote (*LE* 11), and therefore to have experienced Swinburne's mana at first hand would have been especially important to Pound, given his professed aim 'to resuscitate the dead art / Of poetry' (*P* 187). But that was not all: 'I didn't know', Canto 82 continues, 'that he'd been to see Landor.' Pound's meeting with W.S. Blunt, however, gave him the sense, in the words of Canto 81, of having 'gathered from the air a live tradition'. Sunday evenings Pound spent with Victor Plarr (the 'Monsieur Verog' of *Hugh Selwyn Mauberley*), gleaning anecdotes about the nineties poets, some of which are preserved in that poem as one of its more striking examples of mythopoeia masquerading as literary history. Consequently, Pound was at the mercy of those who would tell him what they believed he wanted to hear. Ford, for instance, who had in fact known the Rossettis as a child, and was currently involved with Violet Hunt, the daughter of the Pre-Raphaelite painter Holman Hunt, had a wonderfully inventive memory for this sort of thing, and given enough encouragement would readily tell anybody about the time he met Byron (Aldington 1968: 137).

One of the locations where remembrance of things past

coincided with possibilities of things to come was the London bookshop in Vigo Street owned by Elkin Mathews. Here Pound could browse through volumes of the most recently published poetry and meet not only indigent poets doing the same thing but also established writers and well-heeled book-buyers interested in meeting new talent. As the man who had published *The Yellow Book* with John Lane in the 1890s, Mathews had apostolic connections with that 'tragic generation' of poets, as Yeats was to describe it in a mythopoeic evocation of the period in his *Autobiographies* (London, 1955). And, as a publisher himself, Mathews was persuaded to add Pound to his list: consequently, he published *A Quinzaine for This Yule* in December 1908, *Personae* in April and *Exultations* in October 1909, *Canzoni* in July 1911, *Cathay* in April 1915, and (as a result of anxieties about 'indecencies') what Pound was to call a '*castrato*' edition (*L* 133) of *Lustra* in October 1916 after issuing the unabridged text in a limited edition a few weeks previously. Mathews also published in June 1920, a few months before Pound left London to settle first in Paris and eventually in Rapallo, a culling of his early poems under the title *Umbra*.

It was through Mathews that Pound met Ernest Rhys, a survivor from the nineties who edited the Everyman's Library series for Dent, and who persuaded Dent to publish *The Spirit of Romance* in June 1910. Rhys introduced Pound to the novelist May Sinclair, who introduced him in turn to another novelist, Violet Hunt, through whom he met her most recent lover, Ford Madox Ford, who as editor of the *English Review* published a few of Pound's poems, beginning in June 1909 with 'Sestina: Altaforte'. In theory, 'Apostolic Succession' was a spiritualistic affair, the sort of thing Yeats might have been interested in, and not unrelated to that doctrine of metempsychosis evoked in an uncollected poem of Pound's called 'Histrion', with its claim that 'the souls of all men great / At times pass through us' (*CEP* 71). As a system of symbolic exchange, however, it was always potentially erotic, and among predatory males of the period hem-touching and skirt-lifting could be metonymic of one another. Coventry Patmore's grandson was a far less exciting contact than his estranged wife, the beautiful Brigit Patmore, whom Pound met at 'Immodest' Violet Hunt's house with her lover, the twenty-year-old Richard Aldington. Pound dedicated *Lustra* (1916) to Brigit Patmore (whose Christian name was in fact Ethel) under the Provençal pseudonym 'Vail de Lencour', an act which prompted speculation about his own secret relationship as would-be troubadour with that married lady. He also introduced Aldington to Hilda Doolittle, who, renamed as a romance heroine 'Is-hilda' or 'Ysolt', had been the recipient of a number of love-poems written by Pound and collected as 'Hilda's Book' in the period when he was a postgraduate at Penn and she a drop-out from Bryn Mawr (H.D. 1980: 67–84). Doolittle had assumed when she arrived in London towards the end of 1911 that she was engaged to be married to Pound. But Walter Rummel, a concert pianist who was collaborating with Pound in an adaptation of Provençal poems for voice and piano published subsequently as *Hesternae Rosae* (London, 1913), told her that in fact Pound was now secretly engaged to Dorothy Shakespear. Doolittle married Aldington after their kinship as *Imagistes* had been established by Pound.

And how did Pound come to meet Dorothy Shakespear? Indirectly, through Mathews, who introduced him early in January 1909 to an Australian expatriate poet, James Griffyth Fairfax, author of *The Gates of Sleep* (London, 1906) and *Poems* (London, 1908). Fairfax in turn introduced Pound almost immediately to another Australian expatriate writer from Sydney, Frederic Manning, whose family had sent him to England to be educated under the direction of a clergyman friend of the Shakespear family, Arthur Galton. Manning lived with Galton: when Pound met him in 1909 Galton turned out to be a cornucopia of apostolic lore, and certainly gave the impression (Pound told his mother) of knowing 'everyone since the flood' (Marwil 1988: 23). The year Pound was born, Galton's belletristic studies of Tennyson, Browning, Arnold, Swinburne and Morris were published as *Urbana Scripta* (London, 1885), that 'rather rare book of criticism' Pound was to quote from but not name in a 1917 essay on Landor's *Imaginary Conversations* (*SP* 356). It was with Manning that Pound developed his 'first licherary ComPanionship' in England (Marwil 1983: 15), which resulted in his 'measured praise' of the 'thinking intelligence' manifested in Manning's narrative poem, *The Vigil of Brunhild* (London, 1907), when reviewing it in *Book News Monthly* (Pound 1909: 61). And he used his recent and socially acquired acquaintance with Ford to get Manning's poem 'Persephone' (called subsequently 'Korè') into the December 1909 issue of the *English Review*, which was also to publish Pound's 'answer' to that poem, 'Canzon: The Yearly Slain' (*CEP* 133–4), in January 1910. Pound was at this time immensely impressed also by a book of imaginary conversations Manning was completing, 'a stupendous work', he told his mother in March 1909 (Marwil 1988: 119), which was published as *Scenes and Portraits* (London, 1909). Fairfax took Pound along to a literary gathering at the home of a Knightsbridge (subsequently Mayfair) hostess, Eva Fowler, whose husband manufactured steam ploughs and told that anecdote about the difficulty he'd had transporting them to Abyssinia which is reported at the end of Canto 18. It was at Eva Fowler's late in January 1909 that Pound met 'the most charming woman in London' (Carpenter 1988: 103), Olivia Shakespear, a solicitor's wife who had had an affair in 1896 with the very man Pound most wanted to meet, W.B. Yeats.

Pound was quite a charmer himself, of course, 'always awfully nice', according to Harriet Shaw Weaver (Hutchins 1965: 23), who knew him in connection with the *New Freewoman* (later renamed the *Egoist*), which she supported financially. Joseph Conrad, sixty-one years old and less than happily married, told his American patron John Quinn that Pound had 'many women at his feet', adding wistfully, 'which must be immensely comforting' (Reid 1968: 340). What Hugh Kenner discreetly calls Pound's 'susceptibility' to women ('and theirs to him') was an enduring characteristic of his relations with them, professional or otherwise (Kenner 1971: 266). So it is not surprising that the most charming woman in London should have invited Pound to her Kensington home on a number of occasions at which he met various men of letters who might be expected to entertain him with literary anecdotes or forward his own career as a London bookman. 'I *do* see nearly everyone that matters', Pound was to tell Harriet Monroe when offering his services as London correspondent for a magazine called *Poetry* which she was about to found and edit in Chicago (*L* 44). Among the people Pound met at Olivia Shakespear's was the nineties poet and former editor of the *Savoy*, Arthur Symons, whose book on *The Symbolist Movement in Literature* (London, 1899) is dedicated to Yeats. It also contains a chapter on the poetry of Jules Laforgue which stimulated T.S. Eliot's interest in that writer and thus became part of the genealogy of 'The Love Song of J. Alfred Prufrock', described by Pound as 'the most interesting contribution... had from an American' when sending it to Monroe in October 1914 for publication in *Poetry* (*L* 81).

But the most regular presence at those Shakespear gatherings, apart from Olivia herself, was her daughter Dorothy, in whom Frederic Manning may have been romantically interested for some time before she met Pound. Five years later, in April 1914, Pound and Dorothy Shakespear were married. 'I believe he is in love with her', Manning told Galton, 'but at the same time he is very practical' (Hergenhan 1984: 398). Through Olivia Shakespear the long-awaited meeting took place with Yeats, who was persuaded eventually that he needed Pound as his secretary as well as his mentor and friend. When Pound returned to America for a visit in June 1910 he took with him an invitation to look up Yeats's father, the painter John Butler Yeats, in New York; which he did, and in August that year he met through Yeats *père* the American lawyer and art-collector John Quinn, who became in 1915 the principal patron of those modernist writers and artists for whom Pound acted as an unpaid impresario. That arrangement was fixed up within a year of Pound's marriage to Dorothy Shakespear, whose cousin and close friend, Georgie Hyde-Lees, was to marry W.B. Yeats in October 1917, four or five months after Pound had introduced a selection (made with the assistance of Yeats *fils*) of *Passages from the Letters of John Butler Yeats*. Printed by Elizabeth Corbet Yeats at the Cuala Press in County Dublin, Pound's contribution to this book (first proposed by W.B. Yeats in 1913) was a *quid pro quo* following Yeats's agreement to write the introduction to Pound's Fenollosa-based versions of Japanese Noh plays, published by the same press in September 1916 as *Certain Noble Plays of Japan* (Reid 1968: 242). It is to Pound's credit that he declined to prepare a further selection of the letters of Yeats *père* following his discovery that their author had taken lately to composing 'publishable' letters (ibid.: 292).

Even a brief sketch like this of who met whom, through whose agency, and with what consequences, indicates that a full-length study of the social micro-networks in which literary criticism was produced in England in the early years of this century would reveal the hidden imbrication of critical predilections with socio-sexual opportunism. Within weeks of arriving in London Pound had come to understand something of the social pressures under which so-called 'literary' judgements are made, and the importance (as he phrased it in a letter written to his father in March 1909) of 'being in the gang & being known by the right people' (Carpenter 1988: 107). The point of making friends with 'the two hundred most interesting people' in England, he was to write a few years later, is that 'what these people say comes to pass' (*LE* 372). Having learnt how to let himself be manipulated by the right people for his own benefit, he would now strengthen his position by manipulating others in the expectation of becoming the most powerful reputation broker in London.

In 1917 Pound remembered his university teachers damning England as 'an unscholarly country' from which 'practically no authoritative books on any subject had come out... for many decades' (*SP* 168). But, if the only way of being scholarly was to undergo the teutonic regimen that passed for education in American graduate schools, it occurred to him that there was probably something to be said for the British cult of the gifted amateur. As Pound was to discover during his London years, however, amateurs fell into two categories: the admirable kind – the true *amateurs* – who were uncorrupted by the teutonic craze for specialisation which had ruined American universities, and the despicable kind who failed to take the profession of writing seriously enough. The *amateurs* were represented by an Oxford don, perhaps Sir Herbert Warren (Edwards and Vasse 1957: 177), whom Pound met in 1913, and who, when the table-talk got around to Francis Thompson's *The Hound of Heaven* (1893), casually came out with the (to Pound) devastating criticism that he 'couldn't be bothered to stop for every adjective' (*LE* 214). That don had received the kind of critical education Pound had hoped but failed to receive in America, the kind which appeared to equip its beneficiaries with unerring capacities as arbiters of taste. American conditions, Pound was convinced, could never have 'evoked that swift and profound censure, that scrap of criticism which touches the root and seed of Thompson's every defect' (*PM* 68) – and which, he might have added, happened to coincide with his own recently formulated *Imagiste* directive to 'use no superfluous word, no adjective which does not reveal something' (*LE* 4).

If the *amateur* turned out to be a rarity in Britain and not native to America, there was no shortage of amateurish pseudo-*amateurs* in either country. In Britain, where a 'letterish tradition' promoted 'worship of the bleating amateur' and 'the jolly English belief that it is better to be a duffer at several things than to do anything really well' (Pound 1932: 483; *EP/VA* 90), they were represented at their best by that Shavian beast, the Chesterbelloc. G.K. Chesterton was notorious for his Wildean rewriting of Lord Chesterfield's maxim ('Whatever is worth doing at all, is worth doing well') as 'If a thing is worth doing it is worth doing badly'; and

Hilaire Belloc (according to Ford, who told Pound) had informed the House of Commons that 'there is perhaps nothing an educated man or woman can do which requires less intelligence than the writing of books' (Tytell 1987: 92). The amateurs of Edwardian England were a particularly disarming community in Pound's eyes because their literary interests were an indication of a civilised way of life which refugees from that 'half-savage country', America (*P* 187), crossed the Atlantic to find. The 'young American pilgrim' evoked in Pound's poem 'Moeurs Contemporaines' (1918) is reduced to verbal gaucherie on encountering in London a family in which both parents 'wrote verses', 'the youngest son was in a publisher's office', and 'the friend of the second daughter was undergoing a novel' (*P* 179).

If England was 'a country in love with amateurs', as Pound claimed in a 1914 review of Ford's collected poems, then it was equally a place in which 'the incompetent have such beautiful manners, and personalities so fragile and charming, that one cannot bear to injure their feelings by the introduction of competent criticism' (*LE* 371). The amateurs who controlled the British publishing houses and literary journals, and engaged in belletristic pursuits as men of letters, saw their authority as emanating from their membership of the ruling class to which they belonged, and not from any professionally acquired skills. This gave them the confidence to treat universities as places to pass through rather than as bases to write from, and to subordinate the nurture acquired by learning to the nature conferred by birth. The social code which valorised agreeableness was at odds with the critical code which insisted that sometimes the truth can be unpleasant. Pound certainly felt the strain of trying to professionalise criticism in an environment in which publishing was considered an occupation for gentlemen and writing the prerogative of gifted amateurs, who had never learnt that 'poetry is an art and not a pastime' (*LE* 10) and did not like to be told so, especially not in print. Their most effective form of retaliation was not critical counterattack, which a combative critic like Pound could always handle, but social ostracism, which in that milieu could be devastating: 'it hits me in my dinner invitations, in my weekends', he told Monroe in October 1912, before adding cheerfully: 'Nevertheless it's a good fight' (*L* 47).

As an evaluative critic who aspired to weigh Theocritus and Yeats in the one balance, Pound would have preferred to sever texts from their authors and judge all writing by criteria designed to sift the durable from the transient. But in a world in which publishing was a function of fashionable society – 'a capital where everybody's Aunt Lucy or Uncle George has written something or other' (*LE* 371), and 'a poem Aunt Hepsy liked' was likely to get printed by her sympathetic nephew in the publishing business (ibid.: 17) – the application of rigorous critical standards to the writings of acquaintances or friends and relatives of acquaintances amounted to a breach of social decorum, a violation of the tacit code that charming people who break into print should be treated nicely. Lacking either the inclination or the ability to produce in such circumstances what Henry James had called 'the mere twaddle of graciousness', Pound discovered it was 'impossible to talk about perfection without getting yourself very much disliked' (ibid.: 371). He was caught in a double-bind: if he talked about 'perfection' in that sense he would be excluded from the charmed circle as an uncouth outsider, an 'American', no less, to evoke an Edwardian term of abuse; if he did not, he would be compromised by the social set which was willing to cultivate him as an exotic, and muzzled as a critic. By behaving with what some might call integrity and others tactlessness he found himself within a few years excluded, like Hugh Selwyn Mauberley, from the London world of letters.

Before that happened, various charming men, and especially charming women, exerted pressure on him ever so insidiously to compromise those high standards of his. Concessions were inevitable if he were to have any chance of surviving as a metropolitan critic, particularly when he succeeded in marrying into the social world of literary amateurs with beautiful manners. Since the beginning of 1912 Pound had been wanting to marry Dorothy Shakespear, the daughter of Yeats's lover, Olivia Shakespear, a novelist whose solicitor husband refused to give his consent to the marriage because Pound's income was nowhere near enough to keep Dorothy in the manner to which she was accustomed as a lady of leisure. Over Christmas 1913, while acting as Yeats's secretary at Coleman's Hatch in Sussex, Pound read with Yeats a book which Alexander Pope had dipped into for lore about sylphs and salamanders when augmenting *The Rape of the Lock* in 1714: *Le Comte de Gabalis, ou entretiens sur les sciences secrètes* (Paris, 1670), by the Abbé de Montfauçon de Villars. Pound told Dorothy he baulked at the prospect of putting something so 'delicate' into 'a prophane english vulgo' (*EP/DS* 293); but he managed to get it translated by that 'charming memorial of the XVIIIth Century' (*L* 208), her mother, Olivia Shakespear (Longenbach 1986: 109–10). He arranged for her version of *Le Comte de Gabalis* to be published in five instalments of the *Egoist* from 16 March to 1 June 1914. It appeared over the initials 'M. de V.M.' instead of her own name, and under a title which sounds like a private joke: 'Memoirs of a Charming Person'. The serialisation of the Montfauçon translation took up precious space in five issues of the *Egoist* not because it had anything to do with the modernist movement in literature but because it happened to suit Pound for a couple of reasons. First, it helped firm up his relationship with Yeats, whose enthusiasm for the occult he had learned to feign an interest in, although his corrosive scepticism was not concealed from those spirits who in 1917 told Yeats's mediumistic wife, Georgie Hyde-Lees, bluntly: 'communication impossible while [Pound] is in the house' (Gould 1988: 13). Even before that first sojourn in Sussex as Yeats's secretary he had expected the great man to 'bore [him] to death with psychical research', and he told his mother that he regarded the visit as something he felt obliged to put up with as 'a duty to posterity' (*L* 63). But in fact it was more in the nature of an investment for himself, which paid off when eventually he got Yeats sufficiently on side with the new poetry to make public statements in support of it. As it was still too early to drop Yeats and lose the favourable publicity of his support, there were to be two further winters of secretarial work with Yeats in Sussex, in the course of which, posterity was to discover, the master–pupil relationship gradually shifted in Pound's favour.

The other factor which bears on the presence of the Gabalis translation in the *Egoist* points not to the careerism of Pound's public life but to the desires of his private life. Five days after the second instalment appeared, Olivia Shakespear's daughter married Pound on 20 April 1914. In his first publication as foreign editor of the *Little Review* he described 'Memoirs of a Charming Person' as 'the best translation of Le Comte de Gabalis' (Pound 1917: 5). And, although the name of the translator was not mentioned, the translation itself was shortlisted as one of four publications testifying to the high quality of recent contributions to the *Egoist*: the others were Remy de Gourmont's *The Horses of Diomedes*, Wyndham Lewis's *Tarr*, and James Joyce's *A Portrait of the Artist as a Young Man* (with which, incidentally, Olivia Shakespear's translation was serialised concurrently). Eighteen months after his marriage, Pound brought out in October 1915 an edition of the *Poetical Works of Lionel Johnson*, who was a cousin of Olivia Shakespear's, and in the introduction (dated 1914) to this volume conferred avant-garde respectability on the 1890s poet by claiming that 'no one has written purer Imagisme than he has' (*LE* 362). In the meantime, in a special Imagist number of the *Egoist* published on 1 May 1915, responsibility for surveying the poetry of D.H. Lawrence had been given to 'O. Shakespear', who showed herself *au fait* with Poundian ways of putting things when she picked out the three poems of Lawrence's she thought it would be correct to call ' "imagist," for they each contain two "images," one superimposed upon the other' (Shakespear 1915: 81). Gestures like these may not contribute much to Pound's reputation as a critic, but they no doubt helped convince Henry Hope Shakespear that his bohemian son-in-law was an influential man of letters.

It is clear that the material conditions in which criticism was produced during Pound's years as a metropolitan critic were very different from what he had envisaged as a postgraduate student, when he thought that criticism was simply a matter of arriving at a set of standards and then determining whether or not a particular piece of writing was up to scratch. The longer Pound operated as a critic, the more he came to realise that compromises and trade-offs are part and parcel of the evaluation business. For instance, not all the poems assembled in Pound's first anthology, *Des Imagistes* (1914), are unequivocally *Imagiste*. The one by James Joyce ('I Hear an Army') is Symbolist in its evocative vagueness, and presumably was included not because Pound discovered *Imagiste* precision and clarity in it but because Joyce was recommended to him by Yeats; and, according to Taupin (quoting Aldington quoting Pound), a rather poor poem by Amy Lowell called 'In a Garden' was included in *Des Imagistes* mainly because its author was wealthy: 'Pound needed money for the anthology, and this was a way of procuring it' (Taupin 1985: 82). Pound's recommendation to Harriet Monroe in August 1913 (*L* 59) that 'ten or a dozen' pages of *Poetry* be reserved for a selection of poems from John Gould Fletcher's *Irradiations* (on the grounds that Fletcher was the kind of poet whose strengths were not discernible in isolated poems) is less puzzling once it is recognised that this was a way of pacifying Fletcher, who complained that Pound, after picking his brains and borrowing his books of French poetry, went on to publish in the *New Age* in September and October 1913 a series of articles on recent French poetry called 'The Approach to Paris' (de Chasca 1978: 25–8). It was against precisely this sort of metropolitan deviousness that American expatriates in London cautioned one another: Conrad Aiken recalled being warned by Eliot, shortly after arriving in London, 'that he should never, under any circumstances, in English literary society, discuss his "first-rate" ideas, lest they be stolen, and rushed into print at once, by those jackdaws, those magpies' (Aiken 1963: 276). The story Pound told Monroe in August 1917, however, shifted the focus of his dependence from Fletcher's ideas to Fletcher's books: yes, it was true that he had borrowed the books, but in fact he had had to cut the pages in so many of them that it was doubtful whether Fletcher himself had ever read them (*L* 175–6). And, when Monroe herself objected to Pound's reprinting in *Des Imagistes* (1914) – without seeking her editorial permission – poems first published in *Poetry*, Pound avoided similar problems with his forthcoming *Catholic Anthology* (1915) by including in it one of her own poems ('Letter from Peking'), which in other circumstances he would certainly have rejected (Williams, E. 1977: 42; Carpenter 1988: 282).

Fletcher had inherited wealth, which enabled him to live comfortably, travel, and pay for the publication of books of his own poems. Wealthy children who decided they were writers (and therefore abandoned profitable family businesses and financially secure marriages for a bohemian life in London or Paris) wanted to be accepted for their work, not their money, and were prey to indigent bohemians tempted to praise their work in order to get at their money. Pound's attitude to the poems of Nancy Cunard (the daughter of Lady Maud Cunard), who was to run a highly successful salon in Paris in the thirties, changed from indifference to interest when she took up publishing and became potentially co-optable to his own projects (Tytell 1987: 202). He had met her in 1915, a year before her first poems were printed by Edith Sitwell in *Wheels*, and a decade before Virginia and Leonard Woolf published a book of her poems called *Parallax* (1925). A pedigree like that marked her as a Bloomsbury product, and incapable therefore of contributing creatively to the modernist movement as Pound understood it. But Nancy Cunard was titled and had money. In 1928 she bought from William Bird the printing press he had used when publishing books under the imprint of the Three Mountains Press, and which she in turn used for her own imprint, the Hours

Press. Bird's Three Mountains Press had published *A Draft of XVI Cantos* in 1925, and two years before that a series of books edited by Pound called 'The Inquest', of which the first was his own autobiographical *Indiscretions*. Others in the series included *Women and Men*, by the first London editor to take him seriously, Ford Madox Ford; *The Great American Novel*, by his old literary friend, William Carlos Williams; *In Our Time*, by his most recent protegé, Ernest Hemingway; and a book of prose sketches called *England*, by a certain B.M.G.-Adams, that is, Bride Adams (née Scratton), who appears in Canto 78 under her Provençal pseudonym 'Thiy', and whose husband divorced her for adultery in the year *England* was published, naming Pound (who had known her since 1909, when they met at Yeats's house) as co-respondent. When Nancy Cunard wrote to ask Pound in July 1929 whether she could publish some of his poetry and a book of prose 'in the style of Indiscretions' (Gallup 1983: 451), he offered her a Canto and a book on 'The Probable Music of *Beowulf*', a topic he had first written about in 1918 after hearing Marjorie Kennedy-Fraser sing Hebridean folksongs (*EP/M* 142). The book was announced but never got written, partly because the Hebridean music he had in mind for *Beowulf* looked more improbable the more he tried to make it fit the poem, and partly because he wanted Cantos 17–30 done in a fine edition like the Three Mountains Press edition of Cantos 1–16. As Cunard's deadline approached, the gamble paid off and *A Draft of XXX Cantos* was published in August 1930 by the Hours Press in a beautifully printed limited edition aimed at the bibliophile market, one vellum-bound copy being presented by Pound himself in 1933 to Mussolini, who found it, according to Canto 41, amusing ('divertente').

After the event, trade-offs could always be justified as critically equivalent to losing one or two battles in order to win the war, which is how Pound figured his own relationship to the critical establishment that ran the major review journals. 'When you fell into the hands of those London log-rollers', H.L. Mencken told him in 1937, 'all your native common sense oozed out of you' (Mencken 1961: 411). But Mencken hadn't been there at the time, and so had no idea what it was like to work there. Metropolitan London was an extremely attractive prospect when viewed from an American midwest which seemed provincial and gauche to somebody with Pound's sophisticated tastes. As a place to live in, however, it turned out to be less the cosmopolitan centre he had

expected than a collection of suburbs, intellectually and socially as
well as geographically, each with its discrete ambiance and reputation, and each generating its own kind of suburban prejudices
and snobberies. Some of Pound's contemporaries, like Williams,
took one look at London and returned home for good, finding it
'completely foreign to anything [he] desired' (Williams, W.C.
1951: 117). Others, like Robert McAlmon, made the pilgrimage to
London and then moved on to Paris. McAlmon has described how
he was briefed in London by Wyndham Lewis on the people he
should know and those he should not, and how to read the cultural
significance of borough names like Chelsea, Kensington, and
Bloomsbury, the native habitat of 'Bloomsbuggers' like Roger Fry,
with whom Lewis had quarrelled irreconcilably. 'Intrigue and dis-
trusts and the talk of groups and cliques made up most of the
conversation', McAlmon recalled, adding that that sort of thing
was not peculiar to Lewis but a 'London pastime' (McAlmon 1970:
4). As a New Yorker whose tastes in the arts were European rather
than British, McAlmon found London provincial, although perhaps no worse in that respect than Paris, which Eliot advised him
to treat as 'a place and a tradition, rather than as a congeries of
people, who are mostly futile and time-wasting, except when you
want to pass an evening agreeably' (ibid.: 7).

Pound's first experience of generating and manipulating critical
discourse appears to have been in connection with the production
of his own first book of poems, *A Lume Spento*, printed in Venice
in 1908. In the long term, the small print-run of 150 copies was
designed to ensure the book's status as a collector's item, which is
the fate envisaged for it in an early poem of Pound's called 'Famam
Librosque Cano' (*P* 14–15); but in the short term, as he explained
to his father at the time, the advantage of a small print-run was
that it would not take very long to get rid of the stock, whereupon
he could truthfully announce, ' "First edition" exhausted'. That
phrase itself, he added, would create 'the impression of a larger
circulation', thus making it easier to negotiate a reprint, especially
if favourable reviews could be arranged (Carpenter 1988: 90). 'It
pays to advertise', he told his father. 'What we want is *one big*
hoorah of fore announcements, & one *more* big hoorah of reviews'
(ibid.: 91). A former girl-friend of his father's who was an
immensely popular poet, Ella Wheeler Wilcox, the 'Poetess of Passion', was persuaded – by Pound himself (Wilhelm 1985: 199) –

to review *A Lume Spento*. She did so in a brief and exclamatory fashion ('Success to you, young singer in Venice!'), preoccupied with memories of a dead son of her own who might have grown up, like Homer Pound's boy, to be a poet (*CH* 2–3; Stock 1970: 55). The lack of specificity in Wilcox's comments confirmed Pound's earlier hunch that what were really needed to launch *A Lume Spento* properly were ghosted reviews: 'I shall write a few myself', he told his mother, perhaps recalling that Walt Whitman had written favourable reviews of his own *Leaves of Grass*, 'and get some one to sign 'em' (Stock 1970: 47). One such review is quoted by T.S. Eliot in a promotional pamphlet he wrote at Pound's request and published anonymously (John Quinn paid the bulk of the costs) to boost the American sales of *Lustra* in 1917. The review is attributed to the London *Evening Standard*: it compares Pound to 'a minstrel of Provence at a suburban musical evening', and finds his poetry so 'original, imaginative, passionate, and spiritual' as to be totally unlike 'the trite and decorous verse of most of our decorous poets' (Eliot 1965: 193). Pound calculated that if he could place such 'genuine and faked reviews' in London and New York newspapers then 'Scribner or somebody [could] be brought to see the sense of making a reprint' (Stock 1970: 47). Nobody did, but that hardly matters: for what is revealed in this first and unsuccessful attempt by Pound to market a literary commodity of his own is his conviction that literary texts make their way in the world not by some supposedly intrinsic merit as literature but by claims made on their behalf by criticism. The persistence of that conviction created one of his many disagreements with Amy Lowell about *Imagisme*. 'Advertising is all very well', she told Harriet Monroe in September 1914, 'but one must have some goods to deliver, and the goods must be up to the advertising of them' (Damon 1935: 239). The metaphor she used evokes the world of commerce, but the issue she raised had political implications: she thought Pound had 'never learned the wisdom of Lincoln's adage about "not being able to fool all the people all the time"' (ibid.). But the history of criticism had taught Pound that you can fool enough of the people enough of the time to enable a new way of writing to survive until its potential readership has been educated into appreciating it. He also knew that you sell a product by first stimulating desire for it and then supplying the demand. By 1920 E.E. Cummings was calling him 'one of history's greatest advertisers' (Cummings 1920: 783).

Recognising the prime importance of criticism in the circulation and reception of literary texts, Pound did everything he could to control it by telling people what they ought to say about them, especially about his own poems. Flint's favourable review of Pound's *Ripostes* (1912) in the March 1913 issue of *Poetry and Drama* (*CH* 95–8) was done with Pound's assistance, although (Flint told Robert Frost a few months later) at Flint's own request, because he 'didn't know what to say about the book' (Frost 1964: 87). Friends were also instructed in detail on how to defend him against unsympathetic critics like that professor of classics at the University of Chicago who ridiculed his *Homage to Sextus Propertius* (1919): one such reply-kit was sent to May Sinclair and another to A.R. Orage, each of whom incorporated it in a defence of Pound's versions of the Latin (*L* 211–13; *CH* 158–9, 183–4). This dissemination of favourable accounts of *Homage to Sextus Propertius* was designed to create the illusion (especially in America, where the most adverse criticism had come from) that Pound's latest work was being appreciated already by a discerning readership in London; and those co-opted into the deception went along with it because it helped establish their own reputations as acute critics of one of the most obscure modern poets. By the 1930s such practices had become so much a matter of routine to Pound that he would not have understood why a young American admirer of his poetry, Robert Fitzgerald, had misgivings about reviewing on Pound's instructions the recently published *Guido Cavalcanti: Rime* (1932), edited by Pound, and placing his review either in the *Criterion* (edited by Pound's friend Eliot) or the *New English Weekly* (edited by Pound's friend Orage) (Fitzgerald 1956: 18).

Pound divided people into 'wheels' and 'cubes': wheels 'get things done', but 'you can't lean on 'em' because 'they'll roll out from under you'; cubes, on the other hand, are the 'foundations', because you can not only lean on but build on them (French 1983: 103). Cubes would understand that the ends justify the means: if the only way of breaking the hegemony of a literary critical establishment is by ethically dubious reviewing practices, then these become inevitable, especially if you are convinced that the opposition habitually behaves just as disreputably. Virginia Woolf told Eliot that she and her husband Leonard had 'felt awkward', even felt 'guilt', at reviewing Eliot's *Poems* (1919), which they themselves had published at their Hogarth Press; but neither awkwardness nor guilt had prevented them in the end from reviewing the book, favourably and anonymously, in the *Athenaeum* (Eliot 1988: 309). Pound was willing to double as publisher's reader in recommending that a certain book be published, and periodical reviewer in welcoming what he had already recommended. Both publishers and editors saw benefits in this practice. Publishers liked the guarantee of a favourable review without too much delay, and editors liked to have reviews of the very latest publications: Williams's *The Tempers*, for instance, published in London by Elkin Mathews in September 1913, was reviewed favourably by Pound in *Poetry* (Chicago) in December of that year. In special cases, like Eliot and Joyce, each of whom he regarded as his 'discovery', Pound would review the same book twice, using the opportunity not for diversification but for reiteration: 'Joyce is a writer, GOD-DAMN your eyes, Joyce is a writer, I tell you Joyce etc. etc.' (*L* 179).

The only people short-changed by these practices were readers naive enough to believe that criticism is produced by impartial experts. Pound played games with such readers. When the London edition of *The Poetical Works of Lionel Johnson* (1915) was released in America by Macmillan the prefatory essay by Pound was omitted. Pound reprinted the gist of it, however, in *Poetry* in the form of an anonymous review, in which Pound is praised for his 'excellent criticism' (Pound 1916: 313). There is no such evasiveness in his review for the same journal of his own edition of *Passages from the Letters of John Butler Yeats* (1917), which he says he will 'make no excuse for reviewing' because he has read the book more carefully than 'any other critic or reviewer is likely to do' and therefore is 'more fit to praise it' (Pound 1918: 223). In Pound's circle, as in other circles, one favour deserved another, and resulted in 'log rolling' (*EP/MCA* 266). So in September 1933 when Ford told him he was trying to arrange for *A Draft of XXX Cantos* to be reviewed in the *Transatlantic Review*, he assumed immediately that Ford would commission a favourable review, and asked: 'ANY logs I can roll for you?' (*EP/FMF* 128). That was a private remark; and, although the pair of them had been puffing one another in print for some twenty years, this time Ford declined the offer, saying he was now 'past log rolling', and that in any case it would appear 'too suspect – in the line of "you scratch my back and I'll scratch yours"' (ibid.: 129). In his public statements, however, Pound continued to take the line that 'mutual puffery' (John Churton Collins's term) was a malpractice confined to the literary establishment, which used it in order to protect its own kind. An important consequence of Remy de Gourmont's criticism, he had written in January 1916, is that it signalled 'the end of log-rolling, the end of the British school of criticism for the preservation of orderly and innocuous persons' (*SP* 391). Three months later, however, Pound himself was asking his patron John Quinn whether there was anything he would like to see praised or attacked (Reid 1968: 254). Pound was not opposed to what he called in 1920 'mutual washing' (*EP/WL* 126) provided it wasn't perceived as such by outsiders. There is not much use 'trying to circulate books of controversy or criticism', he told Lewis in 1925, 'unless one is advertising one[']s friends, or their supposedly vendible products' (*EP/WL* 148); so in 1923, when the *Dial* decided it could do without his services as foreign editor, he asked Kate Buss to organise a few 'public laments' because he didn't think there would be any at all unless they were 'engineer'd or faked by [his] friends' (*L* 255).

One way of preserving the benefits of mutual puffery while maintaining credibility among outsiders was to shift the mode of mutual criticism from praise to dispraise, on the grounds that it is better to have one's work kept in the public eye by negative criticism than to have it ignored altogether. 'No one ever praises Osbert Sitwell's poetry', Eliot told Quinn in 1920, 'but all the reviewers mention it, and that is the essential' (Eliot 1988: 358). Pound recognised the publicity-value that a pseudo-attack on a known associate might have in generating rumours of a break between them. 'Am perfectly willing to "attack" you publicly in print now and again', he assured Lewis in 1931 (*EP/WL* 176). That was the year in which he wrote to tell Monroe that 'anybody being a friend of anybody has nothing to do with literary criticism' (*L* 311). Like most readers of that letter, she probably took him to mean that criticism is so important that friendships may well have to be sacrificed to it. But it was equally true for Pound that genuine friendships would survive mutual criticism. He told Williams in 1908 that he hoped he would never 'get so fanatical as to let a man's like or dislike' of his own writings 'interfere with an old friendship or a new one' (*L* 36). The male-bonding exemplified in Pound's relationship with Williams appears to have been equally strong in his relationships with Eliot and Lewis, so strong, in fact, as to have been unaffected even temporarily by such things as Williams's attack on him in *Kora in Hell* (1920) and Lewis's in *Time and Western Man* (1927), or by numerous adverse remarks of his own directed at Eliot, whom he accused in 1930 of having 'arrived at the supreme Eminence among English critics largely through disguising himself as a corpse' (*SP* 53). As one of that select band Lewis called 'the "Men of 1914" ' (Lewis 1937: 9), Pound knew that the revolution in writing they were engineering collectively was too important to be jeopardised by personal tantrums. 'How the hell many points of agreement do you suppose there were between Joyce, W. Lewis, Eliot and yrs. truly in 1917?' he asked a correspondent in 1929 (*L* 300). His public disagreements with Eliot and Lewis in particular were a diversionary tactic to conceal their fundamental solidarity with one another, and to obscure Pound's critical operations as what Van Wyck Brooks called in 1920 'the most unblushing logroller on record' (*CH* 188).

It should be remembered that Pound took on the London literary establishment as an American, and at a time when an English critic could express in print his amazement that anybody could be 'an American, a man of culture and a poet, all at the same time' (Alford 1913: 487). Pound's principal collaborator was another American, T.S. Eliot, who learned a different way of surviving similar prejudices. 'Getting recognised in English letters', Eliot told his mother in 1920, when he had succeeded in doing so, 'is like breaking open a safe' (Eliot 1988: 392). The choice was between using explosives, which was Lewis's approach in his Vorticist journal *Blast*, or putting in the time to learn the combinations of the lock, which was Eliot's preferred method. Pound and Eliot decided they could work together most efficiently by using different means to attain the same end, which was to change literary tastes by changing the discourse of criticism. 'We have collaborated in *literary* criticism', Pound recalled in 1942; 'we have made decisions and taken measures against certain diseases of writing' (*SP* 291). In that critical double-act, Pound was to play the part of American barbarian while Eliot would perfect the art of being more British than the British through what Kenner calls his 'close and knowing mimicry of the respectable' (Kenner 1960: 99). 'You let *me* throw the bricks through the front window', Pound is alleged to have told Eliot. 'You go in at the back door and take the swag' (Carpenter 1988: 264). In the version of this addressed in 1925 to the secretary of the Guggenheim Foundation, a different set of tropes genders Pound as aggressively masculine in comparison with an amorphously 'feminine' Eliot: since Eliot 'wd. never be as hefty a battering ram' as Pound, 'nor as explosive as Lewis', Pound had advised him to 'try a more oceanic and fluid method of sapping the foundations' (Gallup 1970: 76). Accordingly, Eliot learnt how to commute effortlessly as a contributor between avant-garde journals like *Blast* or the *Egoist* or the *Little Review* and establishment journals like the *Athenaeum*, New Statesman and *The Times Literary Supplement*. Pound may well have dictated the terms of the relationship, but Eliot undoubtedly got the better deal when the establishment responded by accommodating Eliot and rejecting Pound. *The Times Literary Supplement* commissioned only one review by Pound (on 19 October 1916, of W.M. Fullerton's *The American Crisis and the War*). This is perhaps not surprising, given Pound's reputation for brick-throwing, and the fact that he had used *The Times Literary Supplement* as his principal source of quotations for those *sottisiers* (or 'fool-columns', as he called them) which he contributed to the *Egoist* in 1914 and 1915. If the publication of *Poems* (1919) confirmed Eliot's status as an important new poet, the publication of his literary essays as *The Sacred Wood* in November 1920 signalled the emergence in London of a highly influential literary critic. Pound felt so out of it all that by the end of December that year he left London for good, whereupon the double-act split up.

Eliot had known for some time that he was becoming a more powerful figure in English letters than Pound would ever be. Shortly before he was offered the assistant editorship of the *Athenaeum*, he told his mother in March 1919 that 'a small and select public' regarded him as 'the best living critic ... in England', and that already he had 'far more *influence* on English letters than any other American has ever had, unless it be Henry James' (Eliot 1988: 280). Nevertheless, he continued to make public declarations of his indebtedness to Pound as a literary critic, especially in the period which culminated critically in *The Sacred Wood* (1920) and poetically in *The Waste Land* (1922). If we ask, therefore, why a comprehensive citation-index of twentieth-century literary criticism would show far more references to Eliot than to Pound, the best answer so far was given in 1960 by Donald Hall, when he observed (in the course of reviewing *Thrones: 96–109 de los Cantares*) that 'Eliot has developed and argued Pound's insights so that they are believed by critics and professors' (*CH* 457). In terms of Pound's own typology of critical functions, Pound is one of the 'inventors', Eliot one of the 'masters' (Pound 1923: 147; cp. *LE* 23).

It is said of Alexander Pope that he never drank tea without a stratagem; and, if we are to believe F.S. Flint, the Museum Street teashop in which Pound discussed with Richard Aldington and Hilda Doolittle ways of getting their poems into print before either of them had written enough to fill the customary slim volume (*L* 288) was the rendezvous at which a *stratégie littéraire* code-named *Imagisme* was planned. It was put into operation so successfully that by the end of June 1915 Pound could boast to T.S. Eliot's father that he had 'engineered a new school of verse now known in England, France and America' (Eliot 1988: 100). Exactly when the conspirators met is not known, but August 1912 seems a likely date, given the fact that Pound went to France in May that year to study Provençal manuscripts and visit places mentioned in troubadour poems, and did not return to London until August. That was the month in which Flint published his lengthy and indispensable survey – the first in English – of various *ismes* which post-*Symboliste* French poets were exploring, such as *Unanisme*, *Néopaganisme*, *Impulsionnisme* and *Futurisme*. 'Contemporary French Poetry' had been commissioned by Harold Monro as editor of the *Poetry Review*, the official journal of the Poetry Society. Before discussing the poetry of important representatives of what he called 'the generation of 1900', Flint dispatched in one sentence fifteen also-rans, including (surprisingly) Guillaume Apollinaire, but also a 'singer of the sufferings of poor children and of the "Urbs" ' by the name of Fernand Divoire (Flint 1912: 362), who was to publish that year a book called *Introduction à l'étude de la stratégie littéraire* (Paris, 1912). As an English observer of the theory and practice of contemporary French poetry Flint was in those days unrivalled, and, although there is no mention of Divoire's book in his 1912 essay, evidence that he knew at least its title is to be found in the draft of an unpublished essay he wrote in French after quarrelling with Pound in July 1915 about the origins of what by then had come to be called Imagism. There he writes that Pound, 'nourrissant en secrète sa petite stratégie littéraire', created *Imagisme* – a 'stupid' word in Flint's opinion – by Frenchifying 'image' and fashionably tacking on an *isme* (Middleton 1965: 40, 44).

Augmented editions of Divoire's book were published in Paris under the title *Stratégie littéraire* in 1924 and 1928. Four years later, in the July 1932 issue of the *Criterion* (to which Pound contributed a commemorative essay on Harold Monro), Flint repeated his claim – this time in English, and in public – that Pound, in manufacturing *Imagisme*, had simply appropriated the word ' "image"

... from T.E. Hulme's table talk' and the *isme* from Flint's own 'notes on contemporary French poetry' written 'for Harold Monro's *Poetry Review*'. The collocation of 'image' with *isme*, he added, 'came to Pound after I had told him about Fernand Divoire's essays on "stratégie littéraire". Pound devised a "stratégie littéraire" ' (Flint 1932: 687). Flint says nothing of the fact that as early as December 1911 Pound was already calling his use of Arnaut Daniel 'strategic' in his development of a 'New Method in Scholarship' (*SP* 26, 21; cp. 43). In Pound's own account of the genesis of the word *Imagisme* the emphasis is slightly different from Flint's, but not at odds with it. Pound had indeed 'made the word ... on a Hulme basis', he confessed to the editor of the *Little Review*, Margaret Anderson, in November 1917, but he had 'carefully made a name that was not & never had been used in France', and which would therefore 'specifically ... distinguish "us" from any of the French groups catalogued by Flint' in the *Poetry Review* (*EP/MCA* 155).

With *Imagisme* decided upon as the name of the commodity, and the marketing of it designed as a Divoirean *stratégie*, Pound moved swiftly to ensure that the first citation in print of this signifier which as yet had no corresponding signified would occur in a book of his own poems, *Ripostes*, published in London in October 1912. The appendix to *Ripostes* includes five poems mischievously and erroneously described as 'The Complete Poetical Works of T.E. Hulme'. They were prefaced by a correspondingly brief note on a group of poets Hulme had been associated with, called by Pound 'the "School of Images", which may or may not have existed', although none of its constituent members had ever known it by that name. 'As for the future', Pound's calculatedly enigmatic note concludes, '*Les Imagistes*, the descendants of the forgotten school of 1909, have that in their keeping' (*P* 251). In September 1912 he sent Harriet Monroe in Chicago three poems by Aldington which she published in the second (November) issue of *Poetry*, together with a note from Pound identifying Aldington as 'one of the "Imagistes", a group of ardent Hellenists who are pursuing interesting experiments in *vers libre*' of the kind which Mallarmé and his followers had attempted. This note was written not to please the twenty-year-old Aldington (who was never consulted about it) but to whet the appetite of the editor of a new poetry journal for a new poetic commodity, of which Pound himself was the sole supplier. The fiction that there was indeed a school of poets calling themselves *Imagistes* was at first sustained entirely by Pound's prose, and by his canniness in not letting his customer have too many of the goods at once, thus creating the illusion of their scarcity. So when in October 1912 he sent some poems by H.D. for publication in *Poetry* he told Monroe that he'd 'had luck again' (*L* 45), as if his securing of H.D.'s poems were the result of separate negotiations after he had managed to get hold of Aldington's. How very fortunate, Monroe was expected to conclude, that she had such a talented foreign correspondent working for her in London, who not only knew about schools of poets nobody else had even heard of but was able to secure examples of their work for *Poetry* at merely the going rates.

Having succeeded in arousing curiosity about *Imagisme*, Pound had to find ways of talking about it which, while combining helpful tips with cryptic observations, would perpetuate that curiosity and prevent his invention from being junked with the *ismes* of yesteryear. The safest way of supplying the demand which Pound himself had created for news about *Imagisme* was to get himself interviewed on the subject by somebody who could be relied upon to be cooperative. For this job he picked F.S. Flint. 'Flint . . . is doing an intelligent article on me chiefly at my own dictation', he reported to Dorothy Shakespear on 8 January 1913 (*EP/DS* 179). What Flint produced was a piece originally entitled 'Les Imagistes: A Note and an Interview' (Middleton 1965: 36–8), which was cut and rewritten by Pound himself before being published over Flint's name in the March 1913 issue of *Poetry* with the title 'Imagisme'. In this process of revision, the three famous principles of *Imagisme* (namely the privileging of 'direct' treatment over *Symboliste* obliquity, and the bans on superfluous words and metronomical rhythms) survive intact. In the original version, they are said to have been 'handed' to the interviewer by Pound himself on an unsigned 'slip of paper' in response to the interviewer's question about the 'code' by which *Imagistes* judge writing: these are the 'principles', Pound is quoted as saying, which 'we' – he and his fellow *Imagistes* – 'have laid down'. Seeing that these principles were indubitably his own, and his alone at this stage, Pound was in something of a dilemma. If they were to be reported as merely his own they might well appear idiosyncratic and lose their intended impact; but anybody recruited to endorse them would almost certainly want to modify or (to use one of his favourite words) 'dilute' them, a hunch later confirmed when *Imagisme* turned into Imagism under the control of that *'Amy*gist' (*L* 288), Amy Lowell. Given the dilemma, his solution was to get himself written out of Flint's text, but to have those *Imagiste* principles he himself had formulated retained verbatim as features allegedly common to a literary movement. His stratagem was to pass off his personal views as those of a group of people of whom (with some justification, given the printed evidence) he could claim later to have been the leader.

Pound's tactical withdrawal from the subject-position in Flint's discourse on *Imagisme* may look like modest self-effacement on his part, but in actual fact it had quite the opposite effect. According to the *stratégie* of the original version, a named interviewer (Flint) was to have reported a conversation with a named representative of the *Imagistes* (Pound), whose replies to the interviewer's questions occupied pronominally the position of consensus ('we'). By this discursive manoeuvre, 'Pound' emerges from Flint's original text as a highly articulate and wholly representative *Imagiste* poet. But, in Pound's corrections to Flint's draft, several of the 'we's' are changed into 'they's' in a pronominal move which redefined the 'Pound' of Flint's text as merely the intermediary between an interviewer and other *Imagiste* poets whose opinions were not sought directly. Whether at Pound's suggestion or Flint's, 'Pound' had disappeared altogether from Flint's text by the time it was published in the March 1913 issue of *Poetry*. There the subject-position ('I') is occupied wholly by Flint as the reporter of a conversation with 'an *imagiste*' (unnamed) who tells Flint how 'they' think poetry ought to be written. It did not escape Pound's notice that by this pronominal arrangement Flint had consigned himself to a position of secondariness in the history of *Imagisme*. 'You will note that Flint writes . . . as one coming to the group not as a founder', Pound pointed out to Monroe on 13 September 1915. 'He does not say "we" but "they" ' (Williams, E. 1977: 39). 'We', Pound makes clear to her, were H.D., Aldington 'and myself'. 'Vorticism', Wyndham Lewis was to remark candidly a year before his death in 1957, 'was what I, personally, did, and said, at a certain period' (Kayman 1986: 63). Anybody acquainted with the documentary files on that founding moment of a modernist poetic which literary historians customarily call Imagism is likely to entertain similar thoughts about Pound and *Imagisme*.

Flint's 1913 article on 'Imagisme' was designed in such a way that the editor of *Poetry* would recognise it as a 'scoop', to use the term Pound himself used when offering her poems by Rabindranath Tagore and Robert Frost (Williams, E. 1977: 67). The elusive *Imagistes*, she would read, 'had not published a manifesto', but now here was Flint actually supplying her with their hitherto unpublished poetic. How could *Poetry* turn down the opportunity to be the first journal in the world to print the *Imagiste* manifesto, especially when it had the opportunity also to publish concurrently an essay by Ezra Pound called 'A Few Don'ts by an Imagiste' (*LE* 4–7), whose recommendations were remarkably consistent with those *Imagiste* principles reported by Flint? But the revelation which Monroe could be counted upon to be grateful for was accompanied by intimations of a mystery that might be resolved in the fullness of time. For the *Imagistes*, according to Flint, 'held . . . a certain "Doctrine of the Image," which they had not committed to writing', on the grounds that 'it did not concern the public, and would provoke useless discussion' (Flint 1913: 199). That statement had also survived intact from Flint's original draft, where it was reprinted as a verbatim quotation from Pound. And again that was a carefully executed and highly successful ploy which makes nonsense of Aldington's claim that Pound had 'the poorest literary strategy [he] ever met with' (Aldington 1925: 311). For nothing is more likely to 'provoke . . . discussion' among people interested in a particular kind of poetry than the intimation that it is based on an occult theory.

When I thought about this passage twenty-odd years ago I was convinced not only that there had indeed been a secret 'Doctrine of the Image', but that I myself knew what it was: it was summed up, I thought, in Hulme's 1909 statement (paraphrasing Henri Bergson) that 'images in verse are not mere decoration, but the very essence of an intuitive language'. Pound's own version of this doctrine of the functional autonomousness of the image is to be found in an essay on 'Vorticism' he published in September 1914, where he asserts that 'the point of Imagisme is that it does not use images *as ornaments*' because 'the image is itself the speech . . . the word beyond formulated language' (Ruthven 1969: 12–13). Since reading Martin Kayman's account of Pound and *Imagisme*, however – which he calls 'How to Write Well and Influence People' (Kayman 1986: 33–65) – I am now persuaded that initially there was no such thing as a 'Doctrine of the Image', and that the purpose of alluding so mysteriously to something that did not exist was to give harmless pleasure to people like me, who would try to guess what it was. The 'Doctrine of the Image' is to be classified, therefore, not with complex aesthetic theories like *Symbolisme* but with advertising gimmicks like 'the ploughman's lunch' in Ian McEwan's film-script with that title (London, 1985), which was a piece of olde English tradition carefully crafted in an adman's office in the 1950s to persuade people to eat in pubs. Both the 'Doctrine of the Image' and 'the ploughman's lunch' exist originally at what Kayman calls '*the level of the signifier*', because 'what [Pound] launched in inventing "Imagisme" was not so much a movement as a *word*' (Kayman 1986: 53, 51). And the purpose of that word was to legitimise his own stylistic desiderata by representing them as shared by a whole group of other writers: his *stratégie*, in short, was to mask subjective criteria in a pseudo-collective aesthetic.

Pound's mystification of an *Imagiste* poetics for publicity purposes was paralleled by his mystification of the principal person co-opted into the conspiracy, Hilda Doolittle. She willingly gave up a name she found embarrassing ('she's shy of her name', Brigit Patmore remembered Pound telling her (Patmore 1968: 64)) by permitting herself to be reinvented by Pound as the enigmatic author-effect, 'H.D. Imagiste'. This was the signature attached on Pound's recommendation to a poem of hers which she says he said ought to be called 'Hermes of the Ways', and which he rewrote according to *Imagiste* principles (H.D. 1980: 18) before sending it as an excellent example of 'the laconic speech of the Imagistes' to Monroe, who published it in the January 1913 issue of *Poetry* (*L* 45). An accompanying note gendered 'H.D.' female, but constructed her as a woman of mystery, 'an American lady resident abroad, whose identity is unknown to the editor'. It is sometimes thought that Pound deprived Hilda Doolittle of her identity in thus depriving her of her name, but she cannot have been altogether displeased with the resulting enigma, because she continued to write over those initials for the rest of her life. Instead of being identified in London as the feckless daughter of the University of Pennsylvania's Professor of Astronomy, the American woman with the funny name, she found herself liberated authorially by the erasure of the name of her father. To reduce 'Hilda Doolittle' to 'H.D.' was to empty the name of history, and to open up the possibility of reinscribing it with secret meanings inaccessible to outsiders, who would be condemned as the profane always are to see without seeing. But the politics of renaming had a private as well as a public dimension, given the history of Hilda and Ezra's romantic involvement with one another. To Pound the 'D' of 'H.D' stood for 'Dryad', a tree-spirit, in memory of intimate moments they had shared up a tree in Professor and Mrs Doolittle's garden; and to Pound's eventual mother-in-law, Olivia Shakespear, 'H.D.' stood for 'hamadryad'.

Although readers of *Poetry* would know nothing of this, Pound calculated that the combination of an enigmatic 'Doctrine of the Image' with an expatriate female *Imagiste* who concealed her identity behind the decent obscurity of initials would be enough to create a lively curiosity about *Imagisme*. His calculation proved to be correct in the case of one subscriber to *Poetry*, Amy Lowell, who experienced a shock of recognition on reading the poems of the mysterious 'H.D.' ('Why, I, too, am an Imagiste' (Damon 1935: 196)), and travelled to London to get to the bottom of the mystery. There she engaged with Pound in a critical power struggle from which each claimed to have emerged victorious. Her version of the story is that she liberated *Imagisme* from cliquishness by reorganising it democratically as Imagism; Pound's version is that Lowell betrayed the principles of *Imagisme* when she rewrote the word as Imagism, and that her democratic tolerance of superfluous words in superfluous poems by superfluous poets transformed *Imagisme* into a parodic excess best described as '*Amy*gism'. Whoever was right, the resultant publicity was good for business. Imagist anthologies edited by Lowell sold well, and Imagism (it seemed sensible to anglicise the word) attracted a great deal of attention. Pound, meanwhile, moved on to another campaign on behalf of another ism of his invention, Vorticism.

As both a poet and a critic, Pound needed space in which to operate, and the medium he chose was those little magazines on shoe-string budgets which came into existence in response to the production of otherwise unpublishable modernist texts. He made his requirements bluntly clear to Margaret Anderson in 1917 when negotiating the terms on which he would act as foreign editor of the *Little Review*: 'I want ... a place where I and T.S. Eliot can appear once a month (or once an "issue") and where James Joyce can appear when he likes, and where Wyndham Lewis can appear if he comes back from the war' (*EP/MCA* 6). Anderson incorporated these words into an announcement of Pound's appointment in the April 1917 issue of the journal, informing readers that by purchasing the *Little Review* and the *Egoist* (another Pound-influenced journal) they would manage to keep 'in touch with the two most important radical organs of contemporary literature' (Anderson 1930: 25).

Radical in their dissent from the cultural consequences of a publishing system controlled by monopoly ownership and mass circulation, the little magazines provided in their review pages a forum for culturally oppositional discourses such as Pound's. Their purpose, Pound stated in 1935, was to 'break a monopoly' (*SP* 242) by conservative editors and publishers of the modes of literary production; and this benign, indeed heroic, construction of Pound's manipulation of the new discursive space created by the little magazines has tended to be reproduced in Pound-influenced accounts of literary history. Pound, however, practised monopoly-breaking in order to set up a monopoly of his own. Willing to write for anybody on practically anything, he aimed at colonising the maximum amount of discursive space both *in propria persona* and by means of a variety of pseudonyms. He tried to dominate the journals he wrote for, sometimes successfully, as in his dealings with the *New Freewoman* and its successor, the *Egoist*. More often, however, editors originally grateful for his assistance would sooner or later resist a mode of co-operation which would move through hectoring and bullying until it came to look increasingly like a takeover, whereupon Pound would move on to the next journal.

Even Harriet Monroe, who had the necessary masochistic temperament for working editorially with Pound – she speaks in her autobiography of the 'rather violent, but on the whole salutary discipline' she experienced 'under the lash' of Pound's criticism (Monroe 1938: 268) – eventually had enough of his help, although their relationship in other respects remained cordial. In response to an essay by Pound on 'Small Magazines' in a 1930 issue of the *English Journal*, however, which complained of her editorial obtuseness, she told the editor that Pound himself was as much to blame as anybody for what had happened: he had simply 'wearied of *Poetry*, of *The Little Review*, of *Blast*, of *The Dial*, even of his own *Exile*', and consequently 'the wrecks of his wild runs strew the path of progress' (Janssens 1968: 121). This pattern of behaviour was so familiar that by the time he volunteered his services to the *Hound & Horn* in 1929 its young editors already had the measure of him. They refused to offer him the contributing editorship he was after, but they printed some of his Cantos and lively letters before letting him go in 1931 when he and they felt they had had quite enough of one another (ibid.: 118–20). In 1932, when he had been in and out of Samuel Putnam's *New Review* as a contributing editor in less than two years, he tried to get a mouthpiece in *Contact*, and was told by Williams 'to go to hell'. Instead, he approached F.R. Leavis, who told Ronald Bottrall that he saw 'no point in giving [Pound] space in *Scrutiny*' because 'he isn't what one feels he ought to be' (ibid.: 120–1). A historian of the *Hound & Horn* concludes that 'Pound gave almost nothing but trouble to "little magazines" from 1930 on' (Greenbaum 1966: 98).

In Pound's London years things were rather different. He managed to act as a contributing editor to three London journals (the *New Freewoman* in 1913, and the *Egoist* and *Blast* in 1914) as well as two Chicago journals (*Poetry* from 1912 to 1917, and the *Little Review* from 1917 to 1921). All but one of these (Lewis's *Blast*) were edited by women: *Poetry* by Harriet Monroe, the *New Freewoman* by Dora Marsden, the *Egoist* by Dora Marsden and Harriet Shaw Weaver, and the *Little Review* by Margaret Anderson and Jane Heap. This phenomenon is clearly not unrelated to that late nineteenth-century 'feminisation of American culture' described by Ann Douglas in her book of that name, which traces the emergence as 'prime consumers of American culture' of those educated churchgoing women who 'edited magazines and wrote books for other women like themselves', and were so successful that 'masculine groups, ministers and authors' came to occupy 'a precarious position in society' (Douglas 1977: 7). The fact that those who wrote for the principal modernist magazines in the early twentieth century tended to be male, and those who edited them female, suggests that the maieutics of modernism are a feminist issue, and that the aggressive masculinity of a Lewis or a Hemingway, or the misogyny of a Hulme or an Eliot, are manifestations of a desire to establish modernism as a masculinist stand against a prevailing feminisation of culture.

Eliot told Pound in April 1915 of his misgivings (which he thought it 'imprudent' to express) about 'the monopolisation of literature by women' (Eliot 1988: 96). When Pound got him appointed in May 1917 as assistant editor of the *Egoist* Eliot hoped to have 'a beneficial influence' on a journal 'run mostly by old maids': what this involved, as he told his father in October that year, was 'a struggle to keep the writing as much as possible in

Male hands' (ibid.: 179, 204). 'The only woman connected with publishing' Eliot found it 'really easy to get on with' was Harriet Shaw Weaver, that 'funny little spinster' who was 'quite nice, and . . . quite intelligent', and to whom he dedicated a volume of his *Selected Essays* in 1932 (ibid.: 348, 181, 300). John Quinn, who in March 1916 had offered to subsidise Pound for two years if he could get editorial control of the *Egoist* (but gave up the idea on Pound's advice when Dora Marsden proved a harder nut to crack than Weaver), negotiated with the two 'female rabbits who pose as the editors' of the *Little Review*, Anderson and Heap, an arrangement whereby he would back Pound financially as foreign editor if they would guarantee Pound five thousand words of his own choice in each issue of their journal (Reid 1968: 249, 444, 284–5). When Quinn finally met Anderson, who describes herself in her autobiography as having been 'extravagantly and disgustingly pretty' in those days, he became sexually interested in her, perhaps not knowing that she was a lesbian (ibid.: 442; cp. 287). Masculinist writers who were not directly hostile to female-bonded editors found them somewhat unnerving. Conrad Aiken, for instance, describes how, after he had made 'the profound mistake' of calling in on the *Little Review* editors and sitting 'stiffly' in their office, he left and went downstairs hearing those 'peals of uncontrollable and derisive female laughter' which Hélène Cixous would later identify as the laugh of the Medusa (Aiken 1963: 218).

In addition to establishing bases in magazines with avowedly literary commitments, Pound was willing to set up outposts in journals specialising in various non-literary isms, such as 'individualism' and 'cerebralism'. The first and only issue of the *Cerebralist* was edited by Edward Hayter Preston in December 1913 to promulgate a philosophy of cerebralism shortly to be explained by its founder, E.C. Grey, in *The Mystery of Sex and Happiness* (London, 1914). It was a philosophy of 'harmony, balance, [and] perfection', based on the proposition that 'both man and womb-man are of uni-sex undetermined, until sexual attraction brings about the oppositeness of Masculine and Feminine' (*EP/DS* 277). Pound's attitude to such matters was largely separatist: he filled his allotted pages in the *Cerebralist* with Flint on novelists and poetry, an essay on *Imagisme* by a mysterious 'R.S.', eleven poems by Aldington and a couple by H.D.'s girlfriend, Frances Gregg. As a sop to Preston, however, he also included a short prose poem of his own called 'Ikon', on the harmonising effects of 'images of beauty', designed for that rarest of readerships, the *Imagiste*-Cerebralists.

The most interesting case of such appropriations occurs in Pound's dealings with the *Egoist*, since before Pound hijacked it for modernism it had been a feminist journal called the *New Freewoman*, edited by Dora Marsden. Politically, she came out of the Women's Social and Political Union (WSPU) founded by the Pankhursts, and had first-hand experience of the breaking of suffragette hunger-strikers by force-feeding, the horrors of which were described in September 1914 by Djuna Barnes, who was fed pea-soup through tubes forced up her nose (Hanscombe and Smyers 1987: 89). In the belief that there was more to feminism than the issue of *Votes for Women* (the title of the WSPU journal), Marsden launched a weekly paper of her own in November 1911 called the *Freewoman*. Subtitled at first 'A Weekly Feminist Review', by May 1912 it had become 'A Weekly Humanist Review', the change signalling Marsden's break with separatist feminism in order to demonstrate 'that the two causes, man's and woman's, are one' (Lidderdale and Nicholson 1970: 46). The *Freewoman* ceased publication in October 1912, which was coincidentally the date of the very first issue of *Poetry* (Chicago). The Freewoman Discussion Circle continued to meet, however, and revived the journal on 15 June 1913 as the *New Freewoman*. It was financed largely by Weaver, the daughter of a well-off Cheshire family, who was a social worker in London's East End before becoming caught up in the establishment of the South London Hospital for Women. Marsden stayed on as editor, with Rebecca West as assistant editor, and for a time it was business as usual, with articles on such matters as labour problems, free love and the supersession of matriarchy by patriarchy.

But two things were to upset the old equilibrium: one was Rebecca West's meeting with Ezra Pound in the summer of 1913 at one of Violet Hunt's literary gatherings, and the other was Marsden's open-door policy for the journal. According to Weaver, West, who had reviewed Pound's *Sonnets and Ballate of Guido Cavalcanti* in the *Freewoman*, and was aware of his activities as literary talent scout for *Poetry*, showed him a copy of the *New Freewoman*, which he proposed 'broadening' by the inclusion of a literary section 'to which he himself would be prepared to contribute regular articles and in which he would secure the collaboration of other young poets and writers' (Hanscombe and Smyers 1987: 168). This proposal, backed by West, was communicated to Marsden, who accepted it. As the latest victim of the womanising H.G. Wells, West was at that time in no state to edit an augmented literary section of the *New Freewoman*: Wells wanted to break off the affair (such as it was: they were not yet lovers), but she didn't, and tried more than once to commit suicide. For Pound it was an opportune moment to use the *New Freewoman* as he was using *Poetry*, that is, as a base from which to campaign critically on behalf of the kind of writing he wanted to see in print. He not only was willing to take on editorial tasks without pay, but managed to persuade another American expatriate, John Gould Fletcher, to put money into the literary pages of the journal. Pound controlled these pages as from 15 August 1913, an event he marked by reprinting from the March 1913 issue of *Poetry* a selection of his own poems.

Henry James, who had made up his mind about militant feminism long ago in his novel *The Bostonians* (1886), declined Pound's request to contribute to the new *New Freewoman*, warning him against becoming its 'bondswoman' (Cournos 1935: 270); but, as it turned out, James needn't have worried. Incredible as it may seem that any feminist would contract out space in a feminist journal to a phallocrat like Pound, it must be remembered that although Marsden wanted to preserve in the titles of the two journals she edited what she called 'differentiation as to gender', she had no time for either the biologism of contemporary feminism ('Why does not someone start a "straight-nose movement"?') or 'the Pankhurst variety' of political activists who in her opinion confused freedom with the right to vote (*NF*, 15 Nov. 1913, p. 203; 1 July 1913, p. 24). Consequently, and dangerously, it was her editorial policy to be programmatically without a programme. '*The New Freewoman* stands for nothing', she wrote in the issue for 15 November 1913: 'it is the flexible frame waiting to be filled with the expression of the constantly shifting tale of the contributors' emotions' (p. 204). Now Pound was certainly willing to fill Marsden's frame and occupy her nothing, but with something more material than emotions: he was to write later of the copulatory sensations he experienced in 'driving any new idea into the great passive vulva of London' (*NPL* viii). Marsden, however, believed that the *New Freewoman* could resist potential seducers: 'Should an influence come in to make it rigid', she added, 'it would drop from our hands immediately'.

But Pound was never a flaccid contributor to anybody's journal, and treated female editors with Casanovan confidence. A couple of days before the first Pound-influenced issue of Marsden's journal was published he wrote to tell Harriet Monroe in Chicago that the *New Freewoman* had been annexed as 'our left wing' (*L* 58). It would go on printing as usual its boring articles and editorials, but its vitality would be in its literary pages. The only remaining problem was its title, which Pound told Joyce was 'unsuitable' (*EP/JJ* 17), presumably because it made it look like some sort of feminist journal. But that too could be fixed. Pound and Aldington were signatories to a letter (printed in the 15 December 1913 issue) from five male contributors requesting a change of name for the journal because its current name failed to communicate its 'character . . . as an organ of individualists of both sexes, and of the individualist principle in every department of life' (p. 244). The Poundian influence, one might say, was becoming rigid, and Marsden should have realised from this tumescence of masculine opinion that she was about to be screwed. But instead she called a meeting of shareholders to discuss the proposal, telling them that the current title 'continues to suggest what the paper is not, and fails to give any indication whatever as to what it is'. The upshot was a unanimous vote in favour of a change of name; and after considering a few of the alternatives (the *Free Voice*, the *Prophet*, the *Revealer*, *Tomorrow*) they agreed to accept Marsden's own choice, the *Egoist* (Lidderdale and Nicholson 1970: 75, 78). And, as if to demonstrate that women would no longer monopolise the journal, Marsden made Aldington – whom Pound regarded as his discovery and (mistakenly, it turned out) disciple – assistant editor for the final issue of the *New Freewoman* on 15 December 1913. Four days later, Pound wrote to Williams: 'Richard is now running the *NF*' (*L* 65).

So by a conjuncture of feminist insouciance and masculinist opportunism the gender-specific *New Freewoman* was erased from patriarchal memory, and with female connivance. When the journal reappeared on 1 January 1914 it did so under the seemingly gender-neutral and Max Stirner-inspired title of the *Egoist* (Levenson 1984: 63–74). But in the wake of George Meredith's novel of that name, and contemporary Nietzschean associations of the word (James Huneker's 1909 collection of essays, *The Egoists*, is subtitled 'A Book of Supermen'), the new name of the journal was at least tacitly masculinist. Certainly, the *Egoist* consolidated its position in androcentric literary history by beginning to serialise on 16

February 1914, at Pound's instigation, one of the unmistakably masculinist classics of modernism, James Joyce's *A Portrait of the Artist as a Young Man*. How Pound set about filling the pages of the journals in which he secured editorial space involves a consideration of his activities as a talent scout and critic of work in progress.

3

The practical critic

Shortly before Pound was to leave Paris for good and settle in Rapallo, he was visited in 1923 by Malcolm Cowley, who observed that in those days Pound was known 'not so much for his own creations as for his advocacy of other writers and his sallies against the stupid public' (Cowley 1951: 119). This was the polite version of Louis Untermeyer's brutal dismissal of Pound as 'a press agent rather than a pioneer' (Untermeyer 1919: 212). Pound's view of his career up to that point, however, was very different indeed, because he liked to believe that he had become a critic more or less by accident – given the imperceptiveness or indifference to genuinely original work displayed by those who controlled the major review journals and publishing houses – and that in any case the criticism he had written in the form of reviews and essays was never intended to be anything more than a temporary truancy from the serious business of writing poetry. 'I have since 1912 abandoned my own work for criticism', he wrote in February 1920, shortly before *Hugh Selwyn Mauberley* was published, 'because during this period I have noted in England an acceptance of the ultra-mediocre' (Henderson 1984: 281). By the end of 1920, however, with Eliot coming to be recognised as the best poet and critic in England, and Joyce's *Ulysses* in the process of being serialised in the *Little Review*, Pound felt he could retire from the fray and get on with his 'REAL work' (*L* 341), namely poetry in the form of the *Cantos*.

But when, in 1927, he was offered and eventually accepted the prestigious *Dial* Award, he at first suspected that he was being overlooked as a poet and celebrated as a critic. For a start, the *Dial* had taken a long time to get around to him since first making the award to Sherwood Anderson in 1921. The 1922 award had gone to Eliot for *The Waste Land* (a judgement Pound himself supported strongly), but in 1923 the recipient had been a mere critic, Van Wyck Brooks. The other award winners, however, were three poets who regarded Pound's poetry as superior to their own: E.E. Cummings (1926), William Carlos Williams (1925), and in 1924, Marianne Moore, whose first book, *Poems* (1921), was published by the Pound-influenced Egoist Press, and who became editor of the *Dial* in 1925. Moore tried a couple of times to commission criticism from Pound in the form of reviews of Cummings and Cheever Dunning, evidently unaware of the fact that her editorial predecessor, Scofield Thayer, had been responsible not only for hiring Pound as Paris correspondent for the *Dial* (at the prompting of Eliot, who had known Thayer at Harvard) but also for firing him in April 1923 and for rejecting Cantos which Pound was under the impression the *Dial* had commissioned (Martin 1986: 48). So when the *Dial* cabled Pound to offer him its 1927 award, and asked him to 'send immediately suitable prose or verse' (ibid.), he assumed from the wording that they were more interested in his prose than in his poems. He therefore told Moore that he could not accept the award, worth $2000, 'except on [his] Cantos or . . . verse as a whole' (Moore 1928: 89). He was able to take this stand and risk losing the money because he and his wife now lived reasonably comfortably on additional income inherited by Dorothy in 1923. The award had to be made for his poetry, he insisted, because his prose was 'mostly stop-gap', consisting of 'attempts to deal with transient states of murky ['Murkn': *L* 289] imbecility or ignorance': it would be 'stupid', therefore, to make the award on the basis of his criticism (ibid.).

All of this was duly conceded and reported by Moore when, after printing an excerpt from Canto 27 in the January 1928 issue of the *Dial*, she announced that Pound had accepted the *Dial* award for 1927. But in the very process of doing so she devoted most of her available space to 'another service of his to letters', notably his work as foreign editor for the *Little Review*, and his critical acuteness in encouraging writers who were not only new (for anybody, even Anatole France, could do that) but good writers into the bargain: 'Mr Pound', she wrote, 'has never made a mistake' (ibid.). Herself of course a beneficiary of such services, Moore concluded that these were the activities which made Pound an appropriate recipient of the *Dial* award as 'one of the most valuable forces in contemporary letters' (ibid.: 90). Until the *Dial* went out of business after the Wall Street collapse in 1929, Moore continued to publish far more of Pound's prose than his poetry. Since nearly all the poetry he wrote was in the form of Cantos which were perceived as obscure in both detail and design, Pound's lively essays became the most accessible part of his writings, and he remained, *malgré lui*, a critic.

Moore's tribute to Pound's triumphs as a talent scout during his London years is one of many which have contributed to the supposition that in literary matters Pound's judgement was always unerring. Williams, for instance, had told her in March 1918 that Pound's most impressive feature was his 'unswerving intelligence in the detection of literary quality' (Williams, W.C. 1957: 42). In October that year Aiken had described him in the *Dial* as a 'King-Maker among poets' (*CH* 145); twenty years later, Ford, who had had a similar reputation in his *English Review* days, was to tease Pound about his 'claim to be the greatest discoverer of literary talent the world has ever seen' (*EP/FMF* 157). Many of these accolades, like Eliot's 'Pound was always a masterly judge of poetry' (Eliot 1946: 329), come from people whose own reputations as writers have benefited considerably from the critical support Pound gave them, although some of them, like Lewis, wondered from time to time about the wisdom of attributing to Pound such extraordinary prescience in these matters. Lewis expressed Groucho-Marxist misgivings about belonging to an exclusive literary club whose membership extended to people like himself when he wrote that he 'entertained a most healthy suspicion of all Pound's enthusiasms – was I not one of them myself?' (Lewis 1937: 284). But by and large Pound has been credited with an inexplicable faculty which enabled him to bypass critical procedures and recognise genius immediately.

The mystification of a critical practice whose processes are held to be inscrutable and always result uncannily in unerring judgements was of course not something which Pound himself, as a critic allegedly endowed with such powers, had anything to gain from demystifying: on the contrary, it made his operations as a critic unassailably authoritative. For Pound, critical prescience was simply a manifestation of the sensibility which enabled him as a poet to be avant-garde. 'Artists are the antennae of the race' (*LE* 58). This Poundian maxim, repeated frequently in his writings (*ABCR* 57, *SP* 199), is the sloganised version of his 1912 conception of the poet as 'the advance guard of the psychologist on the watch for new emotions, new vibrations sensible to faculties as yet ill understood' (*SP* 331). Any poet who was avant-garde in this sense would have no difficulty becoming an avant-garde critic, for as Pound explained to the editor of the *Little Review* in September 1917, to write avant-garde criticism is simply a matter of 'saying things which everybody will believe in three years' time and take as a matter of course in ten' (*L* 179). Observations which are matter-of-fact to a poet-critic will be taken in the fullness of time as evidence of visionary and prophetic powers; for Pound, as for the English Romantic poets, the 'serious' artist (celebrated in a 1913 essay with that title (*LE* 41–57)) is a seer, 'seereeyus' (*L* 380).

Pound took these matters very seriously indeed. After being discharged from St Elizabeths mental hospital in May 1958 he stayed with his daughter and son-in-law at their castle near Merano in Italy. In the garden of Schloss Brunnenburg, Pound had the Gaudier-Brzeska effigy of him, which looks like a miniaturised Easter Island monolith, installed facing the mountains to the west. The purpose of this symbolic placement was not to acknowledge Pound's failure as 'a man on whom the sun has gone down' (Canto 74), but to celebrate his success as an avant-gardist who got ahead and stayed ahead by behaviour which most people thought crazy at the time. Like many events in Pound's life, this one was already textualised. It was scripted by an imaginary dialogue, written in the seventeenth century by Fontenelle, and translated by Pound for the *Egoist* in May 1917. Here the ancient Greek philosopher Strato tells the Italian Renaissance painter Raphael about an incident which took place at Tyre (Brunnenburg is in the Tyrol). After the slaves had killed their masters (as the Italians killed Mussolini), they 'agreed to choose for their king the man who ... should see the sun rise before any one else'. Strato instructed his own loyal slave to endure the ridicule of all those other contestants resolutely facing east by turning his back on them, whereupon he 'saw the first rays of the sun which caught on a lofty tower' to the west (*PD* 135–6) – just as at Brunnenburg the visionary eyes of the Gaudier-Brzeska bust confront the first dawn light on those mountain peaks to the west, named (Hugh Kenner reminds us) *Ziel* and *Mut*, 'purpose' and 'courage' (Kenner 1971: 260). The problem with an avant-garde literature, Pound had written in a 1917 essay attacking provincialism in the arts, is that it is 'always too far ahead of any general consciousness to be of the slightest contemporary use' (*SP* 164). That is why we need 'seereeyus' critics, Village Explainers who will enable us provincials to recognise what it is that's staring us in the face, and why (in the words of the elitist moral which Strato draws from his anecdote) 'the wise should ever turn their backs on the mob' (*PD* 136). Omitted from the list of those who were 'blessed' in *Blast* (1914), 'critics' finally achieved beatification in 1927 when Pound wrote, in his own journal, *Exile*: 'Blessed are they who pick the right artists and makers' (*EP/VA* 199).

Eventually, Pound came to believe that his abandonment of his 'own work for criticism' in 1912 had not been a complete waste of time after all. 'PICKING the rising talent', he was to write in Year 12 of the Fascist era (or 1934 by another calendar), 'is so subtle a process that even the best player attempts it with diffidence' (*LE* 79). Yet if you had the nerve to play the evaluation game the stakes were high, for in addition to the kudos attached to 'picking winners inside the gawden of the muses' (Tyttel 1987: 235), and earning the gratitude of those thus honoured, you could lay claim to the wider social usefulness of a 'critical faculty which' (he told Williams in September 1920) 'can pick you and [Maxwell] Bodenheim, and [Mina] Loy, and [Carl] Sandburg (and in earlier phases [Robert] Frost) out of the muck of liars and shams' (*L* 222). To be seen to have picked the winners after all was cause for a justifiable self-congratulation when reprinting in *Make It New* (1934) essays first published mainly before 1920 on a variety of past masters from Arnaut Daniel to Henry James, but none, surprisingly, on any of those writers he had tipped for a place in an emergent canon of modernist writing. Nevertheless, he wanted it put on record there 'that from 1912 onward for a decade and more' he had been 'instrumental in forcing into print, and *secondarily* in commenting on, certain work now recognized as valid by all competent readers' (*LE* 80).

What made him 'a specialist' in this area, he told Lewis, was his 'flair for "genius" ' (Lewis 1927: 57): in 1914 that 'flair' had been 'at the service of anybody' (*L* 72), although by 1933 he suspected he was losing 'whatever flair there may once have been' (Bornstein 1985: 12). But 'flair', like 'taste', is a word which explains nothing. It merely mystifies the processes by which a critic recognises excellence in literary texts whose own processes of production are similarly mystified by having words like 'genius', 'giftedness' and 'talent' affixed to them. Whatever it was that he meant by 'flair', Pound always insisted that it had nothing to do with his personal likes and dislikes, all of which he considered quite irrelevant to his assessment of any piece of writing. This was what set him apart as a critic, he told Williams in 1920, from Marianne Moore, who had a 'spinsterly aversion' to things she didn't like (*L* 222). Personally, he happened to find D.H. Lawrence's 'middling-sensual erotic verses' somewhat 'disgusting', and was even willing to say so in print when reviewing them in the July 1913 issue of *Poetry* (*LE* 387). But, as he told Monroe in September that year, he could nevertheless '*recognize* certain qualities' (*L* 59) in the writings of a man his own age who appeared to have 'learned the proper treatment of modern subjects' before he himself had managed to do so (*L* 52). This manoeuvre is repeated in his attitude to the writings of Henry Miller, when again Pound attempts to dissociate 'liking' (as a 'subjective' and therefore irrelevant and disposable component in one's transactions with literary texts) from those unspecified but putatively 'objective' considerations which literary critics ought to concern themselves with exclusively. 'Miller has considerable talent', he told a correspondent in 1937, but 'ultimately . . . bores me, as did D.H. Lawrence' (*L* 394). He was careful to add that this was his 'private' view. Likes and dislikes were all very well in private, and perhaps unavoidable, but criticism was to be a far nobler enterprise. For criticism entails a 'duty', as he saw it in October 1956, 'to recognize . . . integrity and . . . merit' in the work of (for instance) Henri Gaudier-Brzeska, Wyndham Lewis and Constantin Brancusi, 'none of whom was making the art that [he], personally, wanted for more than, say, 15% of [his] time' (*EP/VA* 177).

Exactly what it was that he recognised when he read poems written by that 'detestable person' (*L* 52), D.H. Lawrence, he does not say, because he liked to think of himself as possessing those divinatory powers which Ford laid claim to, and which had enabled Ford to recognise Lawrence's talent as early as 1908 merely by glancing at the opening paragraph of that short story which constituted his only evidence for that judgement. In the case of Pound's 'recognition' of Lawrence, what seems to have happened is much less mystifying than he would have us believe. Trusting Ford's judgement of Lawrence as a prose writer, he decided to give Lawrence the benefit of the doubt as a poet. By 1917, when Lawrence had published *Sons and Lovers* (1913) and *The Rainbow* (1915), it was clear to Pound that Ford's initial assessment had been 'justified', although that did not prevent Pound from thinking Lawrence (who 'annoys me') 'inferior . . . to Joyce' as a prose writer (*L* 179). If Pound's own assessment of Lawrence suggests that 'liking' and 'disliking' were not so easily suppressed in the formation of critical judgements as he would have preferred them to be, it was not a possibility he was ever prepared to concede. He told Monroe that, although he personally found the poetry of Robert Frost 'as dull as ditch water, as dull as Wordsworth', he could see nevertheless that Frost was 'set to be "literchure" some day' (Williams, E. 1977: 67), and therefore deserved the favourable reviews Pound gave *A Boy's Will* (1913) in the *Egoist* and *North of Boston* (1914) in *Poetry* (*LE* 382–6).

Given the subsequent history of the reputations of Lawrence and Joyce, and the ways in which those two writers came to be polarised by critical factionalism – the British Leavisites being pro-Lawrence, and American academics largely pro-Joyce – it is amazing that as early as March 1914 Pound should appear to have had such catholicity of taste as to be able to accommodate both of them and declare that 'Lawrence and Joyce are the two strongest prose writers among les jeunes' (*L* 73). Contemporaries who read his criticism tried to determine what his criteria were when defending writers whose work was programmatically different from one another's. How could Pound possibly admire Frost's 'Death of the Hired Man', Fletcher wondered, with its 'echoes of Wordsworth, whom Pound valiantly despised, and of the still more hated Georgians?' (Weintraub 1979: 315). In terms of the *Imagiste* aesthetic which Pound was promulgating at the time, Frost's bucolic garrulousness was an anachronism. Eliot was to observe in 1946 that Pound's literary tastes were 'much more comprehensive than most people realize' (Eliot 1946: 326); but to put it like that is to place the most favourable construction on an eclecticism which admires different things for different reasons and involves no risk-taking whatsoever. Pound made a public acknowledgement of the catholicity of his literary tastes by publishing in November 1915 his *Catholic Anthology*, a book which offended Roman Catholics like Francis Meynell understandably misled by the title (' "Why, why will you needlessly irritate people?" ' his publisher, Elkin Mathews, had asked him (*L* 121)). *Catholic Anthology* contained poems by Pound himself, Hulme, Eliot, Yeats, Williams, Sandburg, Edgar Lee Masters, Orrick Johns, and Maxwell Bodenheim, who had to appear as 'M.B.' in case his German name caused offence in wartime London (*L* 99). It also included poems by a number of other people Pound had reasons for not wanting to irritate: Douglas Goldring, who had been Ford's assistant on the *English Review*; Alice Corbin (Henderson), editorial assistant on *Poetry*; Alfred Kreymborg, who as an editor of the *Glebe* had published the American edition of *Des Imagistes*, and was now editing *Others*; Harriet Monroe, the editor of *Poetry*; Harold Monro, the editor of *Poetry and Drama*; and John Rodker, a trusty who was to take over from Pound as foreign editor of the *Little Review*, and publish *Hugh Selwyn Mauberley* at his Ovid Press in 1920.

What is demonstrated in *Catholic Anthology* is not so much the breadth of Pound's literary tastes as the workings of a literary politics which uses the space at its disposal to keep potentially useful people on side. Years later, Pound would usually justify such ventures by claiming that they had been undertaken to launch an unknown who subsequently become famous – H.D. in *Des Imagistes*, for instance (Williams, E. 1977: 39), or Eliot in *Catholic Anthology* (*LE* 80). But at the time such ventures were undertaken it could be said that Pound was hedging his bets by including such a diverse range of writers. Readers ignorant of the hidden literary politics which determined the selection of items to be included in Pound's anthologies could respond either positively to a surprising breadth of literary taste or negatively to what looked like a mindless eclecticism.

In 1933, after publishing another anthology which posed similar questions, *Profile* (1932), Pound told Ford that 'by the law of averages you . . . discover 97 ducks to every swan and a half' (*EP/FMF* 130). The editors of the *Hound & Horn* might have calculated the incidence of swans much lower, given the number of 'lame duck discoveries' Pound kept trying to foist upon them (Greenbaum 1966: 104). But that is a more accurate representation of how Pound went about the business of separating swans from ducks than what is implied in the myth of his unerring prescience. H.D. remembers Pound as being 'inexpressibly kind to anyone who he felt had the faintest spark of submerged talent' (H.D. 1980: 10). Ready to see promise in a large number of writers, he put himself in the position of being able to claim, in the eventual success of any one of them, to have been the first to spot their quality. Even so, it needs to be asked why, when he was casting his net so widely during his London years, he remained unimpressed by the poetry of Vachel Lindsay, Edward Arlington Robinson, Wallace Stevens and others whose writings became part of the masculinist canon of modernism.

Pound did not work in those optimal conditions which would have given him the time to read widely and reflect deeply before committing a literary judgement to print. He worked in haste and to deadlines, and gambled on what that fictive readership, posterity, would consider to be the best writing of his contemporaries. He saw himself as taking risks, and expected editors and publishers to take risks likewise. In September 1917 he sent to the *Little Review* some poems by Iris Barry and John Rodker which, he explained in a covering note, the editors should not regard as evidence of a willingness on his part to 'compromise' his literary standards. On the contrary, what he was doing was taking 'a bet' on literary promise: he had seen the draft of a novel by Barry (later published as *Splashing into Society* (New York, 1923)), and thought it had 'the chance of being literature'; and he was convinced that Rodker would 'go farther than Richard Aldington'. 'I stake my critical position, or some part of it', he wrote, 'on a belief that both of them *will* do something' (*L* 179). To point out, with the facile wisdom of hindsight, that Pound lost that particular bet, would be to overlook the way in which this episode illuminates that unstable compound of provisionality, risk-taking, best-guessing, self-persuasion and blind faith which characterises all critical judgements of the writing of one's contemporaries. There are no grounds for believing that the bets he took on his famous winners – T.S. Eliot, James Joyce and Wyndham Lewis – were made in any other way.

The completely or relatively unknown writers Pound decided to encourage were perceived by him as 'discoveries', and if the relationship came to anything he would try to assign them to a variety of positions described by such terms as 'protégé', 'disciple', 'neophyte' and 'acolyte'. The metaphor of 'discovery' in such circumstances – as in, 'Have just discovered another Amur'kn', used by Pound of Frost in March 1913 (*L* 49) – was somewhat problematic, implying as it does that writers, like lands remote from the imperial centres, are *terra nullius* until come upon by explorers in the service of exploiters. Even in these terms, however, Frost had been discovered already, in so far as by the time Pound had 'found the man by accident' (*L* 51–2) in March 1913 Frost had already secured a London publisher, David Nott, for his first book of poems, *A Boy's Will*. Pound would go through the ritual of apportioning due credit to others in such cases, but in ways which brought credit on himself. 'I did not discover Mr Joyce', he recalled in 1933. 'Mr Yeats discovered him'; but only, it turned out, as 'a writer of severe and conventional lyrics' quite marginal to what Pound understood by modernism, and not as the author of *Dubliners, A Portrait of the Artist as a Young Man* and *Ulysses* (*EP/JJ* 246). When Pound told Quinn in August 1915 that he had 'more or less discovered' Eliot (Eliot 1971: ix), he no doubt had in mind the fact that Aiken had been showing 'The Love Song of J. Alfred Prufrock' to editors like Harold Monro (who dismissed it as 'absolutely inane') before introducing Pound to that poem and its author (Tytell 1987: 115–16). In his personal dealings with Aiken, Pound made no attempt to underrate Aiken's part in the 'discovery' of Eliot; on the contrary, Aiken was given to understand that that was probably his 'only contribution to the age'. Aiken thought it ludicrous, however, that anybody could claim to have discovered 'the Tsetse', as he called Eliot, since only 'the Tsetse himself could have accomplished that bright and arcane invention' (Aiken 1963: 219). In Pound's subsequent retellings of the story – all of them accurate – Eliot's poetry and Joyce's prose were published where and when they were only as a result of Pound's own perseverance in protracted dealings with editors and publishers; but, in the course of these retellings, details came to be erased from that narrative of the facilitator as hero, and Pound came to be inscribed in literary history as the 'discoverer' of Joyce and Eliot.

Another complicating factor was Pound's proprietorial attitude towards the writers he befriended: increasingly, he came to think of his 'discoveries' as *his* discoveries. So, when the Boston *Transcript* announced in June 1915 that Frost had been published in England 'unheralded, unintroduced, [and] untrumpeted', Pound wrote to inform the editor that he himself had 'done as much to boom Frost as the next man' (*L* 107); and, when 'his' Joyce was (as he saw it) taken over by the Paris publisher of the first edition of *Ulysses* in 1922, Pound was so miffed by the whole business that he declined Sylvia Beach's invitation to attend the book launch (Carpenter 1988: 404). Because Pound believed that critics should not simply pass judgement on writing but involve themselves in its production by both example and a willingness to help other writers, the benefits to be had from a professional association with Pound were considerable. One of the problems he saw in Amy Lowell's plans for bringing out an Imagist anthology of her own was that it would deprive him of what he called his 'machinery for . . . discovering new talent' and 'gathering stray good poems' for publication (*L* 77–8). To any poet trying to get a start in London, Pound seemed well worth knowing, given his contacts with editors and publishers and his willingness to negotiate with them on behalf of worthy newcomers. He was both 'a poet and an impresario', Lewis recalled, which was 'at that time an unexpected combination' (Lewis 1937: 255), and this meant that he spent an increasing, and eventually inordinate, amount of time 'attending to other people's affairs' (*L* 63).

Whether he actually 'liked to be the impresario for younger men', which is what Eliot thought (Eliot 1946: 328), or felt it his duty to look after all those writers he once called 'the *promising young*' (*L* 80) but more regularly (using Ford's term) '*Les Jeunes*' (*EP/FMF* 29), he certainly put an enormous amount of time and effort into promoting other people's careers and living up to the Hebrew meaning of his name Ezra ('helper'). 'I have spent the day in your service', he would write in June 1917 to Battery Officer Wyndham Lewis, who was recovering from trench fever in a casualty clearing station near Boulogne, and therefore had left Pound to deal with gallery owners and attend to the serialisation of Lewis's novel *Tarr* in the *Egoist* (*EP/WL* 81). Days on end were spent trying to sort out James Joyce's complicated affairs, during which Pound came to see the aptness of Lewis's description of him as a 'demon pantechnicon driver' (*EP/JJ* 112–13). Being an American, he was perceived as the P.T. Barnum of London literary life: Lewis commented mockingly on 'the "Pound Circus" ' (Benstock 1987: 22), and Douglas Goldring published some satirical verses about 'Ezra's circle of performing Yanks' (Goldring 1932: 80). Until Pound decided in 1918 that he couldn't 'run the triple ring circus forever' (*EP/MCA* 212), all of the circus animals were well cared for. Pound would read manuscripts and comment on them in detail, and introduce their authors to editors, publishers, potential patrons and one another. He acted as a welfare officer in providing second-hand clothing for indigent protégés, although the more fastidious of these felt as Eliot did that Pound's 'shoes and underwear were almost the only garments which resembled those of other men sufficiently to be worn by them' (Eliot 1946: 328). Medically, he was ready to give advice by post on Lewis's gonorrhoea and Joyce's problems with his eyes and teeth (*EP/WL* 80; *EP/JJ* 100); and his lonelyhearts service offered

Mary Barnard 'a likely lad' who needed 'something above the average to look after him' (Barnard 1984: 117), and proposed to James Laughlin that he might consider marrying that 'fine well grown gal' who happened to be H.D.'s daughter, Perdita (Carpenter 1988: 236). By no means financially secure himself, Pound got his wife to help finance the publication of *Prufrock and Other Observations* in 1917, although 'Eliot never knew it' (*CO/EP* 111).

Accustomed since childhood to the comforts of a big house and a life of private schools, universities and European holidays, Pound had a middle-class view of what constitutes poverty. When Orage observed in 1921 that during his years in London Pound had been 'compelled to live on much less than would support a navvy' (Orage 1974: 145), he was referring only to the money Pound managed to earn from his writings. The average British navvy could not depend as Pound did on cheques sent regularly by his American father, nor would he have married a middle-class woman like Dorothy Shakespear with an annuity and the prospect of an inheritance. 'If I accept more than I need', Pound told Cowley, 'I at once become a sponger' (Cowley 1951: 120). He believed that writers ought to be able to make a living by writing. Whereas Williams became a GP and Wallace Stevens an insurance lawyer, Pound never undertook any kind of regular paid employment which would enable him to pay the rent without being obliged to use that part of his head with which he wrote poems. Eliot took a job with Lloyds Bank because it gave him a regular income and opportunities for interesting work in foreign exchange quite remote from his creative activities, and his employers thought well enough of him to give him three months' paid leave when he needed to convalesce (Eliot 1988: 473). And so, when Pound wrote in July 1916 to ask Lewis if he could suggest 'any bloody way to keep MY income wholly from disappearing' (*EP/WL* 51), the question was not unanswerably rhetorical.

Wartime conditions could have increased Pound's opportunities for reviewing, principally because of the disruptions they caused in the world of London bookmen. Traditionally, that body renewed itself by recruiting bright young gentlemen down from Oxbridge. But by 1915 another institution with a longer tradition and more clout, the army, had decided that bright young gentlemen should be commissioned as officers to lead the lower ranks into German machine-gun fire in France. The consequent decimation of a whole generation of educated men – 'wastage as never before' (*P* 190) –

tightened the control on London literary journalism of those who were too old or unfit or foreign to be enlisted, since that masculinist institution chose not to follow the manufacturing sector in hiring women to replace the missing men. As an American national who suffered from astigmatism, and whose attempt to enlist was mishandled bureaucratically, Pound was preserved from the risk of being killed in action like Hulme and Gaudier-Brzeska. But his reputation among London bookmen as a trouble-maker – too old to be an *enfant terrible*, and not yet distinguished enough to be a *monstre sacré* – meant that financial opportunities which might have come his way in the later years of the war went instead to Eliot, whose tactfulness in handling 'difficult' representatives of different literary factions gave him unique access to both avant-garde and establishment periodicals.

Pound did not like the idea of a major poet wasting his time working in a bank, and embarrassed Eliot in 1922 by trying to make him the beneficiary of a well-intentioned scheme called Bel Esprit, by which thirty people would each be asked to contribute £10 per year in order to establish a fund big enough 'to release ONE proved writer' from Lloyds Bank or its equivalent to get on with their own writing (*L* 238–9). With income tax and death duties either negligible or non-existent, private patronage was still a possibility when modernist writing was being invented. *Poetry*, for instance, was financed by a group of well-off people in Chicago with an interest in the arts and a desire to display that interest conspicuously (Williams, E. 1977: 16–18); and Eliot's *Criterion* was backed financially by Lady Rothermere, who was married to the newspaper magnate, William Randolph Hearst. The value of such people was not only in the cheques they were willing to sign but also in their social connections with other well-placed friends and acquaintances who could be persuaded to take a proselytising interest in the literature they sponsored. The phenomenal commercial success of *Georgian Poetry 1911–12*, which was estimated to have sold eventually 15,000 copies (Ross 1967: 128), was attributable to the influence of its Maecenas, Edward Marsh, in the social circles frequented by those who controlled the reviewing networks constituted by the principal London papers.

If Marsh was to wartime London what Maecenas had been to Augustan Rome, a moral was to be drawn from this 'repeat in history' (*L* 285). For the trouble with Maecenas, in Pound's opinion, was that he had backed the wrong poets, Virgil and

Horace, instead of Propertius (*L* 287). As Propertius *redivivus*, Pound saw the British empire as simply repeating the 'infinite and ineffable imbecility' (*L* 310) of the Roman empire, one manifestation of which were the activities of Edward Marsh, whose patronage of Rupert Brooke and the Georgian poets instead of Pound and the *Imagistes* confirmed Pound's belief that in imperial conditions a Maecenas will always overlook the best poets of his time. If *Poetry* was to become anything more than 'a sheet begging for favours', he told its editor in March 1916, it would need to establish itself as a 'Maecenas, upholding a principle that poetry ought to be decently paid' (*L* 118). State patronage of the arts, as in ancient Alexandria, into which 'art was lifted ... by subsidy' (*PM* 53), is what Pound would have preferred, but in the meantime support for schemes like Bel Esprit would have to depend on 'Maecenism', defined in 1927 as the 'individual desire to stimulate the arts' (*L* 291).

The trick was to turn collectors into patrons by luring them away from a consumerism of safe investments in the celebrated dead, and to get them instead to sponsor the next generation of masterpieces. The man Pound succeeded in persuading to become the Maecenas of modernism in literature was the American lawyer and art collector, John Quinn. He had renewed his acquaintance with Pound – they had first met in New York in August 1910 in the company of W.B. Yeats's father – by protesting against Pound's attack (in the 21 January 1915 issue of the *New Age*) on American collectors who buy 'autograph mss. of William Morris, faked Rembrandts and faked Van Dykes' (*L* 94), instead of works by living artists like Jacob Epstein (Reid 1968: 197–8). As the recent owner of a number of Morris manuscripts, Quinn read Pound's piece as a veiled attack on himself, and pointed out that he had in fact sold most of the manuscripts in his possession in 1912 to the man who endowed the Henry E. Huntington Library in California (ibid.: 123). Replying on 8 March 1915, Pound advanced a notion of patronage which greatly appealed to Quinn: the patron as *artifex* or creator (ibid.: 199–200). In buying from living artists who need money 'to buy tools, time and food', Pound told Quinn, the patron ends up 'building art into the world; he creates' (*L* 97). So Quinn was persuaded to build up his collection of manuscripts of living writers. He had already begun collecting Conrad's manuscripts, and was eventually to acquire from Eliot the original version of *The Waste Land* with Pound's annotations and deletions. It was Quinn who put up the money which enabled Pound to buy space in the *Little Review* and pay contributors to that journal. Pound's part in this deal was to guarantee that the space would not be wasted.

When E.E. Cummings declared that Pound deserved something better from his critics than 'incoherent abuse' or 'inchoate adoration' (Cummings 1920: 783), he indicated the extent to which Pound's critical interventions in literary production polarised the responses of those who experienced or merely observed them. And among those writers who were the focus of Pound's interest as a literary critic, two contrasting types of chronicle survive, one written by the adorers who believe that there would have been no modernist movement in literature but for Pound, and the other by abusers whose principal grievance is that Pound used their writings for careerist purposes of his own.

Cummings aligns himself with the adorers in holding Pound 'responsible for possibly one-half of the most alive poetry and probably all of the least intense prose committed, during the last few years, in the American and English languages' (ibid.: 782). Cummings happened to be reviewing Eliot's *Poems* (1919) at the time, but his assessment of Pound's critical activities had been endorsed independently a month earlier by May Sinclair in her review of Pound's *Quia Pauper Amavi* (1919) in the *North American Review*, where she praised Pound for having 'rendered services to modern international art that in any society less feral than our own would have earned him the gratitude of his contemporaries' (*CH* 178). Such testimonies were still being made in the 1930s by young writers like Ronald Duncan, a student of F.R. Leavis's, who made the pilgrimage to Rapallo and reported that Pound 'taught [him] more in one day than [he] had learned in a year at Cambridge' (Duncan 1968: 158). On behalf of all those writers whose experience of Pound had been similarly enabling, Williams came up with the ultimate accolade: 'before meeting Ezra Pound is like B.C. and A.D.' (Williams, W.C. 1958: 5).

The adorers viewed the abusers as mean-spirited and ungrateful. Ford, another adorer, pitched into such ingrates on his own behalf when reviewing Pound's *Personae* (1926). 'Of all the unlicked cubs whose work I have thrust upon a not too willing world', Ford wrote in January 1927, 'Ezra was the only one who did not subsequently kick me in the face' (*CH* 219). Ford's point had already been developed with considerable bravura by Ernest Hemingway in his own description of Pound as an amazingly generous poet who devoted four-fifths of his time to advancing

> the fortunes, both material and artistic, of his friends. He defends them when they are attacked, he gets them into magazines and out of jail. He loans them money. He sells their pictures. He arranges concerts for them. He writes articles about them. He introduces them to wealthy women. He gets publishers to take their books. He sits up all night with them when they claim to be dying and he witnesses their wills. He advances them hospital expenses and dissuades them from suicide. And in the end a few of them refrain from knifing him at the first opportunity.
>
> (Hemingway 1925: 223)

The expenditure of all that time and energy was in the interests of creating 'a grrrreat littttttterary period' (*L* 235) through the collective achievements of a literary movement, a 'modern experiment' whose 'justification', he told Felix Schelling in July 1922, was *The Waste Land* (*L* 248). The constituent writers of the modernist movement were to be a loose federation rather than a closely knit group, and bonded together more by common antipathies than by an informed understanding of one another's work. To be in the movement was to 'be with *us*', he told Quinn in April 1918, 'rather than with the Poetry Book Shop [of Harold Monro] and the Georgian Anthologies, [Lascelles] Abercrombie, Eddie Marsh, etc.' (*L* 193). Pound's ultimate put-down of somebody, Aldington recalled (while mocking Pound's French pronunciation), was '*Il n'est pas dong le mouvemong*' (Aldington 1968: 133).

Like *Imagisme*, *le mouvement* was a triumph of the signifier, a fiction to confer on individual writers with separate careers in mind the illusion of moving towards a common goal. Ideally, they were to co-operate for what Eliot called their 'reciprocal benefit' (Gallup 1970: 58), although in fact it was far easier to put their writing into the pages of the same journal than to leave them alone together in the same room: Eliot, for instance, did not much care for Ford's work, or Yeats for the work of Eliot or Lewis, and the only writing Joyce appeared to be interested in was his own. To speculate, as Lewis did, on whether Pound was the Baden-Powell of the *mouvement* (because 'he was never satisfied until everything was *organized*' (Lewis 1937: 254)) was to move dangerously close to the abusers' position. Adorationist orthodoxy, however, held that if the world's greatest talent scout had to behave like the world's most famous boy scout then so be it: for as Eliot was to write in 1946, who but Pound could have 'created a situation in which, for the first time, there was a "modern movement in poetry" in which English and American poets collaborated' (Eliot 1946: 330)? And, if you not only had been admitted to Pound's *mouvement* but were in addition a beneficiary of his services, how could you avoid expressing your gratitude to the man?

For an answer to that question we can turn to one of Pound's principal abusers, Richard Aldington, and the story he told Herbert Read in January 1925 of how he and H.D. had been exploited by a self-promoting careerist who used their poems to draw attention to himself:

> Imagism, as written by H.D. and me, was purely our own invention and was not an attempt to put a theory in practice. The 'school' was Ezra's invention. And the first imagist anthology was invented by him in order to claim us as his disciples, a manoeuvre we were too naifs (*sic*) to recognise at the time, being still young enough to trust our friends.
>
> (Aldington 1965: 127)

In this angry reconstruction of the events, Pound is no longer the benign figure made familiar in literary histories of the period – that self-sacrificing worker on behalf of all those writers whose manifest talents were being so unjustly ignored by a corrupt publishing system. On the contrary, Pound's interest in H.D. and Aldington is treated here as evidence of a desire to dominate, a will-to-power. What it felt like to be a protégé of Pound's is given fictionalised treatment in Aldington's novel, *Death of a Hero* (1929), where Pound is 'Upjohn' and Aldington 'George'. Here the relationship is seen as mutually beneficial precisely because it is mutually exploitative: 'Mr. Upjohn desired to make George a disciple, and George was not averse from making use of Mr. Upjohn' (Aldington 1958: 100). Pound had wanted to plant a man he could trust in an editorial capacity on the *Egoist*, and therefore contrived successfully to have Aldington appointed as assistant editor, not knowing that he himself was being manipulated by an ambitious younger man who would edit the journal to his own tastes rather than to Pound's once he was installed in the job.

Not every ambitious young writer Pound came into contact with was quite so skilful as Aldington in counter-manipulative tactics. Harold Monro, who managed to elude Pound's attempts at dominating *Poetry and Drama*, noted in the June 1913 issue of his journal that the newly emergent *Imagistes* were already under 'the formidable dictatorship of Ezra Pound' (Monro 1913: 127). That generous and resourceful nourisher of talent whom Hemingway felt could not be praised highly enough could also be, as Aiken discovered, 'something of a tyrant' to protégés suspected of insubordination (Aiken 1963: 215). Aiken got offside with Pound by not turning up to a *Blast* dinner 'as he had been instructed to do'; it was observed also that he 'had not been too "discreet" in his choice of friends', which meant that he sometimes mixed with people outside Pound's circle (ibid.: 206–7). The power exercised by Pound in these matters took the form which most people encounter inside the nuclear family, where power is invested in acts of kindness, such that resistance is construed as evidence of ingratitude. Trying to work under Pound's gaze could be a daunting experience. Even Eliot felt that Pound could be 'a dominating director' who treated his protégés rather like 'literature machines to be carefully tended and oiled, for the sake of their potential output' (Eliot 1946: 328). Frost complained in July 1913 that Pound kept 'bullying' him to write *vers libre*, threatening to let Frost 'perish of neglect' if he didn't, and behaving as if the mere 'fact that he discovered me gives him the right to see that I live up to his good opinion of me' (Frost 1964: 84). D.H. Lawrence, another 'discovery', was confident enough as a writer to find this sort of thing amusing when telling Edward Garnett in December 1913 about the way in which the '[Ford]–Pound faction seems inclined to lead me round a little as one of their show-dogs' (Lawrence 1932: 172).

Lewis's tactic for avoiding the pressures of working under Pound's 'protective' gaze was first to ask him politely (as he did in 1922) to 'forget [him] for a year' (*EP/WL* 134), and then if Pound persisted (as he did when trying to organise without his consent a special Wyndham Lewis issue of *This Quarter* in 1925) to tell him bluntly that he had no 'mandate to interfere' (ibid.: 150). But Frost suspected that something other than his own welfare was at issue in Pound's overseeing of his career. Noting Pound's 'haste to speak of [his] poetry before anyone' (Weintraub 1979: 311), Frost raises the question of self-interest in Pound's apparently selfless interest in the writings of unpublished or newly published poets. What exactly was being displayed on such occasions – Frost's excellence as a poet, or Pound's excellence as a talent-scout, eager to impress the editor of *Poetry* with yet another 'scoop' (*L* 51)? Frost certainly took the malign view of the case in a fit of uncharacteristic *vers libre* addressed to Pound but sent instead in July 1913 to Flint. (Frost lacked the nerve to have these things out directly with Pound or engage with him about them in print.) In those verses Pound is accused of having 'praised [Frost] arbitrarily' in the course of demonstrating his own 'power' to 'thrust anything upon the world / Were it never so humble...' (Frost 1964: 86). Like Aldington, Frost was ambitious, and his assessment of Pound's intervention in his career is complicated by a deep resentment at being cast in the role of a 'slow of wit' country hick to Pound's city slicker (ibid.: 85).

Both the abuse and the adoration of Pound by those writers he came into contact with are so patently obverse images of one another that neither of them can be taken as an unequivocal representation of what Pound, as some supposedly unitary essence, was 'really' like. Neither constitutes the grounds on which to mount either a wholly favourable or a wholly unfavourable assessment of Pound's operations as a practical critic.

As a man who let it be known that he had educated himself into becoming an expert in the art of poetry, Pound engaged in professional relationships with younger male poets which were coded master/apprentice, with himself habitually assuming the discursive position of mastery. That was a habit established at those Tuesday gatherings which he had organised as a student at the University of Pennsylvania. With the few older writers he could tolerate, such as Ford and Yeats, he would begin more circumspectly, technically occupying the position of apprentice, but gradually undermining the authority he supposedly deferred to, and insinuating himself into the position of mastery. 'In a very short time', Ford recalled, 'he had taken charge of me' (Ford 1931: 131). Douglas Goldring observed a similar takeover of Yeats's 'Mondays' (Goldring 1943: 48).

The game to be played in such circumstances depends on the apprentice's acquiescence in the illusory or real power exercised by the master. Eliot played the game both seriously (when dedicating *The Waste Land* to Pound as 'the best craftsman', *il miglior fabbro*) and facetiously, as when he addresses Pound in his letters as 'cher maître' (*L* 236). Those who refused to play the game on these terms, like Fletcher or Frost, were classified as not fit to play the game at all. But unlike apprentices to other trades, who can expect after working for a specified time under their *fabbro* to qualify as mastercraftsmen themselves, writers who apprenticed themselves to Pound were in danger of being permanently infantilised by this coding of their relationship. Pound's first such apprentice, Williams, was made to feel throughout his writing life that in Pound's eyes he would never know enough to achieve mastery. It may well be thought that that was Williams's problem, not Pound's; but nevertheless it was a problem which Pound had a vested interest in not remedying. Eliot, on the other hand, decided for tactical reasons of his own to operate from the discursive position to which Pound assigned him, and not to comment on Pound's presumption of mastery until Pound had moved on to Paris and Eliot himself had begun his long career as the most distinguished poet and literary critic in England. In October 1923 Eliot told Quinn that he had felt obliged 'to keep an attitude of discipleship' to Pound because Pound was so 'very sensitive and proud', adding inscrutably (in a phrase in which irony contends with generosity) 'as indeed I ought' (Gallup 1970: 77).

Not surprisingly, male poets situated in the position of apprentice to Pound's mastery sometimes perceived it as coded father/son, and experienced it oedipally. In the very same month in which Eliot was confiding to Quinn about the importance of complying with Pound's sense of his own mastery in discipular relationships with other writers, E.E. Cummings was telling his mother that Pound, whom he first met in Paris in 1921, 'sometimes gives me a FatherComplex' (Cummings 1969: 104). To Frost, another sensitive and proud writer Pound tried to bring up by hand, Pound was an intolerable 'father-in-letters' (Weintraub 1979: 312). As 'the father of modernism' (which is how John Crowe Ransom styled him when reviewing *Eleven New Cantos XXXI–XLI* in 1935 (*CH* 294)), Pound was inscribed in a patriarchal version of literary history which made the siring of sons of 'Ez' no more improbable than those seventeenth-century 'sons of Ben' who saw themselves justifiably as the literary progeny of Jonson. Pound's favoured 'sons' were certainly identified as such when he addressed James Laughlin as 'Dilectus Filius' (Carpenter 1988: 529) and Louis Zukofsky as 'Delectus mihi filius', to which Zukofsky responded by addressing Pound as 'Our Farver who Art on Earth' (*EP/LZ*

137–8). But the older he got, and the further he moved away from literary preoccupations, the more likely Pound was to be rejected by young writers like Charles Olson who came to him for paternal guidance as poets, but were so appalled by Pound's Fascist and anti-Semitic attitudes that they decided (as Olson did in 1948) that they could not tolerate 'any longer being a son' to such a man (*CO/EP* xxiii). By that stage, Pound was beginning to sire a new breed of sons – much to the disgust of his daughter, who found them 'sloppy and ignorant' (de Rachewiltz 1971: 293) – like the anti-Semitic Eustace Mullins (self-styled Director of the Aryan League of America) and the notorious John Kasper, a segregationist who worked with the Ku Klux Klan.

If the writer who sought his assistance happened to be a young woman, sexuality was a potentially complicating factor, in which case the master/apprentice code might well be gendered master/mistress. That semiotic instability created problems for women writers who met Pound and could never be certain of knowing exactly what his interest or lack of interest in their work was based upon. Among the last poets with whom Pound continued to be extraordinarily generous with his time was Mary Barnard, who wrote to him from America in 1933 shortly before his forty-eighth birthday, and at a time when he was fast losing interest in writing literary criticism or in talent-scouting for new protégés. 'I have got to the time of life', he had told Parker Tyler in February 1933, 'when, rightly or wrongly, my own work interests me considerably MORE than the poesy of others' – one consequence of which, he suspected, was 'a probable dimming of the critical eye' (Bornstein 1985: 11–12). Mary Barnard was twenty-three when she wrote to Pound in Rapallo, having got on to his poetry partly by way of escape from T.S. Eliot's, which she thought her teachers admired excessively, and partly after reading the account given by Glenn Hughes of Pound's poetry and entrepreneurial activities in *Imagism and the Imagists* (1931). In her literary memoir published in 1984 she writes appreciatively of Pound's correspondence with her (*L* 331, 336–7, 339, 345–8). She also records her awareness that because she was a woman Pound needed to be persuaded that she was serious about writing and not simply filling in time until Mr Right came along. 'Nice gal, likely to marry and give up writing or what Oh?' Pound asked her when responding to the poems she had sent him in October 1933 (*L* 331). In this respect Pound reminded Barnard of Williams: 'They both liked women', she writes in her memoir, 'but whether either of them thought that any woman had it in her to be a really first rate poet I doubt' (Barnard 1984: 312). This remark is especially interesting because it is not made out of any feminist grievance that women poets have been unjustly ignored by men: 'I can't blame them', Barnard adds, 'when I consider our record' (ibid.). She was right of course about Pound, who, under the guise of 'B.H. Dias', had declared himself in August 1918 to be 'not wildly anti-feminist' but still 'to be convinced that any woman ever invented anything in the arts' (*EP/VA* 69).

Such attitudes were encouraged by the masculinist practices of some of the literary groups Pound became involved with in London, especially those organised by Lewis (whose persona, Tarr, thought women 'a lower form of life' (Flory 1980: 72)), and Hulme, who believed that the 'sex element interfered with intellectual talk' (Tytell 1987: 69) and was said to have got Gaudier-Brzeska to make him a brass knuckleduster so that he could 'tame' his women (Carpenter 1988: 231). Although Lewis's *Blast* published on Ford's recommendation that 'clever journalist', Rebecca West (*EP/MCA* 100), the group perceived itself as masculinist, and Pound would certainly have preferred to keep things that way, especially in view of Ford's acknowledgement that literary London regarded a man of letters 'as something less than a man' (Burke 1987: 104). Shortly before the second and final issue of *Blast* was launched in July 1915, Pound told Lewis that his own wife, Dorothy Shakespear, had suggested that the celebratory dinner 'would maintain an higher intellectual altitude if there were a complete & uncontaminated absence of women', and that she herself had offered 'to contribute her own absence to that total & desirable effect' (*EP/WL* 12). As Mary and George Oppen discovered in 1930, Pound had difficulty treating as equals artists who were couples, and would exclude Mary from his conversations with George, thus prompting George to conclude that 'in Pound there is no feminine' (Duplessis 1981: 63).

Sexist fantasies about the place of women in the life of a cultivated man are set out in Pound's scandalously demystificatory tale about a spiritual cult-figure – 'greasy and unpleasant, like most hindoos' (*EP/MCA* 68) – of his London years, Rabindranath Tagore. 'Jodindranath Mawhwor's Occupation' (1917) describes a student of the *Kama Sutra*, Mawhwor (in a southern drawl, 'mah whore'), who lives a life of sensual satisfaction in a comfortable house big enough 'for his women', whom he 'occupies' in the sexual sense made familiar by Shakespeare's *Othello*, 'for generation and pleasure' (*PD* 79, 83). An equally whimsical poem, 'Abu Salammamm – A Song of Empire' (1914), finds in easy sexual access to women optimal conditions for the production of masculinist art: it is described in its epigraph as the sort of patriotic piece Pound would willingly turn out if King George V would give him 'all the food and women [he] wanted' (*P* 237; cp. *PM* 71–2). What place might there be in such a phallocentric conception of artistic production for women as artists? How were young women writers to deal with a man like Pound, who had his effigy carved in marble by Gaudier-Brzeska in the form of a four-foot-high phallus?

In her own transactions with Pound, and as a woman who wanted to become a poet, Mary Barnard perceived herself as inferior by her nature as a woman rather than as inferiorised by the masculinist culture in which she had been educated. On Pound's instruction she studied ancient Greek prosody in the hope that by doing so she would avoid producing what Pound's most recent male apprentice at that time, James Laughlin, was calling ' "girl's stuff" ' (Barnard 1984: 76). She must have known she had escaped at least that particular fate when Laughlin – who had himself been told by Pound that since he would never be a poet he ought to become a publisher (which he did, very successfully, under the imprint of New Directions) – published her work as one of *Five Young American Poets* in 1940. In spite of Barnard's diligence as a dutiful daughter to her poetic father, however, as late as February 1938 Pound was still puzzled as to where she belonged in his stereotypical taxonomy of women writers, asking her whether she was 'going to be lorelai, or matriarch or blue stocking' (ibid.: 116).

Grateful to the end that she had been among 'a number of young women' whose work Pound had taken the trouble to comment on 'if he thought they could perform adequately given proper training', Barnard wanted to make it quite clear that in one important respect she was totally different from some of the others. 'While it is true that [Pound's] interest was more than poetic in some cases', she writes, 'it was not so in all – certainly not in my case' (ibid.: 312). Not that she is inclined to name any names, for she declares in the foreword to her memoirs that she has managed to resist pressures 'to satisfy a public (and editorial) craving for gossip' (ibid.: xvii). Like Iris Sylvia Symes Crump, who wrote under the name of Iris Barry, Mary Barnard maintains a decent reticence at the very moment of encouraging readers to believe that surely some revelation is at hand. Iris Barry was recently out of a convent and barely seventeen years old when she left her post office job in Birmingham to meet Pound in London. He introduced her (apparently as a 'whore') to Wyndham Lewis, by whom she had two children before working as a film critic for the *Daily Mail* and being appointed subsequently as Curator of the Film Library at the Museum of Modern Art in New York (Meyers 1984: 287). Between 1916 and 1917 she was the recipient of an extraordinary series of letters (*L* 124–6, 128–32, 135–49), which combine detailed criticism of her poetry with what in fact constituted Pound's first attempt at drawing up those literary syllabuses for budding poets which were to culminate in *How To Read* (1931). When one of Pound's biographers interviewed her she told him that her relations with Pound were 'severely severed' in 1918 ('and I hope we don't have to go into *that*'): she had 'reasons' for not wanting to see Pound, she added, 'and some of them extremely personal' (Norman 1969: 362). They had last met in April 1939, when Pound visited the USA with the intention of securing an interview with President Roosevelt and correcting his misconceptions about Italian Fascism; but the interview wasn't granted, and before returning to Italy Pound visited the Museum of Modern Art in New York with Mary Barnard to see Iris Barry.

A poem of Barry's published in August 1917 records how a 'junior typist cries ecstatically / On seeing the costly photogravure' of Pound in the frontispiece of *Lustra* (1916), taken by Alvin Langdon Coburn as an allusion to Whistler's self-portrait (Barry 1917: 18); as Yeats had said, ' "*That*'ll sell the book" ' (*L* 147). The masculine pleasures of being 'among beautiful women', 'rested against' by shop girls (an Edwardian euphemism for sexually available young women), and falling under the feminine gaze at a social gathering while 'the new morality' is under discussion, are celebrated in three poems by Pound, 'Tame Cat', 'Shop Girl' and 'The Encounter' (*P* 113, 112, 110). These were republished in that chronicle of lusts, *Lustra* (1916), at a time when London, emptied of young men by trench-warfare in France, had become (Pound was to tell Williams in 1926) 'THE cunt of the world . . . THE land for the male with phallus erectus' (Torrey 1984: 75). As the *Cantos* make clear, young women are appropriate companions in Dionysian activities, but Apollonian creativity is the prerogative of men: 'Anything properly made', the milady of Canto 29 is told, 'is made in your belly or in my mind' (*nel ventre tua, o nella mente mia*).

The braiding of didactic and sexual codes in Pound's literary critical relationships with young women who were themselves sexually attracted to their handsome mentor posed problems first thematised by H.D. In her poem 'Evadne' she describes how she 'first tasted under Apollo's lips / love and love sweetness' (H.D. 1980: 58), experiencing as bewilderment that coding of poetry-making as love-making which Pound identified as the erotic wisdom transmitted secretly by the troubadours in their love poetry, that 'light from Eleusis' which had 'persisted throughout the middle ages and set beauty in the song of Provence and of Italy' (*SP* 53). The Apollo of H.D.'s poem is Pound, whose 'mane of fair hair' (Goldring 1943: 40) resembled the aureola of the sun-god, brushed back as in those early photographs of him taken in profile to reveal the high brow of a highbrow (the first usage of this word logged by the *Oxford English Dictionary* is American and dated 1908). The speaker in 'Evadne' relates to Apollo/Pound not only in discipular fashion as a poet with much to learn from the god of poetry but also erotically as a Dryad (Pound's pet-name for her) who may decide not to frustrate her Apollo as Daphne had done when she metamorphosed into a laurel, 'her thighs in bark' (*P* 196). Similar ambivalences are recorded in a poem of Pound's called 'Tempora', where the Dryad turns up in his courtyard, looking as beautiful as Venus come to reclaim her lover Adonis (Tamuz). But instead of uttering the ritual cry, 'Tamuz. Io! Tamuz!', she asks the giveaway question which identifies her not as the goddess of love but as just another of those 'young poetettes' (*L* 63) who take up too much of his time: ' "May my poems be printed this week?" ' (*P* 110).

Women who were content to remain in 'pleasing attitudes / Of discipleship' (*P* 101) to his mastery were treated by Pound with seemingly boundless generosity, but those who were not, like Gertrude Stein and Amy Lowell, suffered the indignities of an *ad feminam* style of criticism which responded to their strong-mindedness by ridiculing their bodies. So, when Pound calls Gertrude Stein 'an old tub of guts' (Fitch 1983: 128), sexual nausea functions structurally in much the same way as sexual desire functions in his remarks on those women writers he happened to fancy. Stein was of course well-established in Paris before the Village Explainer arrived there from London, and as she was a teacher of prose rather than of poetry she could be ignored. But Lowell arrived from America on Pound's own patch in London as a poet, and proceeded to take over his *Imagisme* as her Imagism. To Ford, who was himself corpulent enough to be called 'fatty Ford' by Pound (Barnard 1984: 152), Lowell was an allegorical figure of excess, 'monstrously fat, monstrously moneyed', as he described her in the October 1919 issue of the *English Review*; but she was also, he added – revealing an anxiety she provoked in phallocratic men of letters – 'disagreeably intelligent' (Damon 1935: 232).

Now, although Pound liked women, he did not like fat women. ' "I hate a dumpy woman" ' is the Byronic epigraph to his poem, 'L'Homme Moyen Sensuel' (*P* 238); and another of his poems disgustedly juxtaposes Isaiah's injunction ('let your soul delight itself in fatness') with the spectacle of an overweight female cabaret dancer who 'pulls up a roll of fat for the pianist' (*P* 163). Physically, Lowell's corpulence was a gross parody of that 'subtle' or 'radiant' body Pound read about in theosophical writings by G.S.R. Mead (Oderman 1986: 144–5). Mystical philosophy taught that because 'the body is inside the soul' (Canto 113), it is discernible as aura, not corpus. In masculinist versions of this doctrine, such as Pound's and Yeats's, the subtle bodies which attract most attention are the supple bodies of sexually desirable young women. Yeats, for example, in a line much admired by Pound, celebrated in Maud Gonne 'the fire that stirs about her when she stirs' (*LE* 14, 53). And an early poem of Pound's called 'A Virginal' records a similar moment of eroticised perception: 'I have picked up magic in her nearness / To sheathe me half in half the things that sheathe her' (*P* 71). The art of representing the subtle body is what 'Sandro [Botticelli] knew, and Jacopo [del Sellaio]', before it was 'lost in the brown meat of Rembrandt / and the raw meat of Rubens' (Canto 80). The ethereal body – 'the body of air clothed in the body of fire' (*LE* 153) – was nowhere discernible in the Rubens-like 'meat' of Amy Lowell, who even as a girl had described herself as 'appaulingly fat' (Damon 1935: 49).

Initially, it looked as if Lowell might eventually shape up. 'When I get through with that girl', Pound told Robert Frost, 'she'll think she was born in free verse' (Norman 1969: 106). That 'girl', incidentally, was some forty years old at the time, and eleven years Pound's senior. 'There are ninety different ways of saying "Damn nigger" ', Pound once remarked; 'it requires knowledge to use the right ones' (*PD* 31). No doubt there are as many ways of saying

'Bloody woman'. Without benefit of feminist theory, Lowell discovered that fat is a feminist issue. At a *Blast* dinner Gaudier-Brzeska amused Pound and himself by imagining what Lowell would look like in the nude (*G-B* 52); her 'telluric mass', assessed by the sculptor in terms of its formal values, is recollected in Canto 77. Having no prospect of ever being called, like the tall and willowy H.D., a Dryad, or being photographed nude in classical 'attitudes' in natural settings (as H.D. was), Lowell settled for being imposing, and was perceived instead as overbearing. A scandalously cigar-smoking phallic woman, she enjoyed being puffed by her publisher in October 1914 as the 'foremost member' of the Imagist group (Damon 1935: 274–5). Like Pound, she was an American in London, and therefore a potential ally in the struggle against American philistinism. She also had money, which obliged her in Pound's view to become a patron of his modernist movement in literature. He even offered her the editorship of the *Egoist* (*L* 70): it was not his to offer, but he offered it nevertheless, believing that Dora Marsden was ready to give it up, and that if Lowell were to move in editorially she would back the journal with her own money. But Lowell was not accustomed to being pushed around by men and told how to spend her money. She saw no reason why she could not go on being an Imagist independently of Pound, and for that she was never forgiven. The Pankhursts might well succeed in obtaining votes for women, but Lowell needed to learn that there is no such thing as 'equal suffrage in a republic of poesy' (*L* 178), and certainly not for a 'Hippopoetess' (*EP/MCA* 116), a term which Pound recalled in 1956 as having been coined by H.D. (Wees 1976: 211). Consequently, Lowell's Imagist writings were categorised by Pound as an ersatz version of the real thing and labelled, maliciously but brilliantly, '*Amy*gist' (*L* 288).

Because the discourse of modernism is dominated by Pound, the literary history of modernism has tended to recapitulate his prejudices, and what was in fact Lowell's independence of Pound still gets treated as a joke. How absurd (we are to understand) that a woman as fat as Amy Lowell could comply with the anorexic aesthetic of *Imagisme* and its dietary phobia about 'superfluous' words. How could any woman that size understand the importance of Maurice Hewlett's prediction that modern poetry would differ from Victorian poetry by being ' "nearer the bone" ' (*LE* 12)? So, when Pound wrote in March 1922 to ask Lowell whether she wished 'to repent and be saved', he did so only to remind her that 'the eye of the needle is narrow' (*L* 237–8), through which she had about as much chance of passing as the proverbial camel. 'Literary' criticism, Pound learned in London, is an aesthetic discourse which encodes a crypto-politics of reputation-mongering. What he failed to concede (although it is revealed so clearly in his 'literary' criticism of Amy Lowell's poetry) is the part played in that crypto-politics by sexual politics.

4
The rhetorical critic

In the guise of 'Z' (the metathesised pronunciation of 'Ez'), Pound published in 1913 a mock-proposal for reducing the amount of time spent reading and writing reviews, based on the assumption that 'only a certain number of things . . . can be said about . . . any work of fiction, poetry or belles lettres' (Pound 1913b: 149). He lists eighteen exemplary 'positions' numerically so that reviewers in future need only print the appropriate number or numbers after the title of the book they would otherwise have to write about. The list ridicules reviewers' clichés like 'the greatest book since', attributing them both to particular journals like the *Spectator* ('this author goes from strength to strength') and also to particular reviewers. 'Epoch-making', for instance, is linked with the name of Lascelles Abercrombie, whom Pound (a swordsman since his Hamilton College days) once challenged to a duel for advocating Wordsworth's poetry as a model for modernists, a challenge Abercrombie avoided by suggesting that they bombard one another with unsold copies of their own books (Stock 1970: 159). 'Never heard of this author' is the position attributed first to Henry James and secondly to Thomas Hardy; Yeats, ranked in third place, represents the evasive reviewer who 'believes the author to be meritorious and possibly excellent, [but] regrets that he has not had time to read the work in question . . . ' Edmund Gosse, Abercrombie and Darrell Figgis each contributes his modicum of fatuity before Pound sends up himself in seventh position: 'someone else has praised this book and . . . therefore it must be bad'.

Pound described himself in *Who's Who, 1920* as a 'constructive critic', and he approved of 'constructive criticism' of his own criticism (*GK* 148). The adjective signals his break with the common view that to criticise something is to find fault with it, destructively, and his sympathy with Felix Schelling's maxim that 'the critic is good when he praises and bad when he blames' (*CC* 322). As a metropolitan critic Pound would try to mediate between academic know-alls ignorant of modern writing, and journalistic know-nothings whose reviews were mere permutations of clichés. Academics, he told Harriet Monroe in August 1917, are 'the only people in America who know enough to get a perspective' on, say, Edgar Lee Masters's *Spoon River Anthology* (1915), which tacitly invites comparison generically with George Crabbe's *The Borough* (1810); but, if those who know about Crabbe are 'so stuck' in their antiquarian ways that they never bother to read Masters, it becomes impossible to obtain 'a level appreciation' of *Spoon River Anthology* (*L* 172). In all such pairings for comparative purposes of old masters with new contenders, literary value is thought of by Pound as something intrinsic to literary texts, and not as something conferred upon them by a particular readership with a particular set of interests in mind. As such, 'excellence' indicates an absolute rather than a relative value. Those texts which are said to manifest it are perceived as transcending the historical circumstances in which they were produced, and as coexisting simultaneously in that condition of adjacency to one another which Eliot called 'tradition' and which André Malraux figured as a *musée imaginaire*. What was needed, Pound had already decided by 1910, was 'a uniform standard of appreciation' (*LE* 362), unimpeded by such distractions as language or nation or epoch (not to mention class or race or gender), which would enable critics to 'weigh Theocritus and Mr Yeats with one balance' (*SR* vi). In his pursuit of the first-rate – a rare though absolute and transhistorical commodity – Pound argued in February 1915 for the development of 'a criticism of poetry based on world-poetry, on the work of maximum excellence' (*LE* 225). From a study of world-poetry 'a Weltliteratur standard' (*L* 62) could be developed to ensure that what Harriet Monroe published in *Poetry* would be 'poetry' and not that provincial substitute for the real thing, 'American poetry' (*L* 43), a category no more plausible in Pound's opinion than 'American chemistry' (*LE* 218).

In order to achieve such aims, Pound had to define poetry in ways which would make his task manageable, and he did so by thinking of it primarily in terms of techniques and experimentation. His criticism concedes the existence of a number of qualities no writer can do without, such as 'impulse', '*virtù*' and 'curiosity'.

But these are treated as manifestations of nature rather than nurture, and as such can be neither induced in people who lack them nor talked about profitably: like 'a sense of verbal consonance', they are 'given' to a writer by 'God, or nature, or ... whatever' (*SP* 340). The 'impulse' is a pre-textual pretext for a poem, 'the precise rendering' (*LE* 9) of which is dependent on technical competence in whichever medium one happens to be working, it being the business of 'technique' to guarantee 'a transmission of the impulse intact' (*L* 60). *Virtù* is that quiddity we call individuality, as a result of which there is never more than 'one Catullus, [or] one Villon' (*SP* 28). It is 'the artist's business to find his own *virtù*' (*SP* 29), and the critic's to recognise it. And, as for 'curiosity' (a reification of another 'natural' faculty), Pound told an interviewer in 1961 that 'you cannot have literature without curiosity' (Bridson 1961: 174).

Pound claimed to have known at the age of fifteen that whereas 'the "Impulse" is with the gods ... technique is a man's own responsibility' (Pound 1913a: 707). This distinction enabled him to redefine writing as technique rather than mystique, and thus to make it available as a pedagogy. This shift of emphasis, however, did not entirely demystify literary production. Pound regarded Horace, for instance, as a writer who had had everything except the 'impulse', for Horace had 'acquired all that is acquirable, without having the root' (*LE* 28). Like Pope in *An Essay on Criticism* (1712), Pound concedes the existence of graces beyond the reach of art, which is why he endorsed the conclusion of a French handbook on poetic technique: '*Mais d'abord il faut être un poète*' (*LE* 7). The point of teaching people the technicalities of writing was not to try to turn non-poets into poets but to enable 'genuine' poets to transmit their impulses more efficiently. In February 1909 he had told Dorothy Shakespear that he was waiting for 'the Great Inspiration' and 'wished above all things to be in readiness, open-minded and waiting, on the Great Day when it should come' (*EP/DS* 3). He certainly impressed upon Eliot the importance of 'experimenting and trying [one's] technique so that it will be ready, like a well-oiled fire-engine, when the moment comes to strain it to the utmost' (Eliot 1948: 16). That is why Pound directed beginners to 'master all known forms and systems of metric' (*LE* 9).

The criteria developed by Pound as poetic theory in a technology of writing were recycled as critical theory in a pedagogy of reading.

Because he saw himself as a poet-critic, and not as a poet who happened also to be a critic, he perceived no problem in treating as timeless and universal a set of criteria developed in fact to meet the requirements of a particular genre (the short lyric poem) at a particular historical moment (the early twentieth century) and in response to a particular literary problem (the need to develop a post-Victorian poetics). It is true that in private correspondence he would occasionally relativise his criteria, as when he advised Louis Zukofsky in December 1931 to 'forget the Donts' because they were unlikely to be any more use to Zukofsky 'as critic 1930 to 1950' than Yeats had been to Pound himself '1910 to 1930' (*EP/LZ* 123); but in public statements he wanted it emphasised nevertheless that he had 'established a critical system, a method' (ibid.: 123), and that if he had 'made any contribution to criticism' he had 'done so by introducing the ideogrammic system', which involved substituting for bland generalities an 'accumulation of . . . concrete examples . . . that insist upon being taken into consideration' (*SP* 303). Dehistoricised at the very moment of their inception, Pound's critical observations on the art of poetry masqueraded not as provisional theories capable of being superseded by better ones but as principles true for all time. The new poetic associated with *Imagisme* could be presented accordingly as at once revolutionary in its break with the bad writing habits of previous generations and traditional in its restitution of those classic qualities which appeared to have withstood the test of time.

Once poetry is defined as technique, and developments in the art are perceived in terms of technical innovation, experimentalism comes to be equated with originality. 'Willingness to experiment is not enough', Pound observed in 1933, 'but unwillingness to experiment' – like any other form of incuriosity – 'is mere death' (*SP* 367). To represent poetry as technical experimentalism, as Wordsworth and Coleridge had done when informing their readers that the poems in the first edition of *Lyrical Ballads* (1798) were published 'as an experiment' (Wordsworth 1926: 934), indicates not only the prestige of scientism in nineteenth- and twentieth-century discourses of the arts but also its status as a ground on which discussion can take place. For to claim that a poem is worth attending to on account of its experimental features is to transform the reading of poetry from a 'feminine' encounter of sensibilities into a 'masculine' technology of communication. The critical function of scientistic metaphors in this context is to permit the writing of poetry to maintain its position in the public gaze by inviting controversy over whether or not an experiment has succeeded. As readers, we are constructed by this strategy not as experiencing subjects of lyrical poems originating in the spontaneous overflow of powerful feelings, but as observers of a verbal experiment, called upon to witness the matching (or mismatching) of a theory with a practice. In other words, experimentalism offers poetry not for experience but for inspection, and aspires to durability by getting itself talked about. The pleasure of the text is subordinated to the cerebrations of scrutiny in a manoeuvre now recognisably masculinist.

If you read through Pound's literary essays and books of literary criticism in search of those dominant assumptions which determine his specific comments on this or that text you discover first that they are relatively few in number and secondly that in the main they are remarkably traditional. A whole etiquette of literary style, expressed positively in terms of recommendations and negatively as what Pound called 'don'ts', is based on a few central concepts like 'economy', 'precision', 'presentation', 'clarity', 'immediacy' and 'newness'.

Take the case of 'economy', for instance, the term which mobilises a functionalist theory of writing, according to which 'each word must have its functioning necessary part' (*EP/FMF* 43). The Aristotelian origins of this criterion are acknowledged in Pound's endorsement of the definition of a perfect work of art as one in which ' "you could neither take from it nor add to it" ' (*GK* 315). If poems are tested accordingly for the substitutability of their parts, Baudelaire comes to be judged inadequate, since 'for a great many of his words and lines other words and lines might be substituted' (*PD* 75). The critical purpose of winkling out the 'replaceable' (*LE* 29) or 'words that do not function' (*ABCR* 47) is to encourage writers to engage in the 'elimination of superfluities' (*P* 202), a process carried to parodic excess in those three lines, four words, and nineteen spaced periods which constitute Pound's poem 'Papyrus' (*P* 112). Privativeness validates minimalism in an *Imagiste* aesthetic which declares it 'better to produce one Image in a lifetime than to produce voluminous works' (*LE* 4), an aesthetic promulgated by a man who had let it be known as early as 1909 that he himself had already 'written and burned two novels and three hundred sonnets' (*CH* 60).

The obverse side of Pound's admiration for a ' "Whistlerian" economy of line' (*EP/VA* 86) is a distaste for 'Keatsian decoration' (ibid.: 187) and all those unmanly practices by which poetry degenerates into 'a sort of embroidery for dilettantes and women' (*SP* 41). By determining 'not [to] use images *as ornaments*' (*G-B* 88), *Imagiste* poets could expect to avoid the vices of '*fioritura*' (*LE* 28) and what Stendhal denounced as 'fustian à la Louis XIV' (*LE* 31). As an *Imagiste* himself, Pound had tried 'to desuetize (de-suetize i.e. take the cold fat out of) current poetry' (*GK* 253), a whimsical etymology directed at the contributors to Amy Lowell's anthology, *Some Imagist Poets* (1915), who claimed to share stylistic principles which had 'fallen into desuetude' (Jones 1972: 135). And the language of criticism was to be invigilated with similar rigour, there being a 'gongorism in critical writing as well as in bad poetry' (*SP* 365). Such concerns were a manifestation in the literary sphere of that Edwardian cult of 'efficiency' which, 'with its antonyms *waste* and *muddle*', Jonathan Rose sees as having 'pervaded discussions of imperial policy, industrial organisation, social legislation, personal hygiene, and religion' (Rose 1986: 117). In the drive to make language more efficient and bring it ' "close to the thing" ' (*SP* 41), various parts of speech came under attack in the modernist period. Lewis wanted to get rid of prepositions and articles, Gertrude Stein of nouns, and Pound of 'the decorative frill adjective' (*L* 91) – both the Shakespearian 'painted' kind (*LE* 12) and those Miltonic 'straddled' adjectives displayed in phrases like ' "addled mosses dank" ' (*L* 91). Pound deplored poems in which each noun was 'chaperoned by . . . adjectives' (*L* 408), and praised poems like H.D.'s in which there was 'no excessive use of adjectives' (*L* 45).

Equally dispensable with was the expletive use of 'do' as an auxiliary verb (' "chooses" is better than "*doth* choose" ' (*L* 402)), which prompted Pound to go through Laurence Binyon's translation of Dante's Inferno 'swatting the "dids" and "doths" ' (*L* 404). Verbs, Pound learned from Fenollosa, should be active rather than passive, and the copula ('to be') substituted wherever possible by an alternative verb which would energise its local context (Fenollosa 1967: 384). Write ' "make" rather than "be" ', he advised Binyon, because 'make' is the 'more active verb' (*L* 404); consequently, Pound's best-known exhortation is not 'be original' but *Make It New* (1934). Such minutiae of style had to be attended to, he told Iris Barry in 1916, because 'a series of . . . minute leakages will sink a poem' (*L* 126). By remedying defects, criticism could work towards reducing the 'number of *blank* words' (*L* 357) in any piece of writing, and by increasing its efficiency help bring about that condensation of energy which is characteristic of great literature, defined as simply 'language charged with meaning to the utmost possible degree' (*LE* 23). A fanciful etymology enabled him to link the German word for 'poetry', *Dichtung*, with *Verdichtung* ('condensation') and epitomise the drive towards economy in writing as 'Dichten = condensare' (*ABCR* 20), the formula itself exemplifying in self-reflexive fashion those 'gists and piths' (*ABCR* 77) with which the *Cantos* are studded, and which were designed to frustrate attempts at reductive summary.

This drive towards economy of expression in poetry is manifest not only in Pound's admiration for such sloganising one-liners as Eliot's 'No *vers* is *libre* for the man who wants to do a good job' (*LE* 12), but also in attempts to produce similarly aphoristic statements himself, like the motto he composed for the *Little Review*: 'the magazine that is read by those who write the others' (*EP/MCA* 119). This development is concurrent with the emergence this century of tabloid journalism, with its displacement of emphasis from time-consuming essays to eye-catching headlines (Tytell 1987: 64). For, if literature is defined in Poundian terms as 'news that STAYS news' (*ABCR* 13), the function of criticism is to produce the headlines which will draw people's attention to it. A poem written by John Donne in the early seventeenth century ('The Extasie') was still news when Pound reprinted it in 1934 with the tendentious caption, 'Platonism believed' (*ABCR* 126). The headlining and billboarding of aesthetic issues was pioneered in *Blast* in 1914, where discontinuous statements printed in bold type are juxtaposed with one another to generate their own interconnections. The effect of such experiments on Pound's own critical prose was to shift attention away from cumulative paragraphs in which a complex argument unfolds and redirect it to the rhythmically energetic and punch-packing individual sentence which is the nuclear unit of 'Poundspeech' (Perloff 1985: 78).

Words which survived elimination as superfluities had in addition to be exactly the right ones for the job in hand. Seeing that 'the touchstone of an art is its precision' (*LE* 48), verbal precision as epitomised in Gustave Flaubert's term, *le mot juste*, was stylistically the ideal which Pound saw his generation as having aimed at (*GK* 49). Glossed by Walter Pater as 'the one word for the one thing' (Pater 1904: 29), *le mot juste* became the shibboleth of English Flaubertians like Ford, from whom Pound learnt 'that poetry should be at least as well written as prose' (*EP/FMF* 26). The fate of *Imagisme* showed the critical importance of calling things by their 'proper' names. *Blast* was ready to go to press embodying a still unidentified ism, a *je ne sais quoi* described unsatisfactorily in April 1914 as 'Futurist, Cubist, Imagiste' (*EP/JJ* 26) before Pound came up with the term 'Vorticism' – 'the right word', he told Quinn, 'if I did find it myself' (*L* 122). Verbal precision, however, is more noticeable in Pound's literary criticism than in either the art criticism he wrote as 'B.H. Dias' or the music criticism as 'William Atheling'. 'Dias' tends to record his visual impressions imagistically, and crams his sentences with rhythmically patterned neologisms as he berates such things as 'the greenery-yallery, or ... grayery-fryery, of the London Group' (*EP/VA* 121). Manifest here – but more extensively in the music criticism of 'Atheling' – is a drift away from that logocentric use of language which privileges difference and thus enables such matters as the *mot juste* to be conceptualised and pursued. Pound's language becomes correspondingly 'logofugal' as he floods his sentences with a mimetically rhythmic babble as yet undisturbed by those differentiations which not only constitute language but enable it in turn to become a precision instrument for recording such differences. Writing on the proms in September 1918, for instance, 'Atheling' moves from 'Pur-up-up, pur-up-up' via 'Tuper-up-up, *skeek*. Followed by up-cheek, up-cheek' to 'Pat-at-ty wump, pat-at-ty wump. Chee-chee-weecheechee WIP' (*EP/M* 124).

Responsibility for maintaining language as a precision instrument, he believed, rests with those 'damned and despised *litterati*' (*LE* 21) on whose linguistic sensitivity any society must depend for its moral and political welfare. 'The *mot juste* is of public utility', he wrote in 1922. 'We are governed by words, the laws are graven words, and literature is the sole means of keeping these words living and accurate' (*EP/JJ* 200). The lesson to be learned from history is that once 'the application of word to thing' becomes 'inexact', then 'the whole machinery of social and of individual thought and order goes to pot' (*LE* 21). The *mot juste*, the exact word, is therefore not just a word but the just word which defines a just society: hence the importance of 'cleaning up ... the WORD' (*PE* 50) and putting an end to 'the befouling of terminology' (*SP* 132). For examples of such befoulings we need look no further than Pound's own use of words like 'free' and 'freedom' in his Fascist years. 'Free expression of opinion', according to the rubric Pound himself wrote to introduce each of his broadcasts from Radio Rome, is not an inalienable right of every citizen but something granted by the Fascist authorities to 'those who are qualified to hold it' (*EPS* xiii). And 'freedom of the press', it turns out, is the freedom to print only what can be 'shown to be of public utility' (Carpenter 1988: 534). The *mot juste* for the first kind of freedom would be 'elitism' and for the second kind 'censorship'.

Pound told René Taupin in 1928 that he was indebted to Flaubert not only for the *mot juste* but also for his conception of 'présentation ou constatation' (*L* 294). As Pound explained in October 1913, the Flaubertian method results in 'constat[at]ion of fact', and 'does not comment' on the materials it simply 'presents'; it thus 'washes its hands of theories' (Pound 1913c: 662). In *Cathay* (1915) Pound translated the work of Chinese poets who had been content 'to set forth their matter without moralizing and without comment' (Pound 1918a: 54). The stylistic ideal exemplified in that poetry is 'to set down things as they are' and 'to find the word that corresponds to the thing . . . instead of making a comment, however brilliant, or an epigram' (*ABCR* 58). The fault which constatation remedies is 'talk *about* the matter' (Pound 1923: 149). *Imagiste* emphasis on the *deixis* of 'presentation' – 'showing and uttering in a given situation at the same time' (Rabaté 1986: 173) – as against the *mimesis* of 'representation' is situated chronologically between Flaubertian constatation on the one hand and Leavis's notion of how poems 'realise' their meanings by enacting them in the linguistic structures of their constitutive utterances.

This privileging of constatation is in support of a 'concrete' or imagistic poetry, and results in the directive to 'go in fear of abstractions' (*LE* 5). A good writer 'seeks out the luminous detail and presents it' (*SP* 23). That 'New Method in Scholarship' Pound first spoke about in 1911 was to be guided by its attentiveness to such details, explicating their implications in order to produce a new kind of knowledge, for 'a few dozen facts of this nature give us intelligence of a period' (*SP* 22). Eliot was to follow this procedure in his enormously influential essay on 'The Metaphysical Poets' (1921), which moves from a study of luminous details – a few conceits in a few seventeenth-century poems – to the cultural generalisation that between Donne's time and Dryden's a 'dissociation of sensibility set in, from which we have never recovered' (Eliot 1932: 288). Cultural analysis of this kind is represented as being grounded incontestably in details of literary style. The method also informs Leavis's essay in *Revaluation* (London, 1936) on misreadings of Keats, which focuses on so-called key-words in key stanzas in key poems by that poet in order to show how late nineteenth-century England came to find itself in the cul-de-sac of aestheticism.

When the principles of 'economy' and 'precision' combine in 'presentation', the result will be a 'hardness' and clean-lined effect which justifies analogies between writing and sculpture: the cut stone is associated with clarity of mind, the modelled with muddle. The binary opposites 'hard' and 'soft' are in Pound's criticism the organising terms in a libidinal economy which pits the 'masculine' virtues of hardness and clarity of outline against such 'feminine' vices as 'softness', 'emotional slither', 'wobbles' and 'slush' (*LE* 12, 7). *Imagisme*, he told Amy Lowell, was to 'stand' for 'hard light, clear edges' (*L* 78); and all modern poetry, in dissociating itself from the 'flaccid varieties' (*LE* 3) that preceded it, should be 'as much like granite as it can be' (*LE* 12), and quite unlike those 'stale creampuffs' he himself had turned out in his pre-*Imagiste* years (*ALS* 4). Literary history recorded earlier instances of the erection of form out of flux. Catullus, for instance, had produced a better rewriting in Latin of a poem by Sappho than her Greek original, because his version was 'harder in outline' (*PD* 60). Seeing that 'the female / Is a chaos' (Canto 29), cosmos is correspondingly male, and the manufacture of those heterocosms we call works of art is therefore a masculine prerogative; for once a man (*vir*) has discovered his *virtù* he can 'proceed to the erection of his microcosmos' (*SP* 29).

Symbolisme, which *Imagisme* set out to supersede, was coded feminine and its characteristics – nuance, metaphoricity and synaesthesia – were labelled 'soft'. 'Nuance', programmed positively in *Symboliste* aesthetics as pleasurably evocative, is perceived negatively by Pound as encouraging a poetry of 'the opalescent word' to which all 'good writing' should be 'opposed' (*LE* 371). Unlike the *mot juste*, which privileges difference by labelling everything separately and distinctly, the opalescent word takes on different meanings for different readers, just as the opal takes on different colours in different lights. Opalescent words are associated with that 'crepuscular spirit in modern poetry' objected to in a pre-

Imagiste poem called 'Revolt', in which Pound expresses his desire to replace the late nineteenth-century poetry of 'shadows' and 'dreams' with a new poetry of 'power' and 'men' (*CEP* 96). Synaesthesia – the exploration of occult correspondences between one sense and another, as when Whistler describes his paintings as 'symphonies' – is treated as a soft option taken by people who 'mess up the perception of one sense by trying to define it in terms of another' (*LE* 7). And metaphoricity, which notoriously subverts the regulatory aspirations of the *mot juste*, and is used in *Symboliste* poetry as a means of resisting rationalistic modes of enquiry which try to explain it away, is tolerated in an *Imagiste* aesthetic only if carefully policed to ensure that there are 'no metaphors that won't permit examination' (*L* 45). So when Fletcher, several of whose poems were called synaesthetically 'colour symphonies', invited Pound to comment on a poem of his which contained the line, 'The palpitant mosaic of the midday light', Pound wrote in the margin: 'how can a mosaic be palpitant?' (de Chasca 1978: 23).

In the urgent task of fabricating a wholly modern poetry, Pound could not accommodate *Symboliste* practices into a repertoire of poetic styles because he identified them as obstacles to the evolution of the modern. The point of being aware of earlier writing was not to imitate it but to get a clearer idea of the direction new developments might take. Because past masters have done certain things 'once for all', he declared, there is no point in 'saying the same thing with less skill and less conviction' (*LE* 10–11). Literature being 'news that STAYS news' (*ABCR* 13), a modern master must describe new things so memorably that they will retain their newness to subsequent generations of writers, thus attaining that 'eternal and irrepressible freshness' which is the hallmark of a truly classic text (*ABCR* xii). No modern writer should behave like those manufacturers of stale erotica referred to in his poem 'Fratres Minores' who are still preoccupied with 'established and natural fact / Long since fully discussed by Ovid' (*P* 148).

As *Imagisme* entered literary history, its achievements became imitable in an equally damaging way, with the result that a young poet had to be told bluntly in 1933 that he could not expect to make 'a dent in the pubk. or highly select consciousness by means of poems writ in the style of 1913/15' (*L* 332). Ford had impressed upon him the importance of trying 'to register [one's] own times in terms of [one's] own time' (Ford 1913: 108), from which Pound concluded that 'no good poetry is ever written in a manner twenty years old' (*LE* 11). What he aimed at in his own writing, and was on the lookout for when reading work submitted for publication by *les jeunes*, was a poetry free of those archaisms in which he himself had 'wallowed' in his 'vealish years' (*L* 50), and which were not to be confused with the legitimate use of functional archaisms (as in 'Langue d'Oc') to designate the 'archaic' sensibility of Provençal poets in comparison with a 'modern' like Propertius (*L* 247). As a literary critic Pound looked for writing in which there would be none of those 'olde' words which Robert Bridges had hoped to recover (*L* 247); none of those inversions of conversational word order to be found in the poems of Henry Newbolt, one of which is immortalised in Canto 80 (' "He stood . . . the door behind" '); and no Wardour Street 'tising and 'twasing, or any other examples of spoken language fossilised into poeticisms.

It was evident to Pound in 1910 that literary criticism was the history of a series of largely unsuccessful attempts 'to find a terminology which will define something' (*SR* 3). And, when asking his readers in 1929 to 'throw out all critics who use vague general terms' (*LE* 37), he had in mind the development of a critical lexicon designed to liberate a younger generation of readers from that 'demoded terminology' which 'bad critics have prolonged' (*LE* 25). He seems to have regarded a critical vocabulary as an amalgam of discrete unit-terms with separate histories rather than as an ensemble of interlinked components in a discursive formation which represents the shared values of a particular interest-group. He himself introduced a few such unit-terms, most of which are rarely encountered nowadays except in writings on his own work. A 'donative' writer, for instance, is one who introduces 'something which was not in the art of his predecessors' (*SP* 25). 'Excernment' is the critical faculty which facilitates a 'general ordering and weeding out' of accumulated literary works (*LE* 75). 'Paideuma', a term he took from the title of the fourth volume (1928) of Leo Frobenius's *Erlebte Erdteile*, is 'the tangle or complex of the inrooted ideas of any period' (*GK* 57), 'the inherited habits of thought, the conditionings, aptitudes of a given race or time' (*SP* 118). 'Dissociation' – as in phrases like *la dissociation des idées* – is a term Pound picked up from Remy de Gourmont and used habitually in the sense of 'discrimination', as when he told Mencken in 1937 that 'the job of a serious writer is to dissociate the *meaning* of one word from that of some other' (*L* 377).

Three of Pound's most outlandish critical terms come together to form a taxonomy of poetry which abandons historical and generic distinctions in order to classify texts according to whether sound and rhythm are foregrounded in them (*melopoeia*), or visual imagery (*phanopoeia*), or whether they engage in free play with the verbality of their constituent words (*logopoeia*). In the first version of the triad, published in the March 1918 issue of the *Little Review*, the second category was called 'imagism' (*SP* 394), and did not emerge as *phanopoeia* until 1923 (Pound 1923: 152). The similarity of this scheme to the one in Coleridge's essay 'On the Principles of Genial Criticism' seems hardly accidental, for Coleridge's 'poetry of the ear' approximates to Pound's *melopoeia*, just as his 'poetry of the eye' does to Pound's *phanopoeia*, and 'poetry of language' to *logopoeia* (Ruthven 1969: 11).

Neither *melopoeia* nor *phanopoeia* is more helpful than the common alternatives, but *logopoeia* seems to be a proto-deconstructive term. Pound introduced it in 1918 when trying to think of what to say about the poetry of Mina Loy, in whose work he could 'detect no emotion whatever'. The effect produced by her poems – *logopoeia* – reminded him of similar traces in Pope, Laforgue, Browning and Eliot of a 'poetry that is akin to nothing but language'. Unable to define it, he settled for evoking it (by the kind of metaphoric impressionism he despised in belletristic writing) as 'a dance of the intelligence among words and ideas and modification of ideas and characters' (*SP* 394). In the 1923 formulation *logopoeia* is defined as 'a play in the shading of the words themselves' (Pound 1923: 152), and claimed to be present in the Latin of Sextus Propertius; and by 1942 it has become 'a play or "dance" among the concomitant meanings, customs, usages, and implied contexts of the words themselves' (*SP* 291). Christine Brooke-Rose thinks that the term 'prefigures the modern notion of *écart* or deviation ... from the expectation aroused syntactically within the text' (Brooke-Rose 1971: 129). Parts of *Homage to Sextus Propertius* (1919) support such a gloss, as when we read of Roman annalists expounding on 'the distentions of Empire' (*P* 207), where the word expected in such a context would be the uninronical 'extensions'. For Richard Sieburth, *logopoeia* 'focuses on the ambiguous process of signification itself', and is simply 'language commenting upon its own possibilities and limitations as language' (Sieburth 1978: 66). If so, then Pound was adept at it long before he managed to identify and tried to name it. On 16 January 1907, for instance, he wrote as a postgraduate student to his head of department at the University of Pennsylvania, Professor Felix Schelling, describing his current research on Giordano Bruno's comedy, *Il Candelaio* (1582), as 'eminently germane' to his other Romance studies (*L* 35). In this poker-faced deployment of an academic cliché, the word 'germane' acquires a Joycean instability, situated as it is between the German name of a professor whose department promoted a Germanic ideal of scholarship, and a reference to a product of Germanic scholarship which filled Pound with 'nausea and disgust', namely *das Privatleben*. 'Germane' glances appropriately at a scholarly method designated 'Germanic', but inappropriately at a scholarly subject-matter designated 'Romance'. Poised indeterminately in the play between similarity (germane/Germanic) and difference (Germanic/Romance), 'germane' articulates a deconstructive moment at which the fixity of a *mot juste* dissolves into the flux of *logopoeia*.

The polysemy of Pound's own surname, which I have discussed elsewhere (Ruthven 1986), ought to have constituted an object-lesson in the instabilities of signification and the resistance of language to closure, given the frequency with which Pound's name circulated in reviews of his work as a unit either of fixity (lb) or fluctuation (£). But Pound as a literary critic was a logocrat committed to the power of naming, and did not think of *logopoeia* as a disease of language which frustrates the drive towards definitiveness in literary criticism. On the contrary, he regarded it as something to be controlled and exploited as a literary device by a Propertius or a Laforgue. It could even be overexploited, as in that 'diarrhoea' of *logopoeia* (*L* 383), *Finnegans Wake*, a text which proceeds by accommodating through its puns and portmanteau words meanings that would have been suppressed in the syntagmatic single-mindedness of 'normal' prose. Pound thought of *logopoeia* as something that would augment his resourcefulness as a poet in the *Cantos* without eroding the certitude of his literary criticism.

A second typology introduced into his 1923 essay 'On Criticism in General' presents a five-fold scheme for classifying writers transhistorically. As such, it abandons those categories of genre, epoch and nation commonly used in such enterprises, and of course ignores the until recently hidden categories of race, class and gender which fascinate more recent taxonomists of writing. By collapsing the categories of time and place, it treats all writers as contemporaneous, as E.M. Forster was shortly to do when imagining 'the English novelists . . . seated together in . . . a sort of British

Museum reading-room – all writing their novels simultaneously' (Forster 1949: 12). Pound's typology of writers is hierarchical. First come the 'inventors', whose pioneering discoveries are perfected by those great writers Pound calls the 'masters'. In third place come the 'diluters', who produce 'more flabby' versions of writings by the inventors and masters, as Imagists produced a 'flabby' version of *Imagisme*. The fourth class, unnamed, are those 'who do more or less good work in the more or less good style of a period'; and in fifth place come the 'starters of crazes, the Ossians, and Gongoras' (Pound 1923: 147–8).

When reissuing this classification-scheme in 1929 as part of 'How To Read', Pound added a sixth category, the belletrists, who bring a particular 'mode to a very high development', but are 'not exactly "great masters" ' (*LE* 24). In the 1929 model, the 'starters of crazes' are moved down into sixth place so that the belletrists can be ranked fifth. Such a reordering should cause no surprise, it being characteristic of idealist anatomies of criticism to give elegance of design priority over the contingencies of history, as anyone can testify who has observed in periodical publications the evolutionary stages of Northrop Frye's *Anatomy of Criticism* (Princeton, 1957). There are of course other problems with Pound's schema, such as the assumption of mutual exclusiveness in the categories, and the implication (in statements like 'the diluters . . . follow . . . the inventors') that the categories are chronologically sequential. In spite of its shortcomings, the scheme aroused the interest of F.W. Bateson, who managed to avoid mentioning Pound's name when proposing in 1950 that the whole of English poetry from Wyatt to Auden might be fitted, generation by generation, into five-fold schemas of 'experimental initiators', 'protagonists of a new style', 'assured masters', 'polished craftsmen', and 'decadents' who were 'reduced to "stunts" to get new effects out of the exhausted tradition' (Bateson 1966: 78). But even by 1929 Pound was unwilling to defend any but his first two categories, which he regarded as essential. For to be familiar with the writings of inventors and masters was to acquire the background necessary to 'evaluate almost any unfamiliar book at first sight' (*LE* 24). It was certainly those two categories – used like Arnoldian 'touchstones' of excellence – that Pound bore in mind when looking for evidence of innovation and mastery in the writings of his contemporaries.

*

To those who experienced it, Pound's style of criticising a piece of writing was a revelation, whether or not they approved of what he said about it in conversation ('Cut this out, shorten this line') or indicated so graphically in his vigorously drawn deletions and corrigenda on their manuscripts, at which he 'slashed with his creative pencil' (H.D. 1980: 18, 40). For here was a critic who, instead of commenting loftily on their beautiful souls or singing voices, looked closely at what poets had actually written, and then made observations such as: this adjective is redundant, the rhythm here is too metronomic, this image is merely decorative, the expression there is too abstract, that word is not the *mot juste*, and so on. Once they had got over the shock of having their manuscripts treated this way, they would either concede Pound's claim that 'only the minute crit. . . . is any good' (*EP/FMF* 65), or never let him read anything of theirs again.

There is no shortage of testimonies, however, from satisfied clients. 'Ezra gave me the first unbiased and objective literary criticism I had ever known', the novelist Phyllis Bottome recalled in 1944, at a time when Pound was being thought of as a Fascist traitor rather than a literary critic (Bottome 1944: 72). She had been a contemporary of his at the University of Pennsylvania, had published her first novel, *Life the Interpreter* (New York and London, 1902) at the age of seventeen, and met up with Pound again in London as a member of the Ford–Hunt circle. She had never qualified as one of his 'discoveries'. Her memoir of 'Ezra Pound – Happy Exile' appeared in the December 1935 issue of *This Week*, seven months after Pound's first published remarks on any work of hers, a novel called *Private Worlds* (London, 1934). Although he had found the book 'readable and workmanlike', Pound said he was not interested in 'discussing it in relation to "the art of the novel"' (Pound 1935b: 48). This is because by then he was through with 'literary' criticism, and moving towards post-aesthetic styles of criticism like the one described below (p. 153) as 'usurocriticism'. He recommended *Private Worlds*, therefore, not for its style but its content: it was 'as good a slide of the psychotherapeutic world as we are likely to get' (ibid.). Or, as he put the matter more pointedly in 1938, every character in the insane asylum depicted in that novel (including the staff) 'was driven off the norm by economic pressure of one sort or another' (*GK* 157). In other words he valued *Private Worlds* not for the quality of its 'writing' but because it revealed the devastating psychological consequences of economic malpractices, just as a year later he 'commended the novels of Graham Seton, of John Hargrave and Henry Wade for specific treatment of live economics' (Pound 1936: 380). In Pound's shift from 'literary' criticism to usurocriticism, a transvaluation of his earlier values occurred: 'what makes for good writing', he had come to believe, was not that attentiveness to stylistic detail which Bottome gratefully learnt from him and said she never forgot, but 'economic awareness' (ibid.).

Another satisfied client, Ernest Hemingway, was not impressed by the maestro's dereliction of Flaubertian principles in the interests of economic awareness. 'Since when are you an economist, pal?' he asked in April 1933 after Pound had tried to educate him in such matters: 'The last I knew you you were a fuckin' bassoon player' (Tytell 1987: 231). That had been in their Paris years (1922–4), when Pound engaged in a variety of extra-literary activities in addition to bassoon playing, such as trying to be a sculptor, writing an opera, and taking boxing-lessons from Hemingway, who remembered Pound as the man he 'liked and trusted most as a critic' in those days, 'the man who believed in the *mot juste*' and taught him 'to distrust adjectives' (Hemingway 1964: 116). Although there are no surviving manuscript copies of Hemingway's short stories worked over by Pound (Hurwitz 1971–2: 476), it is clear from Hemingway's testimony that Pound's procedure was to apply to fiction the critical methods he had designed a decade earlier in connection with *Imagiste* poetry.

In 1917 Pound acknowledged his critical indebtedness to a writer who does not figure prominently in histories of literary criticism, Walter Savage Landor, 'the first analytical critic in English, the first man to go through an English poem line by line marking what was good, what was poor, what was excessive' (*SP* 358). Pound's wording here recalls Landor's stipulation that 'a perfect piece of criticism must exhibit *where* a work is good or bad, *why* it is good or bad; in what degree it is good or bad' (Witemeyer 1977: 155). Pound especially admired Landor's essay on 'The Poems of Catullus', published in *The Last Fruit off an Old Tree* (1853). It shows *inter alia* how inattentive to detail Milton could be in his more magniloquent passages: it points to the faults A.J.A. Waldock was later to collect and analyse in *Paradise Lost and Its Critics* (Cambridge, 1947), a book which Leavis was to co-opt in the 'dislodgement' of Milton from canonical status as an English poet. Poundian in his iconoclastic attitude towards Milton, Landor even writes like Pound from time to time: 'There is many a critic who talks of harmony, and whose ear seems to have been fashioned out of the callus of his foot' (Landor 1853: 245). If Landor had been the innovator of 'almost the only sort of criticism that can profit a later writer' (*SP* 358), Pound would become its master, making it new by redesigning it as a method for criticising living writers and not, as predominantly in Landor's case, the celebrated dead.

In 1946, when Pound feared he might 'go stark screaming hysteric' in the 'hell-hole' of his cell in a part of St Elizabeths hospital reserved for the criminally insane (Carpenter 1988: 733), Eliot was pointing out to readers of *Poetry* that Pound's work as a literary critic was 'inextricably woven with his conversation', so much so that only half of it was represented by his published books and articles: the rest could be known 'only from the testimony of those who have benefited from his conversation or correspondence' (Eliot 1946: 331, 335). A sample of the critic as correspondent is the selection of letters (about one-third of those extant) which Pound wrote to Laurence Binyon in 1938, when new poetry no longer interested him very much, offering what Binyon acknowledged as 'a great number of careful criticisms' of his translation of Dante's *Purgatorio* into English *terza rima* (Binyon 1938: vii). Much more difficult to retrieve is the criticism Pound offered in conversation to people he was in contact with.

The first important writer to invite Pound to 'correct' his work was Yeats, who spent the winter of 1912–13 at Stone Cottage in Sussex, where he invited Pound to join him as his secretary, a position which Pound redefined to include the services of a live-in critic. As the critic at the breakfast table, Pound's confidence was boosted by Yeats's gradual acceptance of Poundian criteria which were first made public in the *Imagiste* manifesto in 1913. Pound at this time thought Yeats the greatest living English poet but in need nevertheless of lessons in writing from a post-*Symboliste* such as himself. The kind of resistance Yeats put up in November 1912 to Pound's removal from his poem 'Fallen Majesty' of the phrase 'as it were' (in the line, 'Once walked a thing that seemed, as it were, a burning cloud') gradually weakened as Yeats began not only to revise his work along Poundian lines but also to talk about the process in a Poundian manner (Williams, E. 1977: 62). He told Lady Gregory on 3 January 1913 that he was now 'writing with new confidence having got Milton off [his] back' (Jeffares 1949: 167), although it is doubtful whether he ever had Milton on his back in the first place, or even thought he had, until Pound told him so. Pound, Yeats went on, had helped him 'to get back to the definite and the concrete away from modern abstractions' (ibid.). One of the poems they worked over together in the company of Sturge Moore eventually became 'The Two Kings'. 'We went at it line by line', Yeats told Lady Gregory early in January 1913 (Ellmann 1967: 66), pointing out that Pound was the better critic of the two, and oblivious of any misgivings Pound himself might have had about providing this sort of service in front of spectators. 'I wish he wouldn't ask me for criticism except when we're alone', he told Dorothy Shakespear on 21 January 1913 (*EP/DS* 183). Yeats made public his indebtedness to Pound's critical abilities when, speaking on 1 March 1914 at a dinner given in his honour by *Poetry*, he told the diners that the 'young man' he had asked to go over all his work with him 'to eliminate the abstract' was Ezra Pound (Stock 1970: 153). When that speech was reported in *Poetry*, Pound's reputation among poets as a critic of poetry was made, helped along by enthusiastic friends like Williams, who told Babette Deutsch in 1936 that Pound 'gave Yeats a hell of a bawling out for some of his inversions and other archaisms of style' (Williams, W.C. 1957: 210).

There were of course problems in telling people what was wrong with their poems instead of writing notes on their drafts. For a start, they could always deny what Pound said he had said, especially if it was something they didn't want to hear. Pound told Flint in July 1915 that a poem called 'A Swan Song' (in Flint's 1909 collection, *In the Net of the Stars*) had been changed for the better as a result of something Pound had said about it. Flint claimed, however, that the principal difference between the 1909 version of his poem and the one called 'The Swan' which Pound published in 1914 in *Des Imagistes* (both are reprinted in Jones 1972: 80, 149) was not stylistic but formal. Flint also said that the earlier version might well be better than the later one, and that in any case 'not... much light' had been generated that evening when Pound 'jabbed at the poem with the stub of a pencil' (Middleton 1965: 41–2).

Part of the problem was the status of Pound's interventions in other people's work: were they to be taken as recommendations or directives? As its title indicates, 'A Few Don'ts by an Imagiste' issues a series of directives which were meant to be obeyed: they developed out of a memo designed to accompany rejection-slips sent out by *Poetry* to aspiring poets in the hope that the next things they set before Pound's 'captious and atrabilious eye' (*L* 79) would be free at least of the kind of faults catalogued as 'don'ts'. When challenged, however, Pound would retreat to a more moderate position. 'I don't mean my slashes are definite improvements', he told Archibald MacLeish in 1926, 'merely a suggested possible elimination or change' (Carpenter 1988: 193). Nevertheless, there came a point at which Pound's gratefully accepted offers of alternative words and phrases made him an unacknowledged collaborator in other people's writings, as was the case in Eliot's poem, 'Whispers of Immortality', to which Pound contributed the line about Donne, 'Who found no substitute for sense' (ibid.: 350-1). He was careful to point out to Binyon that 'collaboration and rewrite à la E.P.' (*L* 402) was not what he had in mind in proposing detailed solutions to local problems in the translation of Dante's *Purgatorio*. 'One can never emend another man's work, or hardly ever', he added. 'One can only put one's finger on the emenda' (*L* 403). Confident writers like Joyce were in no need of such assurances. In November 1926 when Joyce sent him an instalment of what eventually became *Finnegans Wake*, Pound told him that 'nothing short of divine vision or a new cure for the clapp can possibly be worth all the circumambient peripherization' (*L* 276). 'It is possible Pound is right', Joyce told Harriet Shaw Weaver in February 1927, 'but I cannot go back. I never listened to his objections to *Ulysses* . . . but dodged them as tactfully as I could' (*EP/JJ* 229). Equally towering egos, however, resented directives to remove alleged superfluities from their work. Frost, for instance, did not appreciate having a poem of his shortened from fifty words to forty-eight, and accused Pound of having 'spoiled [his] meter, [his] idiom, and idea' (Williams, E. 1977: 64).

How much 'constructive' criticism of his own poetry Pound received cannot be determined, although it is unlikely to have been very much, mainly because of his indifference to the critical judgements of practically everybody except Ford and Eliot. Soliciting comments on Canto 8, he complained to Ford in January 1922 that there was 'no possible way of getting any criticism' of his poetry, adding that 'les jeunes, etc. are no use' (*EP/FMF* 63). Eliot certainly gave him the kind of detailed criticism he sought, removing over twenty personal pronouns from the version of the first of the *ur*-Cantos published in 1917 in the American edition of *Lustra* (Bush 1976: 185-6), thereby earning Pound's gratitude for being 'the only person who proffered criticism instead of general objection' (*L* 173). And he expressed his surprise to Quinn when *Poetry* rejected 'Langue d'Oc' and 'Moeurs Contemporaines' because he himself 'had gone over these poems carefully before Pound sent them; and had applauded them' (Eliot 1988: 223). Pound's view was that as a critic he gave far more than he received. 'I think I have tried to learn from critics', he told Schelling in 1922 (*L* 245), but when he came to count his critical debts to others he could think of only four, which he committed to print in January 1923: to Robert Bridges, for a 'caution against homophones'; to Yeats, for showing that poets should make 'NO compromise with the public'; to Thomas Hardy, for kindling an interest in 'subject' as opposed to 'treatment'; and to Ford, for insisting upon 'a contemporary spoken or at least speakable language' (Pound 1923: 144–5).

Omitted from this list is a critical category Pound may have suppressed, constituted by objections to his own work which he would first resent, then display as evidence of critical stupidity, and finally assimilate into his own repertoire of things to say about poetry. His poem 'Portrait d'une Femme' (*P* 61), for instance, was at first rejected by the *North American Review* on the grounds that in its opening line ('Your mind and you are our Sargasso Sea') Pound had 'used the letter "r" three times', which made the words 'very difficult to pronounce' (*PM* 30). This criticism, which Bridges could have made more plausibly in terms of the sequence of near homophones ('are' – 'our' – '[S]ar-'), had been supported apparently by Tennyson's objection to the 'horrible' sibilants in the opening line of Pope's *The Rape of the Lock* ('What dire Offence from am'rous Causes springs'). This appeal to Tennyson, 'the Tate Gallery among poets' (*LE* 276), merely emphasised in Pound's view the reactionary nature of the original objection, which he displayed in October 1912 as evidence of the 'imbecility' of contemporary editors. But, when invited in 1919 to comment on Eliot's 'Gerontion', Pound objected to the plosives in the second line ('Being read to by a boy') in much the same way as Tennyson had objected to Pope's sibilants. Striking out the words, he wrote: 'b-b-b *Bd* + *bb* consonants and 2 prepositions' (Carpenter 1988: 349). Eliot pondered this objection and then, fortunately, put the words back in the poem.

Pound's habitual transgression of the boundaries between advice and injunction, consultation and collaboration, is displayed most conspicuously in the part he played as a critic in the evolution of that showpiece of the modernist movement in poetry, *The Waste Land* (1922). Eliot modestly told Quinn, when offering him the original manuscript in January 1923, that the point of preserving the draft of *The Waste Land* with Pound's annotations on it was to show 'the difference which his criticism has made to this poem' (Eliot 1988: 572). What posterity would find in Pound's 'blue penciling' on that manuscript, Eliot wrote in 1946 (at a time when it was presumed lost), was 'irrefutable evidence of Pound's critical genius' (Eliot 1946: 330). When the manuscript surfaced again, and was edited in 1971 in the form of a facsimile transcript, it was possible to see evidence of Pound's intervention in both the diction and form of the published poem. For, in giving advice which Eliot took not only on the choice of individual words but also on which sections of the poem to leave in or take out, Pound helped determine what survived for readers to try to make sense of. Whether the original draft was improved by a critical genius (as Eliot always insisted) or ruined by a meddler (as Louis Auchinclos was to claim in 1984) is a purely hypothetical issue. All we can claim in this respect is that a version of the poem untouched by Pound would have had a quite different reception and history from the one in which he was involved.

Anybody who wished to dissent from Grover Smith's view that the Poundianised poem is 'the best of all possible *Waste Lands*' (Smith 1983: 81) would not find it impossible to discover merit in practically anything Eliot agreed to eliminate from the published version. 'When Lil's husband got demobbed', for instance, are words all readers of *The Waste Land* are familiar with, and which sounded colloquially right for half a century before it was revealed that what Eliot himself had in fact written was, 'When Lil's husband was coming back out of the Transport Corps' (Eliot 1971: 13). No doubt Eliot was persuaded by Pound that 'demobbed' was the *mot juste* here: the word had come into circulation in 1919 as the demotic term for soldiers 'demobilised' at the end of the 1914–18 war, and was an appropriate colloquialism to use in a representation of working-class speech. Yet, if the Poundianised lection had not achieved its authority already by custom and currency, the superiority of Eliot's original words might well be established by anybody with a mind to do so. It is not difficult to imagine, for instance, a New Critical reading which would tease out ironic ambiguities in the word 'Transport' (meaning 'ecstasy' as well as 'conveyance'), and discover a creative tension between the 'Corps' mentioned here and the 'corpse' planted in the preceding section of the poem. To enquire into which version of *The Waste Land* is the better poem, or to fantasise about an even better third version made up of the 'best' readings from the other two, is a function of an idealist mode of criticism at odds with those materialist and historicising reading practices which would claim that what has come down to us is not one text in two versions but two texts, each produced in different circumstances for different readerships.

Pound's interventions in Eliot's work extended beyond the microstructures of individual words and lines to such macrostructures as arrangement and form. The order of the poems in *Prufrock and Other Observations* (1917) was proposed by Pound, not Eliot (Langbaum 1985: 170), who told Kenner in 1964 that he 'ascribed great gifts of sequencing' to Pound (Kenner 1988: 728). Presumably that is why Eliot accepted Pound's judgement that *The Waste Land* 'runs from "April..." to "shantih" without a break', and that nothing was to be gained 'by prolonging it three pages further' (*L* 234). That judgement was questioned by Quinn. 'Personally', he told Eliot in 1923, 'I should not have cut out some of the parts that Pound advised you to cut' (Reid 1968: 580), a remark Eliot may have recalled somewhat ruefully on discovering that the Poundianised version of his poem was rather too short for publication in book form, thus prompting him to add notes which would produce the right amount of copy required by the printer (Eliot 1957: 109). But the story Eliot preferred to tell was that Pound, far from vandalising the original *Waste Land*, had in fact used his 'technical mastery and critical ability' to turn 'a jumble of good and bad passages into a poem' (Gallup 1970: 73). In other accounts by Eliot of the genesis of *The Waste Land*, that 'jumble' is described as 'chaotic' (Bush 1983: 70), a word which evokes one of the poem's own cancelled couplets: 'From such chaotic misch-masch potpourri / What are we to expect but poetry?' (Eliot 1971: 41). 'Chaos' was a word with feminine connotations for Pound, who troped his own critical activities in masculinist terms as those of an 'instigator'. And, in yet another set of tropes, Pound is both male midwife and surgeon who delivers a female Eliot of the poem by caesarian section (*L* 234).

Metaphors like these suggest that investigations into Pound's critical engagements with other people's poems need to go beyond aestheticising enquiries into whether or not he improved what he changed, and look instead as Wayne Koestenbaum (1988) has done at the psychosexual and homoerotic implications of such transactions. Many readers think that Pound turned *The Waste Land* (as he tried to turn other people's poems) into a Poundian poem, specifically by cutting out the kind of transitional and discursive passages which Eliot was to make use of in *Four Quartets* (1942), and by juxtaposing the remaining passages in accordance with those 'ideogramic' methods he was experimenting with concurrently in *The Cantos*. But Eliot told an interviewer in 1959 that Pound was 'a marvellous critic' precisely 'because he didn't try to turn you into an imitation of himself' (Eliot 1959: 52–3); or, as he had put it a few years earlier, Pound 'tried first to understand what one was attempting to do, and then tried to help one do it in one's own way' (Eliot 1946: 335). Against this tribute to Pound as the selfless respecter of alterity and heterogeneity, we need to set the evidence of a 'chaotic' manuscript whose author was 'attempting' to represent certain emotional and spiritual preoccupations more or less eliminated as superfluities from a published version which became as a result much more a work of cultural analysis than spiritual autobiography (Gordon 1977: 115–17). Was that the poem Eliot wanted to write, but couldn't do so unaided, or the one Pound thought Eliot ought to write, and ensured that he did?

Pound would not have appreciated being called a rhetorical critic because he thought of rhetoric as a pathology of language, roughly synonymous with 'verbiage', and symptomatic of evasiveness. 'Rhetoric', he wrote in 1916, 'is the art of dressing up some unimportant matter so as to fool the audience for the time being' (*G-B* 83); Yeats was to be praised, accordingly, for having 'stripped English poetry of its perdamnable rhetoric' (*LE* 11). This is a usage commonly encountered among modernists who had read Verlaine's poem, 'L'Art poétique', and responded favourably to its injunction, 'Prends l'éloquence et tords son coup', which is reproduced by Eliot as 'wring the neck of rhetoric' (Eliot 1917a: 151). But rhetoric is traditionally the art of verbal persuasion, and as such is an appropriate word to apply to that ensemble of stylistic devices and critical strategies used by Pound in order to bring readers around to his way of seeing things.

The ventriloquial agility of Pound's critical style is not altogether

The rhetorical critic

surprising in a writer whose poetry sets the pluralities of personae above the univocity of a singular personality. His speaking voice, as Iris Barry remembered it from his London years, was distinguished by its polyglot features: 'the base of American mingled with a dozen assorted "English Society" and Cockney accents inserted in mockery, French, Spanish and Greek exclamations, strange cries and catcalls, the whole very oddly inflected, with dramatic pauses and *diminuendos*' (Barry 1931: 159). Pound's prose correspondingly vocalises its constituent words and rhythms. As a subject-in-process in language, Pound let his writing accommodate a multiplicity of idiolects, acquiring mastery over language by keeping open house to different varieties of it, and enjoying the effects produced by the collocations and clashes of different registers. And, when the end came to that mastery, he experienced it not as something willingly surrendered or even involuntarily lost but as something taken away from him and replaced by silence. 'I did not enter into silence', he remarked on his eightieth birthday, momentarily on parole; 'silence captured me' (Torrey 1984: 277).

Locutions from a variety of discursive domains invade the space of a Poundian paragraph and are entertained there in a variety of moods, ranging from seriousness to mockery. Academese will inaugurate a sentence with the word 'Compare', be brushed aside ('pardon the professorial tone'), but immediately reassert itself for the remainder of the sentence ('whereof I seem unable to divest myself') (*LE* 233). The voice of a London socialite is to be heard in his description of Yeats's poems as 'ripping' (*EP/MCA* 24) and Rabindranath Tagore's as '*the* sensation of the winter' (*L* 44), although the world of 'the mondaine London clientèle' (*L* 184) is distanced when he describes a private viewing at the Goupil Gallery as 'a very brilliant occasion', but puts the phrase in quotation marks and adds the preceding rider, 'as they say in the *Times*' (*EP/VA* 184). The ubiquitous hill-billy of Pound's later prose puts in an appearance to congratulate Joyce on the early chapters of *Ulysses*: 'I recon' this here work o' yourn is some concarn'd litterchure... an' I'm a jedge' (*EP/JJ* 129). This is poles apart from the Wildeanism which dismisses Edmund Gosse in 1920 for having 'all the qualities of a critic, except insight and the capacity to discriminate' (Henderson 1984: 275). It is equally far removed from the elaborately staged Shavianism directed in the same essay against the American responsible to the Wilson government for preventing the circulation of 'obscene' mail like copies of the *Little*

Review containing instalments of *Ulysses*: 'in the United States, there is a person without literary culture named Lamar, who is employed in the deep recesses of the postal administration, to prohibit the mailing of our best novels' (ibid.).

Clashes of register generate characteristically 'Poundian' effects. A sentence which begins with the words, 'This is the proper tone to use when dealing with elderly', exhibits a decorousness which is deliberately abandoned when the patiently expected noun required to complete the sentence turns out to be 'muttonheads' (*MN* 240). The lexeme 'Milton's god is a' mismatches its complementary lexeme 'fussy old man with a hobby' (*SR* 165) in order to break the decorum of Milton criticism, just as the decorum of music criticism is broken when invaded by the discourse of athletics in the sentence, 'We believe 22¼ minutes is a speed record for performance of the Liszt B minor sonata' (*EP/M* 238). Absolute constructions ('nothing but', 'only', etc.) combine frequently with exaggerated observations (such as, 'Eliot is now paralyzed from the neck up' (*CO/EP* 85)) to produce amusingly outrageous statements like 'Orage was the sole editor of any London weekly who encouraged mental activity' (Pound 1918b: 35). Absolute constructions served Pound's purposes especially well because they conferred an air of certitude on his judgements, and enabled him to avoid the hesitancies created by modifiers and parodied in his statement that 'the history of literature as taught in many institutions (? all) is nothing more (hardly more) than a stratified record of snobisms' (*SP* 368). Stylistic mannerisms from a variety of sources coexist eclectically to enlist other authorial presences in a critical attack. Cummings's use of the split word (what rhetoricians call 'tmesis') is co-opted in phrases like 'the public (so) libraries (called)' (*I* 10) and 'absobloodylootly nothing' (*EPS* 230). A Jamesian use of ironic quotation marks is responsible for both 'the London so-called "school" of Economics' (Pound 1935a: 534) and 'the London School of "Economics" ' (*GK* 234), an institution elsewhere renamed 'the London School of Falsehood' (Pound 1936b: 315).

What powered the criticism was a carefully nurtured irascibility barely containable except in the more spectacular forms of imprecation. This was the characteristic which led MacLeish to address Pound in 1926 as 'Ezrascibilissimus' (MacLeish 1983: 188), and Eliot to depict him as the apoplectic 'Appleplex' (Eliot 1917). Eschewing blandness, Pound liked a book to be an 'irritant' (*LE*

173), and thrived on a hostile review, because 'that sort of thing occasionally draws down the muse if I read it before dinner' (*EP/DS* 118). Denunciations were to him what daffodils were to Wordsworth. Mencken explained the abusiveness in terms of 'Puritan pressure', which had turned Pound into 'a mere bellower' (*CH* 142). But I incline to Carpenter's view that what the acerbic qualities of Pound's prose reveal – especially in his letters – is not uncontrollable anger but 'a caricature of rage' (Carpenter 1988: 295). The invective violence is offered more as spectacle than threat, and in view of its generic affinities with flyting it has less in common with murder than with all-in wrestling. Those who knew Pound understood this. 'Lawd how you cuss and rave', Eliot replied in 1922 after receiving a typical tirade (Eliot 1988: 612). William M. Reedy told Babette Deutsch that he 'revelled' in Pound's 'ingenuity of insult', which he countered with 'ribald joshing' of his own (Raffel 1985: 86). But, for every American who enjoyed (as Aiken did) 'the pleasure of quarreling' with Pound (ibid.: 97), there was a Briton who thought it ungentlemanly of Pound to make differences of opinion 'as caustic as possible' (*GK* 169), and who was ready (as Aldington was in 1913) to attribute Pound's insulting behaviour to the fact that 'he is an American, and probably doesn't know any better' (Williams, E. 1977: 82).

To the vocal mimicries of his critical style Pound added expressionistic effects made possible by his typewriter, which enabled him to replicate symbolically the gestures of an almost inarticulable rage. His attack in 1917 on the *Little Review*'s 'BLOODY goddamndamnblastedbitchbornsonofaputridseahorse of a foetid and stinkerous printer' is very much print-dependent, and would lose its force if handwritten (*EP/MCA* 181). Pound himself had had some six years earlier a memorable encounter with a gestural critic in the person of Ford, who had been so appalled by the archaisms in *Canzoni* (1911) as to roll on the floor, thus prompting Pound immediately to begin 'using the living tongue' in his poems (*SP* 432). Pound's own contribution to gestural criticism of the unsublimated kind was to try to embarrass Amy Lowell (whose poems on the sensual pleasures of bathing appear to have provoked in her contemporaries a great deal of ribald mirth) by bringing into the restaurant at which she was giving a dinner to celebrate the publication of *Des Imagistes* a large tub and announcing the existence of a new school of poetry, the *Nagistes* (Carpenter 1988: 253).

That kind of buffoonery was far from his usual practice of ridiculing people he had no time for by ridiculing their names. *Nomina sunt consequentia rerum* was the formula he took from Aquinas (*G-B* 92) to prop up a consequentialist theory of naming which claims that correct names reveal the true natures of things. Except in allegorical fictions, where they habitually reveal natures, proper names tend to be thought of as quite arbitrary. But Pound himself inherited a surname with several different referents (a unit of weight, a unit of currency, an enclosure, a stretch of water, the action of striking violently, and so on): what was the true *res* of which 'Pound' was the *consequentia*? To ' "call things by their right names" ' (*SP* 99) was for Pound a critical obligation which began as an aesthetics of the *mot juste* and broadened into the Confucian ethic of *cheng ming*. In these terms, false names are to be exposed because they conceal unsavoury natures best revealed in a diagnostic rewriting of them. By vandalising an accepted name scatologically, Pound was able to substitute paradigmatic morphemes of an allegedly revelatory nature which acts of deceit or squeamishness had obscured. 'Consequentially', the correct name for 'Bloomsbury' was 'bloomsbuggery', on account of the goings-on of 'arsethete[s]' like Clive Bell and other 'bloomsbuggahs', including of course the 'shitwell[s]' (*EP/WL* 302, 177, 172, 127). The subterfuge of these disparaging pseudo-etymologies is characteristically logocentric, for what is claimed to be the true meaning of a name is invented in fact after the event, *nachträglich*. This is done by substituting for an otherwise inscrutable name a supplement which is then credited with the authenticity and explanatory powers of an origin.

The genre Pound was most at ease in as a critic turned out to be the essay rather than the book, although if he had had his own way it would have been neither. Ideally he would have preferred a situation in which poets (say) were criticised only by other poets, and preferably in the form of poems which 'answer' other poems, as the *Cantos* 'answer' Browning's *Sordello* (1840), it being still Pound's contention as late as 1933 that 'the critical sense shows more in composition than in a critical essay' (*SP* 367). Twenty years earlier he had praised verse parody as 'the best criticism' because it 'sifts the durable from the apparent' (*L* 47) without doing the slightest damage to masterpieces like Edward Fitzgerald's *The Rubáiyát of Omar Khayyám* (1859), which 'has survived hundreds of parodies' (*ABCR* 53). He praised parodies of his own poems when they focused on technicalities as cleverly as those by Aldington did, and wrote in 'The Lake Isle' (*P* 117) a parody of Yeats's 'The Lake Isle of Innisfree' which Yeats wanted to include in his *Oxford Book of English Verse* (Carpenter 1988: 304). The attraction of answer-poems and parodies was that they dispensed with those interfering intermediaries between poem and reader, critics, and their obfuscatory discourse, criticism.

Two other critical genres, the *sottisier* and the anthology, were prized for similar reasons. In *Who's Who 1915* Pound listed among his recreations 'searching *The Times* for evidences of incredible stupidity': from these he put together in various issues of the *Egoist* in 1914 and 1915 'the sort of fool-column that the French call a *sottisier*' (*LE* 17). These were reproduced on the assumption that some statements are so self-evidently stupid that refutation is unnecessary because all you need do is quote them. The *sottisier* in the 1 July 1914 issue of the *Egoist* reproduces from *The Times Literary Supplement* the statement, 'If Homer is authentic, so is Milton, though with a slight difference', and adds: 'Yes, a *slight* difference'. By May 1918, however, ironical appendages had disappeared, and the corresponding entry reads simply: 'John Milton was a great poet. – *The Times*'. This is coterie criticism at its most confident, barely intelligible outside an in-group which knows without needing to have it explained that 'Milton' is the signifier of stylistic excesses: it was a name which 'summed up', Fletcher recognised, Pound's 'three chief hatreds ... superfluity of adjectives, inversions, and rhetoric' (Fletcher 1937: 59). 'These sottisiers are often the first parts of a live mag. that people read', Pound wrote in 1929, advising a correspondent to 'run [a] sottisier confined to literary criticism', taking its materials from '*Poetry* and the main literary reviews, Sunday supplements, etc.' (*L* 302). As a critical genre its lineage was impeccable: 'Flaubert published his *sottisier*' (*SP* 302) in the form of a dictionary of received ideas appended to his novel *Bouvard et Pécuchet* (1881). As a critical method it worked on the assumption that 'to indict one need only cite' (Sieburth 1978: 121), and came out of the same anti-critical syndrome which promoted the idea that 'the text itself' is somehow its own best commentator.

The generic monument to that particular ideology of the text is the anthology, which Pound saw as a means of evading problems of critical discourse by substituting the 'presentation' of texts-in-themselves for the representation of them in critical commentaries.

'My criticism', he wrote in 1910, 'has consisted in selection rather than in presentation of opinion' (*SR* vii–viii). He came to regard Confucius as the supreme example of the critic-as-anthologist, the man who (according to tradition but not modern sinologists) had eliminated superfluities from a collection of three thousand odes by preserving the 'best' three hundred (Canto 53). The business of a critic, Pound observed in 1917, is not 'to write huge tomes "about" this, that, and the other' but 'to dig out the fine thing forgotten' (*SP* 168). This was a lesson never learnt in the 1930s by that *Scrutiny* 'school of "critics" ' who wrote in a 'ridiculous dialect' and believed 'that their books about books about writing' would 'breed a "better taste" than would a familiarity with the great poets' (*SP* 201). Criticism would achieve the desideratum of minimal intervention if it became primarily deictic, content to point in a particular direction and say by way of marginal annotation, ' "There digge" ' (*L* 347). If the text 'itself' is its own best commentator, who needs 'Jojo's opinion of Jimjim's explanation' of it (*LE* 66)? That conviction was still intact in one of the last pieces of prose Pound ever published, his 1966 memorial words on Eliot, where he declines invitations 'to write "about" the poet' with the blunt injunction: 'READ HIM' (*SP* 434). The aim of such discursive reticence was to rid criticism of a vice comparable to 'rhetoric' in poetry, variously called 'palaver' or 'yatter' (*SP* 324, 366). But like other forms of minimalism, criticism-by-anthologising is profoundly authoritarian in its assumption that the very act of selecting this rather than that text needs no justification and is a value in itself. Against whatever benefits are to be had from those silent acts of witnessing and recognition made possible by the anthologist's method of 'presenting' texts without commentary we need to set the disadvantages which follow the pre-emption of a discursive space in which selections might be defended and questioned. Pound continued to stand by the practice of anthologising as a critical act in spite of problems he encountered with every anthology he edited, an experience which might have persuaded him that neither meaning nor value is ever so self-evident in the case of literary texts as to obviate the need for opportunities to discuss them.

Pound's unwillingness or inability to undertake reasoned criticism alarmed sympathetic readers like Orage, who complained in 1918 that Pound was 'indiscriminating in his praise as well as in his censure' (Orage 1974: 154). Pound was well aware that his strength lay more in the energy of his assertions – his rhetoric – than in the subtlety of his argument. In 1913 he told Monroe the amusing story of how a Penn friend, L. Burtron Hessler, had once advised a seminar 'that it might as well agree with [Pound] in the first place because it was bound to do so in the end out of sheer exhaustion' (*L* 54). Forty years later, however, the same conviction that certain things are beyond argument sounded more sinister when Pound told listeners to his Radio Rome talks: 'I am not trying to prove anything, I am just telling you' (*EPS* 245).

Such foreclosures of dissent are structurally at odds with those many books and articles of his which present themselves as occasional in their provenance, hurried in their execution, and provisional in their refusal to marmorealise their constituent sentences, arrange their component sections into artful symmetries and asymmetries, or proceed inexorably towards that climactic kind of closure which is read as the signifier of an unshakeable certitude. The problem of closure in fact generates a good deal of the text of Pound's 1916 book on Gaudier-Brzeska, which is designed to look unfinished, and therefore to represent that dynamism of process which Pound preferred to the stasis of Gaudier-Brzeska's completed marble bust of him. The fifteenth section of that book opens with the confession that 'it is difficult to stop writing' (*G-B* 125); several pages and four sections later, Pound is still requesting 'the reader's indulgence' to add another set of observations (*G-B* 134). *Guide to Kulchur* (1938) similarly puts itself together by taking itself apart. A vade-mecum with a difference, it is aware in its mockingly reductive title of its unlikeness to the customary Baedeker for culture-vultures whose sensibilities would be offended on encountering the word 'culture' so crudely misspelled. (Readers of the first American edition, entitled simply *Culture*, were spared at least that outrage.) In deconstructing guidebooks to grandiose topics, *Guide to Kulchur* continuously undermines its own authority, drawing attention to its 'ridiculous title' and classifying itself as 'a stunt piece' (*GK* 183). In its persistent risk-taking and open acknowledgement of the possibility that a rereading of a few other books might have made it quite different from what it is (*GK* 33), *Guide to Kulchur* is an amazingly open-ended production to have come from a writer usually thought of as by that stage unremittingly authoritarian. And if nothing else it points up the hazards of trying to educe political conclusions about writers from the evidence of their literary styles and forms.

Pound was habitually apologetic about his prose style. 'My prose is bad', he confessed to Monroe in 1913, 'but on ne peut pas pontifier and have style simultaneously' (*L* 50). A year later, reflecting on the difficulties of trying to produce deathless prose to deadlines in order to pay the rent, Pound complained that 'one can't "get the punch" into one's article, because of "the pressure of time"' (*EP/VA* 190). Such disclaimers betray the anxieties of a man who had spent some years 'trying to write English as Tacitus wrote Latin' (*L* 137), and who suspected that prose was a belletristic art-form he would never master (*SP* 23). As a student he had been impressed by J.W. Mackail's 'gush' (Pound 1919: 24) about the prose style of Tacitus, a writer who employed 'every artifice of style' and a 'daring use of vivid words and elliptical constructions' in order to avoid 'the old balance of the sentence', and who established 'a new historical manner' which 'never ... says a thing in a certain way because it is the way in which the ordinary rules of style would prescribe that it should be said' (Mackail 1896: 209–10). And while writing *The Spirit of Romance* in 1909 Pound was still hoping to develop 'a prose style as concise as [Robert Louis] Stevenson's' (Carpenter 1988: 125). But the material circumstances of his life as a London literary journalist – an experience which by 1917 had turned him into 'a highly mechanized typing volcano' capable of emitting 'an article a day for a month' (*EP/WL* 104, 99) – removed any residual hopes he may have entertained of reproducing Tacitean rhythms in English prose and being admired for a belletristic style of writing. So instead of trying to write 'nice, orderly, old-fashioned prose' (*G-B* 82), and 'screw[ing] about like Tacitus to get his thought crowded into the least possible space' (*LE* 50), Pound settled instead for an extempory mode of 'stop-gap' prose designed 'to deal with transient states of Murkn imbecility or ignorance' (*L* 289). What he developed in the process was a prose style which exhibited that 'complete mastery of mordant and unforgettable phrase' which Mackail had found in Tacitus' *Agricola* (Mackail 1896: 212), and which helps to make Pound's literary criticism by far the most lively and provocative written this century.

5

The vanishing critic

For some years before Pound finally left London for Paris, he had come to regret his 1912 decision to abandon his 'own work for criticism' and the multifarious duties associated with the practice of criticism as he understood it. There were too many weeks in his life like the one in March 1916 when, in addition to his reviewing commitments, he was still acting as executor to the Gaudier-Brzeska estate, overseeing the packing up of a Vorticist exhibition for display in New York, making a selection for publication of the letters of Yeats *père*, and helping with the production of a play by Yeats *fils* (*L* 120). By January 1918 he was telling the editor of the *Little Review* that he was 'bored to death with being any kind of an editor': as a poet, he wanted to get on with his 'long poem', *The Cantos*, and as a scholar, to cultivate his *passéisme* in peace by having time 'to hear the music of a lost dynasty' (*L* 187). This would involve, of course, stopping up his ears against the siren-songs of current dynasties, and eventually losing contact altogether with what was going on around him, in the manner of his own Hugh Selwyn Mauberley.

He had gone to 'deah old Lundon' originally because it was 'the place for poesy' and the city where critical standards were such as 'to make one feel the vanity of all art except the highest' (*L* 41–2). There was never a week in London 'without some new thing of interest', he wrote in 1913, 'no fortnight in which some new and interesting personality is not whirled up against one' (Pound 1913: 300): he would soon have the word he was looking for when describing London in December of that year as 'The Vortex' (*L* 65). London was full of people carrying 'particles of knowledge and gossip, wearing you away little by little' in a process described rather more negatively in his poem 'Portrait d'une Femme' (*P* 61), which is a study of a woman without qualities, who exists as a mere function of her metropolitan ambiance, and has become a Sargasso Sea of cultural debris. By September 1920 the only thing preventing him from shifting to Paris appeared to be 'masochism' (*L* 223); terminally through with London, he stayed briefly at the Hotel Terminus in St Raphael before settling in Paris (*EP/FMF* 50), where he added for the benefit of a *New York Herald* interviewer a further and political reason for his departure from London: 'the decay of the British Empire', which was 'too depressing a spectacle to witness at close range' (Stock 1970: 235). For a Europhile like Pound, born in a half-savage country, 'exile' to Europe was a sort of homecoming, a *nostos* scripted as inevitable for American intellectuals of his own and the preceding generation of Henry James and James McNeill Whistler. Pound's farewell to England was as decisive as his earlier farewell to America. It had been a narrow escape from that sinking island and the city he would identify as 'Sodom on Thames' (*EP/MCA* 314) or alternatively 'Gomorrah on Thames', where he had never managed to 'find any Englishman who knew anything' (*GK* 228). As history continued to be rewritten negatively in his memory, he would quote with approval on Radio Rome in March 1943 Hemingway's designation of him in 1922 as 'the ONLY American who ever got out of England alive' (*EPS* 245). In order to escape alive he had tried, unsuccessfully, to fake his own death. The editors of the *Little Review* had received a letter allegedly from his wife (but in John Rodker's handwriting) announcing Pound's death, plus photographs of a 'death mask' of Pound made by Nancy Cox McCormack; but they refused to go along with the hoax, much to his annoyance (*EP/MCA* 283; *EP/WL* 133). 'Please don't contradict report of my demise if it has the luck to spread', he asked Williams in May 1922. 'I want a little quiet' (*L* 244). So in 1925 when Ethel Moorhead and Ernest Walsh were preparing the first issue (dedicated to Pound) of their journal *This Quarter*, they solicited from Hemingway 'an appreciation ... to be written as though Pound were dead' (Hemingway 1925: 221).

The narratives generated by Pound about his departure from London to Paris construct that episode in various ways. Some give us to understand that he left of his own accord because he had better things to do with his time; others encourage us to believe that he was given the push by people with a vested interest in getting rid of him; and there are still others which seem to reveal that he behaved in such a way as to ensure that he would be given the push, thus enabling him to represent himself as the victim of a conspiracy. Situating himself oppositionally to established journals, Pound was reluctant to blunt the cutting edge of his criticism by accommodating himself to their practices as Eliot was to do. Yet at the same time he would never refuse on principle a commission from such journals. Whenever he was dismissed subsequently for trying to sell them a product they did not want, he would see in such episodes evidence of persecution. His brief career as a drama critic, first for the *Athenaeum* and later for the *Outlook*, typifies a recurrent problem. That the editors of both journals should have fired him after a relatively short time is less surprising than that they should ever have hired as a drama critic in the first place a man who was to tell readers of the *Dial* in March 1923 that if, like him, they needed ' "poetic" or "literary" satisfaction', they would come to understand, as he did, that ' "the theatre" in general is no good, that plays are no good' (Pound 1923a: 277). When Middleton Murry decided that drama criticism was not Pound's forte he did not, as Pound told Quinn, give him 'the *chuck*' (Reid 1968: 437), but offered to keep him on instead as a book-reviewer for the *Athenaeum*. That offer was unacceptable to Pound, because by that stage he had scripted himself in such a way as to expect doors to be slammed in his face. Sympathetic friends like May Sinclair were persuaded not only to see things that way too but to say so in print: in May 1920 she wrote in the *North American Review* that 'with one exception, every serious and self-respecting magazine' was now 'closed to this most serious and self-respecting artist' (*CH* 180). The exception was presumably the *New Age*, whose editor told his readers on 13 January 1921 that 'much of the Press has been deliberately closed by cabal' to Pound (*CH* 200).

Pound never seemed to understand that even sympathetic editors could have misgivings about the tone as well as the content of some of his articles. 'Every time I print anything of his', Eliot confided to Quinn in October 1923, just as the *Criterion* was getting itself established, 'it nearly sinks the paper' (Gallup 1970: 77). Pound cherished letters like the one sent him on 22 October 1914 by the editor of the *Quarterly Review*, G.W. Prothero, pointing out that he could not 'open the columns of the *Q.R.* – at any rate, at present – to any one associated publicly with such a publication as *Blast*' because 'it stamps a man too disadvantageously' (Stock 1970: 162). This was the reputable journal which had published, in October 1913, a reputable essay by Pound on Provençal troubadours (*LE* 94–108). He displayed Prothero's letter as proudly as a war-wound at the end of his 1919 essay on Remy de Gourmont (*LE* 357–8). It had been a godsend when he first received it, for it improved his credibility with the *Blast* group he had attached himself to, some of whose members, according to Lewis, wondered why a man so given to 'fire-eating propagandist utterances' as Pound was had never got around to writing anything more experimental than 'a series of pastiches of old french or old italian poetry' (Lewis 1927: 55). So among Pound's contributions to the July 1915 issue was a poem which castigates 'Cowardly editors' like Prothero who 'threaten' to 'cut down [his] wage' if he refuses to 'sing their cant' (*CEP* 284). Pound told Quinn in February 1918 that his *New Age* articles on art would have to be signed pseudonymously ('B.H. Dias') because 'E.P. would be hopelessly suspect of Vorticist Propaganda' (*EP/VA* xxii). He was convinced that every time he was fired or refused a job it was not on account of any actual or presumed incompetence on his part but because his criticism was so devastatingly subversive that the powers that be had conspired to silence him. Even Orage, he recalled in 1933, the 'outcast editor' of that 'rebellious paper', the *New Age*, for which he wrote art criticism as 'B.H. Dias', had found him eventually too hot to handle, and had been obliged 'to limit [him] to criticism of music' – published again pseudonymously, in this case as 'William Atheling' – 'as no other topic was safe' (*SP* 199). This account overlooks the fact that in October 1920 Pound had been 'grateful for [the] chance to kill B.H. Dias' (*EP/VA* 245), an opportunity afforded by a reduction in the format of the *New Age*, which had been constrained by newsprint rationing in 1918, and was only half the size it had been in 1914 (Carswell 1978: 144). But Pound preferred to present himself melodramatically as a dangerous man to be associated with, and told Quinn that the promotional pamphlet written by Eliot in 1917 and called *Ezra Pound: His Metric and Poetry* (Eliot 1965: 162–82) ought to be published either pseudonymously 'with a nom-de-swank' or simply anonymously (as indeed it was) because it would harm Eliot's career to be associated with Pound publicly (*L* 191–2; cp. Reid 1968: 280). 'Don't breathe my satanic name', he told Mary Barnard when she was thinking of applying for a Guggenheim award in 1934 (*L* 345).

Pound's contretemps with Macmillan, the publisher of Palgrave's best-selling *Golden Treasury* (1861), illustrates his ability to present even his gaffes as evidence of victimisation, and to incorporate those involved into a demonology of oppression. To propose a new anthology of poetry 'to replace that doddard Palgrave' (*LE* 18) was a plausible if somewhat tactlessly phrased undertaking, seeing that everybody believed a poetry renascence was in progress. To conceive of the anthology as requiring ten volumes, however, was quite unrealistic, especially when there was a war on (Oxford University Press was also to reject Pound's proposal on account of wartime economies). But to suggest to Macmillan – and through an agent – that they replace their own best-selling anthology, and then be surprised because they didn't jump at the opportunity, was either a naive or disingenuous thing to do. Macmillan's rejection, however, like Prothero's, became documentary evidence for the conspiracy theory revealed in January 1929 to readers of the *New York Herald Tribune Books*: 'From that day onward no book of [his] received a British imprimatur' until his *Selected Poems* (1928), which Eliot 'castrated' by excluding from it that homage to sex, *Homage to Sextus Propertius* (*LE* 18). Conveniently omitted from this persecution narrative was the collection of his poems published in June 1920 as *Umbra* by the still loyal Elkin Mathews.

Pound went to Paris expecting to find 'Paris', and found himself instead in an anglophone ghetto of self-exiled American artists and writers. Whereas in London he had been an interesting exotic, first courted and then dumped by the literary establishment, in Paris he was just another of those Americans who were there, in Robert McAlmon's phrase, 'being geniuses together'. In Paris the American *salons* were well established: Natalie Barney had been there since 1902, and Gertrude Stein since 1903. Furthermore, they were run by women who, unlike some of the London hostesses he had encountered (such as 'the Lady Valentine' of *Hugh Selwyn Mauberley*), knew what they were doing, and took writing seriously. Stein in particular saw herself as the central American exponent in Paris of avant-garde experimentalism, complete with disciples like Sherwood Anderson and Ernest Hemingway (Benstock 1987: 15–16). It was difficult for Pound to appear as anything other than a parvenu, a reject from literary London although an American nevertheless. By November 1922 he was complaining already of the 'enervation' of a Paris represented by Marcel Proust in comparison with the 'male' vitality of Gabriele d'Annunzio's Italy (Carpenter 1988: 426); and in any case, as he was to tell Cowley in 1923, there were too many 'distractions' in Paris for a man who wanted to write an opera and complete *The Cantos* (Cowley 1951: 122). The fiscal strength of the pound sterling and the American dollar in postwar Europe made it sensible for Pound to stay there, although an old antipathy towards Germanic ways of doing things kept him away from the least expensive European capital at that time, Berlin, where Robert McAlmon calculated the absurdly low cost of living by reporting that a mere ten cents American would buy you 'a deck of "snow", enough cocaine for quite too much excitement' (McAlmon 1970: 96). The refuge from Paris he finally chose was that 'navel of the world' (Reck 1967: 48), the Italian coastal town of Rapallo: having been 'rejuv[e]nated by 15 years in going to Paris', he told Lewis in December 1924, he had 'added another ten of life, by quitting same . . . ' (*EP/WL* 138). Canto 77 recalls Yeats, who visited Rapallo in 1928, looking across the bay and murmuring, 'Sligo in Heaven', an anecdote Eliot must have remembered in 1934 when he wrote to Pound: 'I will arise & go NOW, & go to Rappaloo . . .' (Carpenter 1988: 484). But as a Mediterranean version of that escapist's dream, the Lake Isle of Innisfree, Rapallo was by no means an ideal location for a bookman like Pound. For although the Rapallo Tennis Club no doubt had its moments (it was there, for instance, that Pound first met Adrian Stokes in 1926), its potential as a focus of artistic talent was severely limited in comparison with the average Yeats 'evening' in London or gathering *chez* Natalie Barney in Paris. From now on Pound's contacts with the English-speaking literary world would be dependent on visitors to Rapallo and the efficiency of the post office in processing his burgeoning correspondence.

However much of a new lease of life Pound may have got as a poet by leaving both 'a decadent wallow like London' and 'an enervated centre like Paris' (Pound 1922: 549), his departure from London in particular signalled the beginning of the end of his career as a literary critic. Turning his back on England, he suppressed his curiosity about the work of other writers still living there. 'I am not the least interested in the fortunes of any writer in England save yourself', he told Eliot in March 1922 when turning down an invitation to become involved editorially in the *Criterion* (Eliot 1988: 512). Yet the very conditions which make life in a metropolis intolerable to writers who think they just want to be left alone to get on with their own work are precisely those which attract them there in the first place. Pound's restlessness took him geographically from one marginal position in America to another in Italy via a couple of centres, London and Paris. The first margin he had occupied involuntarily as an accident of birth, and as soon as he was able to he 'left the virgin republic' of America for Europe, as Fletcher had done, 'as a duckling departs from a hen' (Pound 1913d: 111), relocating himself in a metropolitan literary centre. But eventually the attractions of the centre reconstituted themselves as 'distractions', and Pound came to believe that the optimal environment for his real work was Rapallo, far from the madding crowd. He made that move out of a mistaken conviction that margins occupied voluntarily are more enabling than those to which one is assigned. For a literary critic of the sort Pound set out to be in London, however, all margins are equally disabling. The cultural conditions which attract *aficionados* of the centre register themselves daily in barely perceptible ways, and constitute the hidden processes by which shifts of allegiance and other changes occur. The print culture generated by a publishing centre like London floats on an oral culture created by people who depend on it for their livelihood, and who meet in pubs or cafés or more intimate locations to regale one another with that mixture of speculation and fact which is disparaged as gossip but which nevertheless constitutes the news behind the news. The feuds and the factions, the intrigues and the in-fighting, the machinations of one-upmanship, the economic and erotic foundations of reputation-mongering, the conspiratorial exclusions, the cult-figures and the camp-followers, the groupings and the groupies, all constitute an oral culture of rumour about unpublished and published authors which preconditions the knowingness of metropolitan critics and informs their allegedly 'literary' judgements in ways which make non-metropolitan critics correspondingly provincial. Only a fraction of this indispensable lore ends up explicitly in print, but it is the kind of information a metropolitan critic needs to have, if only for the benefit of being in a position to decide what, if anything, to do about it. When Pound left London for Paris and finally Rapallo he sacrificed the exhilarations of being in the thick of things. If he tried to stay in touch he would become merely another provincial critic trying to read between the lines of the print culture in the diminishing hope of discovering what was really going on in the metropolis. Better, perhaps, to forget about it altogether, and take up more fundamental matters, like economics and banking.

*

By the 1930s Pound's reputation as the literary critic who had discovered Eliot and Joyce and various other writers became increasingly irksome as something to live up to. Although he was out of touch with contemporary writing, it was assumed nevertheless by admiring young poets and inquisitive journalists that he would somehow know all about it, and be able to identify the next generation of important writers any time he was asked. Those poets he thought well enough of to represent in 1933 in his *Active Anthology* (Basil Bunting, Louis Zukofsky, George Oppen and D.G. Bridson) were not, however, the ones generally admired in Britain in the 1930s, such as W.H. Auden, Stephen Spender, Louis MacNeice and C. Day Lewis, all of whom were lumped together in 1946 as that composite left-wing beast, 'MacSpaunday', by the right-wing poet, Roy Campbell (Alexander 1982: 199). All of them were published in Britain by Faber & Faber, and in that respect reflected the critical tastes of its poetry editor, T.S. Eliot. *Active Anthology* also included work by old friends and former discoveries of his, such as Williams, Marianne Moore and Eliot, but its primary critical purpose was to present the newcomers, 'mostly ill known in England, in whose verse a development appears ... to be taking place' (*AA* 5). Self-exiled from London for over a decade by now, Pound discovered he could *'not* share the Auden craze' (*L* 312), and told Laughlin in 1933: 'This Spender Auden / particularly Spender bizniz ... beats me' (Carpenter 1988: 483). 'Surely Bunting and Bridson must be better than Eliot's deorlings', he told a correspondent in 1934 (*L* 334), but he had neither the time nor the inclination to argue the case. Sometimes he would construe his failure to recognise talent in currently fashionable English poets as evidence that there was in fact no talent there to be recognised. What did it matter that 'Auden and Bottrall (*not* Spender)' were 'among young England's best dozen' (*L* 334–5) if Auden was simply the James Elroy Flecker of his time (*L* 312)? By 1937 Pound was wondering whether truly innovative writing had come to an end a decade earlier in 1927 (the year in which his own short-lived journal, *Exile*, was published) or even further back in the '1917/19' issues of the *Little Review*, since which time there had been in his opinion 'very little news ... on the literary frontier' (*SP* 422). But in 1933 he had been disturbed by increasing evidence that he may have lost his touch as a talent scout. For who apart from Pound himself was interested in such *Exile* 'discoveries' as

Charles Rakoski, Whittaker Chambers, and Ralph Cheever Dunning? What he identified in February 1933 as 'a probable dimming of the critical eye' he attributed to his being more involved now in his 'own work' than 'the poesy of others' (Bornstein 1985: 11-12). But by and large he preferred to attribute his mistakes to the generation gap. 'One CAN'T select the next generation as one selects one's own', he had decided by January 1934 (*L* 334), after doubting a year earlier whether 'there is any recorded case of a writer of [his] advanced age knowing what the better members of the next generation... were driving at' (Bornstein 1985: 7). That was basically the same attitude Yeats had taken five years earlier when discussing Pound's own work in *A Packet for Ezra Pound* (1929), but it was surely belied by the success of Eliot (who was only three years younger than Pound) as poetry editor of Faber & Faber in making the choices which seemed to be the right ones for the generation of the thirties.

'I still know a real book when I see one', Pound would boast on Radio Rome in May 1942 (*EPS* 129), by which time he had learnt how to mask his ignorance of contemporary writing by mentioning hardly any names at all and letting this be taken as evidence of his critical fastidiousness. On his visit to the USA in 1939, for example, he told reporters that Cummings was the only poet in America (Carpenter 1988: 559); and, when asked in the 1950s what he thought of contemporary American poetry, he replied that there wasn't any (Reck 1967: 115). As his researches into the economic conditions in which the arts are produced led him deeper into subjects like monetary reform, banking history and Fascist politics, 'literature', as an autonomous entity existing in a supposedly politics-free space, no longer engaged him as it had done in the past. He was not interested, he told Laughlin in 1935, in 'yawpin' 'bout licherchoor' (Carpenter 1988: 117). His pragmatic reason for saying this was that as a man accustomed to the position of mastery in literary critical discussions he did not want to have his authority as the 'Ezuversity' challenged by bright young visitors to Rapallo more familiar with contemporary writing than he himself was. But the more important reason was that he was in the process of moving away from a narrowly literary criticism towards a 'kulchural' criticism described and illustrated in *Guide to Kulchur* (1938). Privately, Eliot had also given up on literature and literary criticism in the course of evolving that right-wing cultural critique displayed in *After Strange Gods* (London, 1933).

Throughout the intensely politicised 1930s the *Criterion* was to retain its subtitle, 'A Literary Review', in spite of Eliot's editorial claim as far back as 1927 that 'every "literary" review worth its salt has a political interest' (Eliot 1927: 283); had that not been the case, the *Criterion* could never have accommodated those essays of Pound's which it would take a stretch of the imagination to describe as literary. Such contradictions persisted in the 1930s, and with consequences for Pound's own publishing career as a critic. By June 1934, for instance, Eliot was confiding to Paul Elmer More that 'pure literary criticism' had 'ceased to interest [him]' (Kojecký 1971: 78), while at the same time, and on behalf of Faber & Faber (who had Pound on their list principally as a poet), he did all he could to ensure that the contents of a couple of books of prose on that list, *Make It New* (1934) and *Polite Essays* (1937), were predominantly works of literary criticism.

By the middle of the 1930s Pound had come to believe that the moment of literature had passed. 'The vitality of thought now (1935) is in econ[omics]', he wrote in April that year to 'Bib' Ibbotson, the man who had taught him Anglo-Saxon at Hamilton College thirty-odd years earlier (*EP/I* 18). What is surprising about Pound's 'abandonment' of literary criticism for what he himself regarded as economic analysis is that it took so long to come into effect. When discussing Camoens as long ago as 1910 he had been aware of the possibility of looking at the arts as 'a by-product of trade or a secretion of commercial prosperity', although he had seen that kind of approach as something to supplement rather than replace the conception of art as 'the inevitable expression of genius' (*SR* 233). Years spent in London trying to make a living by writing gave him ample experience of that ἀνάγκη of modernity' (as he called it in August 1918) 'cash necessity', indifference to which made Henry James inferior as a novelist to Balzac (*LE* 300). Episodes such as Macmillan's rejection of his proposal for an alternative to Palgrave's *Golden Treasury*, which they themselves published, proved to him that the bottom line in that decision had been their investment in the expensive electro-plate from which that popular anthology was reprinted (*LE* 18). 'Whatever economic passions I now have', Pound was to recall in 1933, 'began *ab initio* from having crimes against living art thrust under my perceptions' (*SP* 200–1).

The possibility of theorising in economic terms a nexus of problems associated with the production of non-commercial writing (jeopardised by impecuniousness) and the circulation of it (blocked by tariff laws, copyright laws and the mass-circulation interests of monopoly capitalism) did not present itself, however, until 1919. That was the year in which Orage first introduced him to Major C.H. Douglas, the inventor of an economic theory called Social Credit, and the author of a book on *Economic Democracy* which the *New Age* was currently serialising. Pound reviewed Douglas's book favourably in the April 1920 issue of the *Little Review*, noting especially the contribution made by Social Credit towards 'a more humane standard of life' and 'the prevention of new wars... blown up out of economic villainies at the whim and instigation of small bodies of irresponsible individuals' (Pound 1920: 42). By the summer of 1921, when he came to review Douglas's next book (*Credit Power and Democracy*) in Williams's journal *Contact*, he had begun to consider the consequences of economic theory for literary production, and declared (no doubt with his own Hugh Selwyn Mauberley in mind) that 'the symbolist position, artistic aloofness from world affairs, is no good *now*' (Pound 1921: 1). What was needed instead was an understanding of the real foundations – economics – without which the study of history is 'mere bunk' (*GK* 259) and the study of literature just so much aestheticist chit-chat. What made Douglas particularly attractive was that he was 'the first economist to include creative art and writing in an economic scheme' (*SP* 202). As such, he gave not only painters and sculptors (whose basic materials can be prohibitively expensive) but also poets 'a definite reason for being interested in economics; namely, that a better economic system would release more energy for invention and design' (ibid.). To be knowledgeable about economics therefore became *de rigueur* for writers 'with intellectual aspiration'; the rest would discover to their embarrassment that 'intelligent conversation, Salonfähigkeit now includes economic culture' (Pound 1935: 331).

To the extent that Pound continued to think at all about literature in the late 1930s, he was moving towards what might be called a 'symptomatic' criticism. From his reading of Leo Frobenius he derived the concept of *Kultursymptome*, which enabled him to see (as he phrased it in a 1938 essay on Frobenius) that 'art can be a symptom' (Rabaté 1986: 48), and not merely – as supposed in aestheticising discourses – an end in itself. 'The one thing you shd. not do', he wrote that year, 'is to suppose that when something is wrong with the arts, it is wrong with the arts ONLY' (*GK* 60).

According to this type of analysis – formulated by Pound in a Europe which had just come through a Depression and expected war to break out sooner rather than later – writing was in trouble because the economic system was at fault in condoning 'usury', defined as the making of money out of money alone, irrespective of productivity. What Pound pieced together from his investigations into such matters as banking history and the origin and distribution of money was a primitivistic scenario in which a 'natural' (agrarian) economy based on the abundance of nature and payment for productivity was displaced by an 'unnatural' (usurious) economy administered by banks and similar institutions which profit by making money out of money. Usury thus became for Pound the Original Sin which, by corrupting the benefits to be had from a 'natural' economy, deferred endlessly the prospects of a just society. He was much taken with Dante's assignment of usurers and sodomites to the same circle of the Inferno, on the grounds that both activities were ' "contrary to natural increase" ' (*SP* 61): 'buggaring' was therefore the *mot juste* for describing that 'system of usury' in which he saw Eliot as trapped (*L* 370). And, since Pound regarded the banks as being run predominantly by Jewish families, anti-Semitism became a crucial component in a conspiracy theory which saw the western democracies as totally under the control of an international set of Jewish financiers who manipulated recessions and wars in order to profit from interest on loans. Believing that the Spanish Civil War had occurred so that '$1 of petrol [could] be sold for $5' (Carpenter 1988: 554), Pound refused to contribute to Nancy Cunard's *Authors Take Sides on the Spanish War* (1937) because 'the kikes were financing on both sides' (Tytell 1987: 245). 'Usurers provoke wars to impose monopolies in their own interests', he wrote in 1944, 'so that they can get the world by the throat' (*SP* 310). That was the corrupt system which Pound saw as being challenged in their different ways by Nazi Germany and Fascist Italy. Fascist Italy under Mussolini seemed to be implementing Douglasite reforms, but was blind to the menace of Jewish bankers; Nazi Germany under Hitler was on to the Jewish 'problem', but was misguidedly conducting an old-style pogrom instead of gunning for the international 'usurocrats', who had set Britain at war with Germany and were to set America at war with Italy.

The conjuncture of what Pound called his 'usury axis' (*GK* 41) with a symptomatic style of reading created the possibility of a new kind of criticism which Pound merely adumbrated and to which, surprisingly, he gave no name. It involved uncovering in various art forms (especially painting and architecture) the monetary policies of the societies in which they had been produced, just as Marxist criticism uncovers the crypto-politics and feminist criticism the gender-bias in cultural representations. As Pound described it on Radio Rome in July 1942, it was to be an art criticism of the future, practised by those skilled in telling 'how far the TOLERANCE of usury prevailed, or did not prevail when a given picture was painted' (*EPS* 193). Privately, he himself had been trying for some time to become one of those 'finer and future critics of art' (*GK* 27), having told a correspondent in January 1938 of his ability to 'tell the bank-rate and component of tolerance for usury in any epoch by the quality of *line* in painting' (*L* 397). 'With Usura the line grows thick', we read in Canto 45, which was first published in February 1936. 'Blobby and messy' art appears whenever 'the ethical estimate of usury' is low or non-existent, he wrote in August 1937: 'the kind of thought which distinguishes good from evil, down into the details of commerce, rises into the quality of line in paintings and into the clear definition of the word written' (*SP* 90). What I call 'usurocriticism' reads the visual arts in the same way as John Ruskin read Gothic architecture, when he discovered in its forms evidence of a social order both morally and spiritually superior to what came afterwards. Usurocriticism operates by placing economics in the position Ruskin placed religion, and then producing a symptomatic account of painting and architecture which calibrates the contemporary tolerance of usurious banking practices. For Pound as for Ruskin, what is 'seen' by such methods is not a representation of a true or false religion on the one hand, or of a sound or corrupt economics on the other, but the structural replication of those phenomena in a particular medium (painting or architecture) symptomatically. As with all catastrophe theories, usurocriticism can date the fall it chronicles. Some time after 1500 – 1527, according to Canto 46 – 'art thickened' and 'design went to hell', and architecture began to develop baroque extravagances. As 'the Church slumped into a toleration of usury' (*SP* 243), the result was Protestantism, defined as 'a usury politic' (*L* 439) and developed by people who had '*lost* the sense of mental and spiritual *rottenness*' (*L* 385).

If Pound discovered usury as a systemic trace in literary texts, he said comparatively little about it. When 'the festering mind of

Calvin' spread 'moral syphilis' throughout Europe, there was some literary evidence of the consequences: 'it shows in England's versification', for instance, because 'these things move parallel', in a homologous system of relationships (*SP* 235). Perhaps he thought of 'rhetoric' as linguistic evidence of usurious excess, although his distinction between 'Guido [Cavalcanti]'s precise interpretive metaphor, and the Petrarchan fustian and ornament' (*LE* 162) was not made in terms of banking practices, and if it had been would have required Pound to antedate the fall into usury. In his literary criticism Pound occasionally conceives of usury as systemic, as when he writes that 'Hardy's plots all imply monetary pressure' (*GK* 289); but, when he praises Joyce's *Ulysses* for its exposure of 'the capitalist system, the HELL made in great cities by the usury system' (*EPS* 141), he is conceiving of usury as something merely thematisable by literature. His description of crime fiction in 1944 as a diversionary tactic for concealing 'the great underlying crime... of the usurocratic system itself' (*SP* 311) and his attacks on 'the dominant usury that... keeps good books out of print' (*L* 349) bring his writing much closer to the politicising modes of recent left-wing criticism than the mystical formalism of usurocriticism, which seeks in shapes and lines the symptoms of monetary corruption. Perhaps, as Christine Brooke-Rose suggests, he was reaching towards that 'synthesis between money and language as corruptible exchange' explored by a later generation of French theorists associated with *Tel Quel*, and which now informs poststructuralist discussions of these matters in Pound's own writings (Brooke-Rose 1971: 235–6).

In the 1950s, when Pound was incarcerated in a mental hospital in Washington and widely regarded as a Fascist traitor who had saved his neck by successfully pretending to be insane, Eliot was to refashion Pound as the poet and bookman he had been some thirty or forty years earlier, and write an influential introduction to what was in fact a depoliticised collection of Pound's essays published by Faber & Faber in 1954 under what a still very political Pound called the 'narsty title' of *Literary Essays* (Carpenter 1988: 816). Coming some three years after Paige's Faber & Faber edition of *The Letters of Ezra Pound* (1951) – which similarly avoids Pound's politics by selecting for the most part letters of 'literary' interest – Eliot's edition of Pound's *Literary Essays* was nevertheless a crucial stage in the reinvention of Pound as a major poet-critic in the

English tradition of Coleridge and Arnold to which Eliot had earlier assigned himself in *The Sacred Wood* (1920).

Literary Essays makes it clear that much of Pound's best literary criticism was literary journalism: it was hastily written, repetitive, often outrageous, and 'occasional' in the sense that it was prompted by particular sets of circumstances in which Pound decided to intervene. He himself propagated the view that his journalism was merely a 'divagation' from his real work as a poet: some of it was collected under the title *Pavannes and Divagations* (1958). He liked to think of it as hard work done for money: 'Am doing art and music critiques under pseudonyms', he told his father in January 1918, 'paying the rent' (*EP/M* 57; cp. *EP/MCA* 212). But it was, he added, 'rather entertaining work', to which he responded entertainingly. The assumption that criticism which is written for money cannot be taken as seriously as poetry which is not is a curious snobbery, especially when repeated by admirers of Pound's poetry, many of whom pay their own rent indirectly by equally mercenary activities. The mystification of poets as ethereal creatures who should not be expected to demean themselves by writing mere criticism for money is profoundly at odds with the strategies first made explicit by Wordsworth and Coleridge in their prefaces to *Lyrical Ballads*, which were designed – like Pound's journalistic reviewing – to create the taste for a new style of writing, a new conception of what the arts might aspire to. We should be grateful that Pound responded so engagingly and energetically to new writing in the literary journalism he professed to despise.

In the process of becoming *persona non grata* in the world of English letters, on account of his right-wing politics and 'unliterary' interests in economics and monetary reform, Pound acquired a new status among teachers of modern literature as an interesting has-been. Maurice Lesemann, commissioned in 1927 to write on 'Mr. Pound and the Younger Generation', reported in *Poetry* that he found 'no curiosity about [Pound] among young people who read or write poetry' (Torrey 1984: 124). The few who contested that verdict were likely to be protégés like Louis Zukofsky, who in 1932 dedicated an anthology of 'objectivist' poetry to Pound because he was 'still for the poets of our time the most important' (Zukofsky 1932: 27). But while *les jeunes* were becoming increasingly indifferent to Pound as a poet who appeared on the evidence of his *Cantos* to have lost his way, he was in the process of being reinvented by literary historians and writers of dissertations as a data bank of information about the modern movement in literature. They were to seek him out as he himself had sought out people like Victor Plarr and Elkin Mathews for literary anecdotes. Writings he had contributed to an avant-garde movement in literature were suddenly being exhibited and analysed as documents in the history of that movement. And, after some resentment at this shift of interest away from what he was currently doing towards what he had once done, he gradually came to accept the historicity of that remote period before Year 1 (according to his private calendar) of the Pound Era, 1921, and in particular 'that decade or so' marked by the efflorescence of *Imagisme* and Vorticism, when the men of 1914 had 'tried to get the arts sorted out' (*GK* 49).

His immediate critical problem was to contain and control that interest which was legitimated by changing institutional attitudes in the USA towards literary studies in general and American literary studies in particular. For by the late 1920s American literature had become academically respectable in the USA as a subject for research. The importance of a professional commitment to the native product is polemically stated in *The Reinterpretation of American Literature* (1928), a collection of essays edited by Norman Foerster, who was soon to publish in *The American Scholar* (1929) an attack in humanist terms – Foerster had been a student of Irving Babbitt's, and was an old New Humanist – on that crippling of literary studies by philology which Pound himself had castigated twenty-odd years earlier as symptomatic of the teutonisation of American intellectual life. The fact that Pound was an expatriate who by that time had not lived in the USA for over twenty years and had no intention of ever again living there permanently did not affect his status for academic purposes as an American writer, especially not in the 1920s, when so many hard-drinking representatives of what Gertrude Stein was to call the lost generation were leaving America for the prohibition-free pleasures of cultural life in Paris, that 'paradise of artists irrespective of their merit', as Pound had described it in October 1920 (Pound 1920a: 406). After all, Pound had remained an American citizen throughout his self-imposed exile: while admittedly living in London, he had acted as foreign editor for American literary magazines like *Poetry* and the *Little Review*, and had been instrumental in the publication of American poets like H.D. and T.S. Eliot.

If American expatriate writing in Paris was the most recent phenomenon for a newly emergent American literary studies to come to grips with in the late 1920s it was still in too volatile a condition for academic treatment. Much more suitable in that respect was the American poetry 'renascence' of the previous decade centred on Harriet Monroe's *Poetry*, which academic speculators could open up as a new subdivision in the realm of literary study, ripe (as they say) for development. All of this was occurring at a time when Pound was fast losing interest in purely 'literary' criticism. Having intervened so successfully in the production of that poetry renascence, he had to decide whether he should try to intervene also in the reproduction of it as literary history, especially when he began to be consulted by those who were going to determine what the new subdivision would look like. Consequently, requests for his memoirs − or 'meeemoires', as Pound called them, to signal his misgivings about that self-indulgent genre − created a dilemma. On the one hand he felt that he ought to decline such requests, because (as he told James Laughlin) 'when a man writes his meeemoires that's a sign that he's finished' (Laughlin 1986: 314). But if he did so he would forfeit the opportunity to fashion the past by trying to ensure that his own version of it would be preserved as an official history. In this respect, the contrast between his dealings with an American professor, Glenn Hughes, and a French doctoral student, René Taupin, is most instructive.

Hughes and Pound had careerist interests in one another, although different ends in view: Hughes saw Pound as a potentially valuable source for an academic book he was writing on the Imagist movement in poetry; Pound saw Hughes − who was a Professor of English at the University of Washington and had tried in 1925 to interest Aldington in taking a job there (Doyle 1989: 101) − as a potentially valuable contact with the American academy. Hughes's preliminary enquiry on 7 September 1927 prompted a brusque but not wholly dismissive reply from Pound, who made it clear that it 'wd. not interest [him] in the least to write [his] literary autobiography' (*L* 288). The reason he gave was that he had no room in his mental life for retrospection. Yet only a few years earlier he had found time to publish in the *New Age* between May and August 1920 a dozen articles on his relatives and early childhood, which he thought of highly enough to reprint in book form as *Indiscretions* (1923). 'Reminiscence bores me exceedingly', he concluded his letter to Hughes after briefly setting him straight on the subject of who was an Imagist (Aldington and H.D.) and who was not (Fletcher, Flint, Ford, Lawrence, Lowell and Williams). On 7 August

1928 Aldington told Pound that Hughes would be staying with him shortly, because he had obtained a Guggenheim Fellowship to visit Europe and ' "write a book on Imagism . . . with the collaboration of the principal poets concerned" ' (Stock 1965: 123). Aldington saw the importance of trying to 'keep a fairly tight hand' on Hughes 'to prevent "contamination" '; he did not want Hughes to pick up any other account of the history of Imagism than the 'official version' which Aldington, H.D. and Pound could agree on, and which Flint and Fletcher would accept. 'The principal thing', Aldington went on, 'is for you and I to agree and put the dope on Hughes' – which meant conceding that 'Hulme was a sort of distant ancestor', and agreeing that 'Amy [Lowell] only came in as an after-thought' (ibid.). By this time, however, Pound had already put the dope on Taupin about *Imagisme* and its derivatives, and had other uses for Hughes, who as editor of the University of Washington Chapbooks was persuaded by Aldington to publish Pound's translation of Confucius' *Ta Hio: The Great Learning* in April 1928 (Doyle 1989: 114). Perhaps Hughes thought of this as a trade-off, hoping that a few more reminiscences of the heyday of Imagism might thereby be elicited from this reluctant eye-witness whose version of events differed considerably from the one he himself was piecing together. Pound informed Mary Barnard in 1934 that he'd told Hughes 'to go to HELL' (Barnard 1984: 73). 'Mebbe it sour'd him', Pound added, for, when Hughes eventually published what was to be the first book on *Imagism and the Imagists* (1931), it was clear that the story it told had not been dictated by Pound. Aldington came out rather well as a 'rebel' whose poetry (together with H.D.'s) is called 'the purest expression' of Imagism (Hughes 1931: xi, 37). There was some consolation, however, in the gossip communicated by Zukofsky (after he himself had failed to get a Guggenheim award) that the Secretary of the Guggenheim Foundation believed 'Glenn Hughes wouldn't do anything of value' (*EP/LZ* 95). Hughes did not, of course, go to quite the lengths Amy Lowell had gone in playing down the influence of Pound on Imagist poetry: she had tried to erase Pound from literary history by omitting him altogether from her survey of *Tendencies in Modern American Poetry* (Boston, 1917), and certainly not for the reason given by Jane Heap, namely that Pound could not be classified as a 'tendency' because he was so indisputably 'a force' in modern poetry (Heap 1917: 16). A 'mere skimming' of Lowell's book convinced Pound that its author had 'a vaterersatz . . . or perhaps an

Ezra-ersatz', and that it was 'a great lark from the ironic point of view' (*EP/MCA* 154).

In spite of what Aldington told Pound, Hughes ended up taking the pro-Lowell line that Pound's involvement with Imagism had been only marginal. *Des Imagistes*, edited by Pound in 1914, was unquestionably the earliest Imagist anthology; but it included poems by several people 'who had no particular interest in imagism' as Hughes understood the term (Hughes 1931: viii). And, because he perceived Pound's involvement in the movement as principally that of an 'organizer, propagandist and aesthetic philosopher' (ibid.), Hughes decided that the practice of Imagist poetry was best represented by those who contributed to the three Imagist anthologies published under Amy Lowell's direction as *Some Imagist Poets* (Boston, 1915, 1916 and 1917). These had come into existence as a result of Pound's break with Lowell, and consequently no poem of his was published in any of them. Nor was his work represented in 'Aldington's Imagist mortology 1930' (*EP/LZ* 45), better known as *Imagist Anthology 1930* (London, 1930), in a foreword to which Ford refers whimsically to 'the – alas, late – Mr Ezra Pound' (Ford 1930: x). In Hughes's reconstruction of the events, Pound had deserted Imagism characteristically for his next brief enthusiasm, Vorticism, before removing himself even further from Imagist preoccupations. By doing so, he had written himself out of any history of modern poetry conceived of as the history of Imagism, a questionable identification nowadays, but one which is innocently assumed in the elision between the title of Hughes's book, *Imagism and the Imagists*, and its subtitle, 'A Study in Modern Poetry'.

Pound's response to René Taupin's enquiries, nine months after Hughes had made his overtures, was at once more expansive and more authoritative. Taupin was working on his Sorbonne doctorate when he wrote enquiring whether Pound had invented *Imagisme* after reading H.D.'s poems. Correcting Taupin's misconception that the poems had preceded the theory, Pound sketched out (in a letter written from Vienna in May 1928) his own version of the relationship between French *Symbolisme* and Anglo-American poetry, dating it from his own arrival in London in 1908. He also expressed a willingness to discuss these matters in person with Taupin in either Vienna or Rapallo, but there is no record of the two of them having met at that stage. Nevertheless, the Sorbonne dissertation which Taupin went on to publish as *L'Influence du sym-*

bolisme français sur la poésie américaine (de 1910 à 1920) (Paris, 1929) was greatly influenced by Pound in both its conception and its interpretation of events. Taupin assumes, for instance, that Anglo-American poetry was not very interesting either before or after *Imagisme*, and, furthermore, that the central figure in the *Imagiste* movement was Pound. Unquestioningly, Taupin assimilated such details as Pound's definition of Futurism as 'accelerated Impressionism' (Taupin 1985: 284); he also repeated Pound's undervaluation of James G. Huneker as a mediator of French writing to Americans – 'more of a moralist', according to Taupin, 'than a true literary critic' (ibid.: 47). Taupin's book opens with a quotation from Pound, and concludes that the business of renewing American poetry in the twentieth century was achieved by 'the Imagists, led by Pound' (ibid.: 250). Quoted and paraphrased throughout the book, Pound occupies two-thirds of the chapter (shared with H.D., Aldington and Flint) on the 'first' *Imagistes*. Amy Lowell is classified as a *Symboliste*, not an *Imagiste*, on the grounds that although she 'publicized' and 'monopolized' *Imagisme* she also 'denatured' it because 'she was never an Imagist in Pound's sense' (ibid.: 151).

Although he felt that Taupin had overemphasised the matter of 'influence', and consequently had made 'the error of sposin one NEVER thinks of anything for oneself' (*EP/LZ* 94), Pound could hardly have fared better if the book had been written by one of his protégés as a promotional stunt. Its polemical value in representing the modernist era as fundamentally the Pound era was exploited by Pound in a Harvard journal, the *Hound & Horn*, whose name derived from a couple of lines in an early poem of his, which 'Bid[s] the world's hounds come to horn' and hunt 'the white stag, Fame' (*P* 25). In a 1930 issue of the *Hound & Horn* (or 'Bitch and Bugle', as he liked to call it) Pound modestly reveals that according to 'a recent work published in Paris' – no title or author is mentioned – he had already 'done something toward bringing sound French writing into America' (Pound 1930: 115). The editors knew the book he was referring to, for they commissioned a lengthy review of it by Yvor Winters, who objected forcibly in nativist terms to Taupin's 'basic assumption that American poetry untouched by French influence is bad or negligible and that all of the influences imported by Mr. Pound and Mr. Eliot from France are about equally good' (Winters 1931: 616). A response to this review by Louis Zukofsky, plus a reply by Winters, were type-set but never printed (*EP/LZ* 106); meanwhile, Taupin had secured a position at Columbia University, where he met Zukofsky. The extent of Pound's input into Taupin's book can be gauged from his lengthy letter of May 1928 (*L* 292–5); but that letter was not available to Winters, of course, and Pound had nothing to gain by telling anybody about it. He preferred to let Taupin's book be received as the objective work of an outsider and an academic who, although disagreeing with Pound on one or two details (such as the extent of Hulme's influence on *Imagisme* (Taupin 1985: 81, 83, 133)), nevertheless accepted Pound's construction of the modernist movement in poetry, and the centrality of Pound himself in that construction. If they had got it right at the Sorbonne, what did it matter if a local axe-grinder like Louis Untermeyer had wilfully underestimated Pound's achievements in *The New Era in American Poetry* (1919)? Thanks to Taupin's houndsmanship, the white stag fame was now his. And what did it matter either if Taupin considered him too unsystematic to rank as a critic in the French sense? For even Taupin, in spite of his gallic scorn for muddling through, never doubted that Pound's critical writings were 'the educating force for poetry in the United States', and that Pound had managed to invent – without benefit of French 'system' – 'a poetic criticism, a practical criticism' of which T.S. Eliot had become by the late 1920s 'the true master' (Taupin 1985: 212–13). So in Taupin's account Pound emerges not only as the major theorist and practitioner of modernist American poetry but also as the *éminence grise* of modern criticism in English.

Pound not only contributed indirectly towards the formation of that pedagogic practice of close reading which came to be known in the USA as the New Criticism, but was also instrumental, quite inadvertently, in provoking the first and extremely damaging attack on it to be given wide publicity in the media. The occasion was the award to Pound in February 1949 of the Bollingen Prize for Poetry, which had been established by the Library of Congress in Washington in March 1948 on the initiative of Allen Tate. The prize was to be awarded annually for the best book of verse by an American author published during the preceding calendar year. On 20 February 1949 it was announced that the prize had been awarded to Pound for *The Pisan Cantos*, published by New Directions. The committee responsible for making the award had as its secretary the poetry consultant to the Library of Congress, Leonie

Adams, and consisted of three other women (Louise Bogan, Katherine Garrison Chapin and Katherine Anne Porter) and nine men (Aiken, Auden, Eliot, Paul Green, Robert Lowell, Karl Shapiro, Theodore Spencer, Tate and Willard Thorp). It appears that before the award was made a ballot was taken twice, with Pound gaining a clear majority each time. In the second (February) ballot he secured ten of the thirteen votes, with one abstention (Green) and one death, Spencer, who had voted for Pound the first time.

The only person to vote against awarding the prize to Pound was a Jewish returned service-man, Karl Shapiro. What made *The Pisan Cantos* (in Eric Homberger's phrase) 'safe for democracy' (*CH* 27) was a joint statement signed by everybody except Shapiro, in which the committee indicated its awareness that 'objections' might be made to their giving such a prize to a man 'situated' (in their delicate phrasing) 'as is Mr. Pound', or in other words, to a man formally charged with treason and declared insane (McGuire 1982: 210). Nevertheless, they had done what they had done in the conviction that 'to permit other considerations than that of poetic achievement to sway the decision would destroy the significance of the award and would in principle deny the validity of that objective perception of value on which any civilized society must rest' (ibid.). Five days later, on 25 February 1949, Shapiro explained to readers of the *Baltimore Sun* that he had voted against Pound because he believed that literary criticism should go beyond merely aesthetic considerations; and that, while *The Pisan Cantos* was undoubtedly 'a work of extremely high order', no truly democratic society should give a literary prize to 'a confessed Fascist and a violent anti-Semite' (Young 1980: 321). Shapiro understood only too well that his dissenting vote was not simply one of those differences of opinion condoned by the accommodationist practices of liberal humanism (in which begging to differ – 'yes, but' – is perceived as the guarantee of free enquiry). On the contrary, it represented a direct confrontation with a politically suspect and institutionally dominant critical ideology. Pound's supporters on that committee had exhibited, by the way they voted, their compliance with a style of literary evaluation which operates by depoliticising literary texts. There was nothing mysterious or miraculous about their consensus: they had voted as they did, Shapiro declared, because intellectually they had all been processed discursively, whether they knew it or not, in the same ideological formation as that 'coterie of writers called the "new critics" ' (ibid.). In the end, they had conceived it as their proper task to set *The Pisan Cantos* alongside the only other volume of poems published in 1948 they were interested in, Williams's *Paterson (Book Two)*, and to exercise their literary judgement in assessing the purely literary merits of each text.

Four of the male poets on that committee who voted for Pound – Auden, Eliot, Lowell and Tate – each had personal though different reasons for taking a decision which would reaffirm and therefore perpetuate a mode of criticism which deemed politics irrelevant to poetry. Lowell, for instance, had been given a one-year prison sentence for the stand he had taken as a conscientious objector during the recent war against Nazi Germany. Tate was aligned politically with those Southern Agrarians whose right-wing views had been under attack in the USA since the 1930s by liberals who labelled them reactionary and by Marxists as Fascist. Eliot, a self-exiled American like Pound, was so embarrassed by the anti-democratic and anti-Semitic views he had expressed in *After Strange Gods* (London, 1934) – a book based on lectures delivered at the University of Virginia in the foundational year of Nazi Germany, 1933 – that he would never allow it to be reprinted. And Auden, who had lived in the USA since 1939, had begun already the process of suppressing or ideologically revising left-wing poems he had written during what he had come to call, famously, that 'low, dishonest decade', the 1930s. Five months after the Bollingen Prize was awarded to *The Pisan Cantos*, the first British edition was published in July 1949 in an even larger print-run than the American edition (1,976 as against 1,525 copies) by Faber & Faber, of which Eliot was a director. (Auden had been on the Faber & Faber list since 1930, and Lowell was to be added in 1950 with his *Poems 1938–1949*.) Eliot's literary friendship with Pound was already legendary, and the publishing house Eliot worked for had had Pound's poetry on its list for the last twenty years or so. None of this appears to have troubled the Bollingen Prize committee in 1949, it being no doubt assumed at the time that Eliot as a literary critic would transcend his business interests in the same way that Pound as a poet had managed to transcend his Fascist politics.

The scandal went public in the pages of the *Saturday Review of Literature* for 11 and 18 June 1949 when the president of the Poetry Society of America, Robert Hillyer, attacked Pound as a non-poet and the Bollingen Prize committee as a set of Eliotic New Critics, representatives of a critical mafia which controlled a few 'esoteric literary reviews' (Young 1980: 322). Among these was the *Kenyon Review*, edited by John Crowe Ransom, whose book on *The New Criticism* (published by New Directions in 1941) had provided a journalistically handy name for the writings of various critics who opposed what nowadays would be called the 'old' historicism of literary studies in the universities. Hillyer was currently a colleague of Ransom's at Kenyon, where institutional struggles for the control of English studies resulted on the one hand in Ransom's defence of 'The New Criticism' in the autumn 1948 issue of the *Kenyon Review*, and on the other hand in an article in the *Kenyon Collegian* for 30 September 1949 by a Kenyon student, D.H. Lobdell, which reads Hillyer's double-barrelled attack on 'treason's strange fruit' and 'poetry's new priesthood' as an attempt to 'loosen the strangle-hold on American letters held these many years by mad Ezra Pound, T.S. Eliot and other high priests of incomprehensibility worshipped by the "New Critics" ' (Young 1980: 324). Ransom, off campus at the time as visiting professor at Indiana University, was inclined to dismiss the whole affair as a piece of silly season journalism. But Tate took it seriously, and in the resulting fall-out, Hillyer resigned from Kenyon College and Congress ruled that its Library should stop awarding prizes. As a result, the Bollingen Prize for poetry was administered by Yale University and awarded in 1950 to Wallace Stevens, who had been more discreet than Pound in his 'pro-Mussolini' stance when defending Italy's 'right to take Ethiopia from the coons' (Stevens 1967: 289–90). There was no outcry in 1961 when Noel Stock was awarded a Bollingen Fellowship for the purposes of 'classifying and editing the letters of Ezra Pound stored at Schloss Brunnenburg, Tirolo, Italy' (McGuire 1982: 326).

Tate had a low opinion of Pound as a critic: when reviewing *How To Read* he had concluded that the justification of its thesis was 'not [Pound's] arguments, but his poetry' (Tate 1932: 108). To Pound, Tate (like Ransom) belonged to 'that gang of southern morons' who had 'allus been in opposition' to him (*EP/FMF* 146). Yet Pound's legacy to American New Criticism was acknowledged in 1951 by one of its leading practitioners, Cleanth Brooks. After mentioning 'vulgarizations' of criticism in such places as 'the columns of the *Saturday Review of Literature*', Brooks praised Pound for the 'specific and positive help' he had given to several writers ('in one sense the most important kind of criticism that there can be'), and then observed that Poundian criticism shared with formalism 'the same intense concern with the text' and 'the same concern with "technical problems"' (Brooks, C. 1951: 77–8). He might have added other common factors too, notably the New Critical appropriation of Pound's use of *personae* in his poems (as a means of representing a dispersed subjectivity) for a critical persona-theory whose purpose is to demonstrate that all great literature is 'impersonal'. And he might have added also that a New Critical reading practice predicated on the generic supremacy of poetry and the importance of unravelling ambiguities in texts respected for their ability to mean more than they seem to say got considerable support from Pound's definition of great literature as 'simply language charged with meaning to the utmost possible degree' (*LE* 23). But the interesting thing about Brooks's tribute is that the Pound it acknowledges is the pre-1920 critic and not the more recent one, who (as John Paul Russo notes) 'advocated didacticism, statement in poetry, antimetaphorical language, antiambiguousness – all of which were at odds with New Critical assumptions' (Russo 1988: 225).

Brooks's Pound is filtered through Eliot in the same way that Leavis's Pound is. Leavis took *How To Read* seriously enough to publish a response to it which comes to the patronising conclusion that Pound did not understand the importance of the issues he raised (Leavis 1932: 49). 'What is Leavis?' Pound asked John Drummond in February 1932 on receipt of *How To Teach Reading* (*L* 321). He appears to have written a letter about it which Leavis had not been 'man enough to answer' (*L* 335), although this had not prevented Leavis from making use of information contained in that letter. 'I spose thet is the yitt coming thru', he added, anticipating the anti-Semitic strain in a *New English Weekly* attack on the 'Leavites' of *Scrutiny* (Heppenstall 1933: 209). Leavis kept the letter – the only one he received from Pound – but did not hand it over to D.D. Paige (editor of the 1951 *Letters*) because of its disparaging manner of referring to Eliot (Leavis 1951: 77). As he makes clear in *New Bearings in English Poetry* (London, 1932), Leavis thought *Hugh Selwyn Mauberley* a masterpiece but the *Cantos* (of which he couldn't have seen more than the first thirty) a failure; but Pound seems to have ignored that book too. It certainly did not occur to him at the time that reputation-making in the literary world was in the process of shifting from the review-pages of metropolitan literary magazines into the universities, several of which were beginning to publish critical journals of their own. Leavisite criticism was concerned with the Englishness of English literature, and from that perspective Pound was a comparatist with eccentric interests in (for example) Cavalcanti and Daniel rather than Dante. Even if he happened upon the 'right' foreigner, like Remy de Gourmont, he was inclined to pick the 'wrong' book, translating erotica like *Physique de l'amour* (Paris, 1903) instead of the 'central' text, *Le Problème du style* (Paris, 1902), which Eliot had assimilated in *The Sacred Wood*. This is the book of Eliot's which Leavis said he bought just after it first came out in 1920 and read every year, because to do so was to understand 'what the disinterested and effective application of intelligence to literature looks like' (Leavis 1947: 58). As for the canonical English writers, Pound's low opinion of Milton and Tennyson happened to accord with Leavis's, but because Pound disliked them for less cogent reasons than Eliot he could be ignored.

Pound's reputation as a literary critic suffered because he never published anything comparable to *The Sacred Wood*: 'there is no one book', Donald Davie observes, 'not even any two or three books, that can be pointed to as constituting the *corpus* or the *canon* of Pound's criticism' (Davie 1984: 423). Nevertheless, its indirect influence on British practical criticism is as pervasive as its equally mediated influence on American New Criticism. These things were happening, of course, at a time when Pound had decided that literature was much less absorbing than economics or politics. Consequently, just at the time when Leavisite literary criticism was consolidating itself in the quarterly journal *Scrutiny*, Pound was being regarded as an American who had once been a poet but now lived obscurely in Fascist Italy pursuing unliterary interests, one by-product of which was that rag-bag of macaronic odds and ends he called *The Cantos*.

Leavisite criticism was still going strong in Britain long after the demise of *Scrutiny* in 1953. In America, New Criticism was also to survive the Cold War years of the 1950s until a younger generation, radicalised by the Vietnam war of the 1960s and enabled by neo-Marxist theory to articulate their political disaffection, brought about a change in the public sphere, one manifestation of which was an interest in uncovering the hidden political agendas of an academy which prided itself on being apolitical. Those battles were not to be fought until the 1970s, by which time the New Criticism had consolidated its hegemony in literary studies by presenting itself not as a critical theory which might be contested, but simply as the best available way of learning how to read and respond adequately to literature.

As what the *New York Times* called on 1 January 1950 'L'Affaire Pound' came to lose its newsworthiness, Pound's writings began a fresh career in the domain of literary studies as an academic subject in their own right. Pound's literary criticism continued to be read as ancillary to his poems in academic courses on modern poetry, and that relationship was not upset with the establishment in the 1950s of what Pound himself referred to disparagingly as 'the Pound Industry' (Brooke-Rose 1971: 1). Remembering the pittances he himself had earned for his writings, Pound was to complain to one of his biographers about 'the Univs. of Calif. Oxon etc. subsidizing parasites on [his] work' (Norman 1969: 464–5), although the scholarly and critical studies published by academic presses in support of the curricularisation of Pound's poetry can only have benefited sales of his books. The academic production of a 'Pound' disinfected of political opprobrium began in 1950 (1951 in Britain) with the publication of D.D. Paige's edition of *The Letters*, the most recent of which (dated 12 March 1941) was written nine months before the Japanese bombed Pearl Harbor and America declared war on Italy. Paige said that even as late as 1953 he was wary of letting it be widely known that he had worked on Pound because 'a lot of people considered that you were a traitor, too' (Norman 1969: 434). Another young man willing to take that risk was a Canadian admirer of *The Pisan Cantos*, Hugh Kenner, who had been introduced to Pound at St Elizabeths by Marshall McLuhan. Kenner subsequently wrote the book (with its Poundian dedication to McLuhan: ' "A catalogue, his jewels of conversation" ') which Faber & Faber published in 1951 as *The Poetry of Ezra Pound*. Pound had wanted it called *The Rose in the Steel Dust*, a Poundian image used eventually by Walter Baumann for the title of his 1967 book on the *Cantos*. 'Definitely AIMED at Yale grad/school etc', Pound commented while conceding the usefulness of Kenner's book, 'if you MUST get all yr/ information at 2nd. hand' (Carpenter 1988: 799). It was a mean remark, given the difficulty in 1950 of getting any first-hand information about Pound, or even copies of his out-of-print books. The efflorescence of Pound studies seeded by Kenner's book was so successful in redeeming Pound's reputation as a major poet that within a decade of its occurrence the Bollingen Prize controversy had become such a dead issue that it could be recycled as a subject for academic study, just as in the 1980s it was possible to attend seminars and read symposia on *l'affaire Heidegger* or the 'case' of Paul de Man's wartime journalism. In 1959 there appeared *A Casebook on Ezra Pound*, which reprints what it calls on its cover 'pro and con selections' from texts generated by the award of the Bollingen Prize to Pound, and which is 'intended to be used as controlled source material for the Freshman English Course'. It ends by listing topics for research exercises, including the depoliticising give-away: 'Pound's Beliefs vs. the Quality or Worth of His Poetry' (O'Connor and Stone 1959: 179).

By 1972, however, when the University of California Press had published Kenner's major book with the colonising title, *The Pound Era* (1971), and the University of Maine issued the first volume of a journal devoted entirely to Pound scholarship, *Paideuma*, the Bollingen Prize affair had come to be thought of as the kind of thing which Pound (who died that year) might have included in his annals of American stupidity. Much of Pound's writing had been made available again in reprints and new editions, including important collections of his criticism, such as Eliot's edition of Pound's *Literary Essays* in 1954 and Noel Stock's gathering of non-literary pieces in *Impact* (1960), a volume which was to be supplemented in 1973 by William Cookson's edition of Pound's *Selected Prose 1909–1965*. John Edwards, whose 1952 dissertation on Pound's London years was unfortunately never published, produced *A Preliminary Checklist of the Writings of Ezra Pound* in 1953 and edited the *Pound Newsletter* from 1954 to 1956 in the course of preparing with William Vasse the first *Annotated Index to* The Cantos of Ezra Pound (1957); and a similar service for the shorter poems collected as *Personae* (1926) was attempted in 1969 by a certain K.K. Ruthven. The first version of Donald Gallup's indispensable *Bibliography* appeared in 1963, was revised twenty years later, and is still being added to. Gary Lane produced a concordance to *Personae* in 1972, and Robert Dilligan and others a concordance to the *Cantos* in 1979.

The critical activities which accompanied and were part of this massive investment of time and energy in the writings of one writer and his associates magnified the metadiscursive problem – first posed by Kenner's 1951 book – of how to write about Pound in a non-ventriloquial manner. For Pound's dominance as a literary critic is nowhere more evident than in the writings of many of his admirers. This situation continued into the late 1970s, when it became clear to British Poundians that critical developments which had superseded the New Criticism needed to be introduced into Pound studies if it were not to remain the intellectual ghetto it had become. The importance of reading the Pound text against the grain of the kind of commentary it invites is displayed in *Ezra Pound: Tactics for Reading*, a volume of essays edited in 1982 by Ian F.A. Bell. In his own book, *Critic as Scientist*, Bell distances himself significantly from unreconstructed Poundians who, content with a mere 'miming of the master', continued to produce a 'Poundian commentary' which 'perpetuates the ideology of its subject and becomes a self-sealing paradigm' (Bell 1981: 230). Such moves were made not in order to dislodge Pound from his position as a canonical author in the history of Anglo-American modernism, but to enable readers to understand more clearly the nature of that achievement by liberating them from what Martin Kayman calls 'self-validating and universalising categories of explanation that come from an ahistorical reading' (Kayman 1986: 133). In this way the Pound text came to be rescued from its marginalised status as the sacred writ of acolytes, pedants, cranks and uncritical enthusiasts, and introduced into the domain of contemporary critical debate, where the discursive conventions are very different indeed from those on display in the Bollingen affair.

In the domain of 'literature', where the texts labelled 'Pound' had circulated earlier, those cold warriors called New Critics had been able to admire the tireless experimentalism and technical virtuosity of Pound's writing, worry a bit about its obscurity, but dismiss the nutty ideas and politically offensive attitudes as extra-literary irrelevances, it being a well-known fact at the time that you can admire *The Divine Comedy* or *Paradise Lost* for their poetry alone without necessarily being troubled by the Christian ideologies which shape them. The ritual manoeuvre in such circumstances after the 'scandal' of the Bollingen affair was to dissociate oneself from Pound's Fascism and anti-Semitism by prolegomenal expressions of moral outrage, after which it could be business as usual: *Quellenforschung*, annotation, exegesis, evaluation and the correction of other critics' errors. When Pound's broadcasts from Fascist Rome led to his indictment for treason, the Pound text was shunted out of the domain of literature and into the domain of law, where a different set of discursive conventions operated. Here the 'same' writings could be construed as evidence of the beliefs of their author, and scanned for Fascist sympathies and anti-American sentiments. Suspecting that the prosecution might win its case, Pound's defence attorney agreed – with Pound's connivance – that the poet was mentally too unstable to stand trial, whereupon the Pound text was shifted yet again, this time out of the domain of law and into the domain of psychiatry. Once this had occurred, stylistic and syntactical features which, in the domain of literature, were admired as evidence of innovatory boldness could be read in the domain of psychiatry as symptoms of defective powers of reasoning; and what *littérateurs* identified as mercurially brilliant shifts of subject-matter were read as signs of a disturbing inability to keep to the point.

The Bollingen affair occurred before Michel Foucault had demonstrated that the issues we debate so heatedly do not exist 'before' or 'outside' discourse, but on the contrary are constituted by the kind of discourse we choose in order to debate them. In the domain of critical theory, where politicising discourses get their purchase on texts by discrediting the procedures of New Criticism, the question of Pound's politics is foregrounded because of the kudos currently attached to the pan-political position ('everything is politics'). As no discursive domain is ever the 'natural' one for a text to occupy, the Pound text is likely to be as transient an inhabitant of the domain of critical theory as it has been of the domains of law and psychiatry. But, since that is where it happens to be at the moment, we may as well take advantage of the fact. The discursive reproduction of 'our' Pound is a consequence of the conjuncture of two interpretative conventions: the privileging of politicising over aestheticising reading-practices, and the eduction of an authorial identity out of textual diversities. A diachronic study of the discursive production of different 'Pounds' for different readerships on different occasions – from the earliest reviews of Pound's poems to a book such as this – would contribute greatly to our understanding of the institutionalisation of Anglo-American modernism inside literary studies this century. One place to start such an enquiry is with Pound's own attempts at controlling the discursive reproduction of literary texts produced by his contemporaries. But in order to do that we need to take Pound seriously as a critic.

Bibliography

Names and publication details of frequently cited works are listed in the Abbreviations on pp. xiv–xvi.

Ackroyd, P. (1980) *Ezra Pound and His World*, London: Thames & Hudson.
Aiken, C. (1963) *Ushant: An Essay*, London: Allen.
Aldington, R. (1925) 'A letter', *This Quarter* 1, 2: 311–15.
—— (1958) *Death of a Hero* [1929], London: Four Square Books.
—— (1965) 'Letter to Herbert Read [1925]', in A. Kershaw and F.-J. Temple (eds) *Richard Aldington: An Intimate Portrait*, Carbondale, Ill.: Southern Illinois University Press, p. 127.
—— (1968) *Life for Life's Sake* [1941], London: Cassell.
Alexander, P. (1982) *Roy Campbell: A Critical Biography*, Oxford: Oxford University Press.
Alford, J. (1913) 'American poetry', *P&D* 1, 4: 487–8.
Amdur, A.S. (1936) *The Poetry of Ezra Pound*, Cambridge, Mass.: Harvard University Press.
Anderson, M. (1930) *My Thirty Years' War*, London: Knopf.
Auchinclos, L. (1984) '*The Waste Land* without Pound', *New York Review of Books* 31, 15: 46.
Barnard, M. (1984) *Assault on Mount Helicon*, Berkeley, Calif.: University of California Press.
Barry, I. (1917) 'At the Ministry', *LR* 4, 4: 18.
—— (1931) 'The Ezra Pound period', *Bookman* 74, 2: 159–71.
Bateson, F.W. (1966) *English Poetry: A Critical Introduction* [1950], 2nd edn, London: Longman.
Baumann, W. (1967) *The Rose in the Steel Dust: An Examination of the Cantos of Ezra Pound*, Berne: Francke Verlag.
Bell, I.F.A. (1981) *Critic as Scientist: The Modernist Poetics of Ezra Pound*, London: Methuen.
—— (1982) (ed.) *Ezra Pound: Tactics for Reading*, London: Vision Press.
Benstock, S. (1987) *Women of the Left Bank*, London: Virago Press.
Berryman, J.B. (1983) *Circe's Craft: Ezra Pound's* Hugh Selwyn Mauberley, Ann Arbor, Mich.: UMI Research Press.

Bibliography

Binyon, L. (1938) *Dante's* Purgatorio *with a Translation into English Triple Rhyme*, London: Macmillan.
Bornstein, G. (1985) 'Eight letters from Ezra Pound to Parker Tyler', *Michigan Quarterly Review* 24, 1: 1–17.
Bottome, P. (1944) *From the Life*, London: Faber & Faber.
Boyd, E.L. (1974) 'Ezra Pound at Wabash College', *JML* 4, 1: 43–54.
Bridson, D.G. (1961) 'An interview with Ezra Pound', in J. Laughlin (ed.) *New Directions 17 in Prose and Poetry*, Norfolk, Conn.: New Directions, pp. 159–84.
Brooke-Rose, C. (1971) *A ZBC of Ezra Pound*, London: Faber & Faber.
Brooks, C. (1951) 'The formalist critics', *Kenyon Review* 13, 1: 72–81.
Brooks, D. (1984) 'A letter from Ezra Pound to Etienne Gilson', *Helix* 19–20: 29–33.
Brown, J.L. (1971) 'Ezra Pound, comparatist', *Yearbook of Comparative and General Literature* 20: 37–47.
Burke, C. (1987) 'Getting spliced: modernism and sexual difference', *American Quarterly* 39, 1: 98–121.
Bush, R. (1976) *The Genesis of Ezra Pound's* Cantos, Princeton, NJ: Princeton University Press.
—— (1983) *T.S. Eliot: A Study in Character and Style*, New York and Oxford: Oxford University Press.
Carpenter, H. (1988) *A Serious Character: The Life of Ezra Pound*, London: Faber & Faber.
Carswell, J. (1978) *Lives and Letters*, London: Faber & Faber.
Cory, D. (1968) 'Ezra Pound, a memoir', *Encounter* 30, 5: 30–9.
Cournos, J. (1935) *Autobiography*, New York: Putnam.
Cowley, M. (1951) *Exile's Return*, New York: Viking Press.
Coyle, M. (1988) ' "A profounder didacticism": Ruskin, Orage and Pound's reception of Social Credit', *Paideuma* 17, 1: 7–28.
Cummings, E.E. (1920) 'T.S. Eliot', *Dial* 68, 6: 781–4.
—— (1969) *Selected Letters*, ed. F.W. Dupee and G. Stade, New York: Harcourt, Brace & World.
Damon, S.F. (1935) *Amy Lowell: A Chronicle*, Boston: Houghton Mifflin.
Davie, D. (1980) *Trying To Explain*, Manchester: Carcanet.
—— (1984) 'The critics who made us: Ezra Pound', *SeR* 92, 3: 421–32.
de Chasca, E.S. (1978) *John Gould Fletcher and Imagism*, Columbia, Mo.: University of Missouri Press.
de Nagy, N.C. (1966) *Ezra Pound's Poetics and Literary Tradition: The Critical Decade*, Berne: Francke Verlag.
de Rachewiltz, M. (1971) *Discretions*, London: Faber & Faber.
Dilligan, R.J., Parins, J.W. and Bender, T.K. (1981) *A Concordance to Ezra Pound's* Cantos, New York: Garland Press.
Douglas, A. (1977) *The Feminization of American Culture*, New York: Knopf.
Douglas, P. (1989) 'Modernism and science: the case of Pound's *ABC of Reading*', *Paideuma* 18, 1–2: 187–96.
Doyle, C. (1989) *Richard Aldington: A Biography*, London: Macmillan.
Duncan, R. (1968) *All Men Are Islands*, London: Hart-Davis.
DuPlessis, R.B. (1981) 'Oppen and Pound', *Paideuma* 10, 1: 59–83.
Edwards, J. (1952) 'A critical biography of Ezra Pound, 1885–1922',

Bibliography

unpublished Ph.D. dissertation, Berkeley, Calif.: University of California.
—— (1953) *A Preliminary Checklist of the Writings of Ezra Pound*, intro. N.H. Pearson, New Haven, Conn.: Kirgo Books.
Edwards, J. and Vasse, W. (1957) *Annotated Index to* The Cantos *of Ezra Pound*, Berkeley, Calif.: University of California Press.
Eliot, T.S. (1916) 'Mr. Leacock serious', *New Statesman* 7, 173: 404–5.
—— (1917) 'Eeldrop and Appleplex', *LR* 4, 1: 7–11.
—— (1917a) 'Reflections on contemporary poetry – III', *Egoist* 4, 10: 151.
—— (1918) 'Observations', *Egoist* 5, 5: 69–70.
—— (1918a) 'Studies in contemporary criticism – II', *Egoist* 5, 10: 131–3.
—— (1927) 'A commentary: politique d'abord', *Criterion* 5, 3: 283–6.
—— (1928) 'Isolated superiority', *Dial* 84, 1: 4–7.
—— (1928a) *The Sacred Wood* [1920], London: Methuen.
—— (1932) *Selected Essays*, London: Faber & Faber.
—— (1946) 'Ezra Pound', *Poetry* 68, 6: 326–38.
—— (1948) 'Introduction: 1928', in T.S. Eliot (ed.) *Ezra Pound: Selected Poems*, London: Faber & Faber, pp. 7–21.
—— (1957) *On Poetry and Poets*, London: Faber & Faber.
—— (1959) '[Interview:] The art of poetry: I', *PR* 21: 47–70.
—— (1965) *To Criticize the Critic*, London: Faber & Faber.
—— (1971) The Waste Land: *A Facsimile and Transcript of the Original Drafts including the Annotations of Ezra Pound*, ed. V. Eliot, London: Faber & Faber.
—— (1988) *The Letters of T.S. Eliot*, ed. V. Eliot, vol. 1 1898–1822, London: Faber & Faber.
Ellmann, R. (1967) *Eminent Domain*, New York: Oxford University Press.
Fenollosa, E. (1967) 'The Chinese written character as a medium for poetry', in E. Pound, *Instigations* [1920], Freeport, NY: Books for Libraries Press, pp. 357–88.
Fitch, N.R. (1983) *Sylvia Beach and the Lost Generation*, New York: Norton.
Fitzgerald, R. (1956) 'Gloom and gold in Ezra Pound', *Encounter* 7, 1: 16–22.
Fletcher, J.G. (1937) *Life Is My Song*, New York: Farrar & Rinehart.
Flint, F.S. (1912) 'Contemporary French poetry', *Poetry Review* 1, 8: 355–414.
—— (1913) 'Imagisme', *Poetry* 1, 6: 198–200.
—— (1932) 'Verse chronicle', *Criterion* 11, 45: 684–9.
Flory, W.S. (1980) *Ezra Pound and* The Cantos, New Haven, Conn.: Yale University Press.
Ford, F.M. (1913) 'The poet's eye [I-II]', *NF* 1, 6: 107–10.
—— (1930) 'Those were the days', in *Imagist Anthology 1930*, forewords by F.M. Ford and G. Hughes, London: Chatto & Windus, pp. ix–xvi.
—— (1931) *Return to Yesterday*, London: Gollancz.
—— (1937) *Portraits from Life*, Chicago: Regnery.
Forster, E.M. (1949) *Aspects of the Novel* [1927], London: Arnold.
French, W. (1983), 'For "gentle graceful Dorothy", a tardy obit', *Paideuma* 12, 1: 89–112.

Frost, R. (1964) *Selected Letters*, ed. L. Thompson, New York: Holt, Rinehart & Winston.
Gallup, D. (1970) 'T.S. Eliot & Ezra Pound: collaborators in letters', *Poetry Australia* 32: 58–81.
—— (1983) *Ezra Pound: A Bibliography*, Charlottesville, Va.: University of Virginia Press.
Goldring, D. (1932) 'A triumphal ode', in S. Vines (ed.) *Whips & Scorpions*, New York: Wishart, p. 80.
—— (1943) *South Lodge*, London: Constable.
Goodwin, K.L. (1967) *The Influence of Ezra Pound*, London: Oxford University Press.
—— (1968) 'Ezra Pound's influence on literary criticism', *Modern Language Quarterly* 29, 4: 423–38.
Gordon, L. (1977) *Eliot's Early Years*, Oxford: Oxford University Press.
Gould, W. (1988) 'Gratitude to the unknown instructors', *The Times Higher Education Supplement* 793: 13.
Graff, G. (1987) *Professing Literature*, Chicago: University of Chicago Press.
Greenbaum, L. (1966) *The Hound & Horn: The History of a Literary Quarterly*, The Hague: Mouton.
Gross, J. (1969) *The Rise and Fall of the Man of Letters*, London: Weidenfeld & Nicolson.
Grover, P. (1978) (ed.) *Ezra Pound: The London Years*, New York: AMS Press.
H.D. (1980) *End To Torment: A Memoir of Ezra Pound*, ed. N.H. Pearson and M. King, Manchester: Carcanet.
Hanscombe, G. and Smyers, V.L. (1987) *Writing for Their Lives: The Modernist Women 1910–1940*, London: Women's Press.
Harris, N. (1979) 'Aesthetics and/or politics: Ezra Pound's late critical prose', *Centennial Review of Arts and Sciences* 23, 1: 1–19.
—— (1983) 'A map of Ezra Pound's literary criticism', *SoR* 19, 3: 548–72.
Hartman, C.O. (1977) 'Condensation: the critical vocabulary of Pound and Eliot', *College English* 39, 2: 179–90.
Heap, J. (1917) 'Notes on books and plays', *LR* 4, 8: 15–22.
Hemingway, E. (1925) 'Homage to Ezra', *This Quarter* 1, 1: 221–5.
—— (1964) *A Moveable Feast*, New York: Scribner.
Henderson, A. (1984) 'Pound's contributions to *L'Art libre* (1920)', *Paideuma* 13, 2: 271–83.
Heppenstall, R. (1933) 'Let the poets get clear', *NEW* 3, 9: 208–10.
Hergenhan, L. (1984) 'Ezra Pound, Frederic Manning and James Griffyth Fairfax', *Australian Literary Studies* 11, 3: 395–400.
Hoogstraat, J. (1988) ' "Akin to nothing but language": Pound, Laforgue, and logopoeia', *ELH* 55, 1: 259–85.
Hughes, G. (1931) *Imagism and the Imagists*, Stanford, Calif.: Stanford University Press.
Huneker, J. (1909) *Egoists: A Book of Supermen*, New York: Scribner.
Hurwitz, H.M. (1971–2) 'Hemingway's tutor, Ezra Pound', *Modern Fiction Studies* 17, 4: 469–82.
Hutchins, P. (1965) *Ezra Pound's Kensington*, London: Faber & Faber.
—— (1968) 'Ezra Pound and Thomas Hardy', *SoR* 4,1: 90–104.

Bibliography

Janssens, G.A.M. (1968) *The American Literary Review*, The Hague: Mouton.
Jeffares, A.N. (1949) *W.B. Yeats: Man and Poet*, London: Routledge & Kegan Paul.
Jones, P. (1972) (ed. and intro.) *Imagist Poetry*, Harmondsworth: Penguin.
Kayman, M.A. (1986) *The Modernism of Ezra Pound: The Science of Poetry*, New York: St Martin's Press.
Kelly, L. (1986) 'Guide to Kulchur: the book as ball of light', *Paideuma* 15, 2-3: 279-90.
Kenner, H. (1951) *The Poetry of Ezra Pound*, London: Faber & Faber.
—— (1960) *The Invisible Poet: T.S. Eliot*, London: Allen.
—— (1971) *The Pound Era*, Berkeley, Calif.: University of California Press.
—— (1975) *A Homemade World*, New York: Morrow.
—— (1988) 'Self-similarity, fractals, Cantos', *ELH* 55, 3: 721-30.
Koestenbaum, W. (1988) '*The Waste Land*: T.S. Eliot's and Ezra Pound's collaboration on hysteria', *Twentieth Century Literature* 34, 2: 113-39.
Kojecký, R. (1971) *T.S. Eliot's Social Criticism*, London: Faber & Faber.
Korn, M. (1983) 'The poet as critic', in *Ezra Pound: Purpose/Form/Meaning*, London: Middlesex Polytechnic Press, pp. 32-60.
Landor, W. (1853) *The Last Fruit off an Old Tree*, London: Moxon.
Lane, G. (1972) *A Concordance to Personae: The Collected Shorter Poems of Ezra Pound*, New York: Haskell House.
Langbaum, R. (1985) 'Pound and Eliot', in G. Bornstein (ed.) *Ezra Pound Among the Poets*, Chicago: University of Chicago Press, pp. 168-94.
Laughlin, J. (1985) 'E.P.: the lighter side', *Paideuma* 14, 2-3: 367-75.
—— (1986) 'Walking around a water-butt', *PR* 100: 309-18.
Lawrence, D.H. (1932) *The Letters of D.H. Lawrence*, ed. and intro. A. Huxley, London: Heinemann.
Leavis, F.R. (1932) *How To Teach Reading: A Primer for Ezra Pound*, Cambridge: Minority Press.
—— (1947) 'Approaches to T.S. Eliot', *Scrutiny* 15, 1: 56-67.
—— (1948) *The Great Tradition*, London: Chatto & Windus.
—— (1951) 'Pound in his letters', *Scrutiny* 18, 1: 74-7.
Leigh, J. (1986) ' "An odd sort of post-graduate course": Ezra Pound's first course in modern poetry discovered', *Paideuma* 15, 2-3: 143-5.
Levenson, M.H. (1984) *A Genealogy of Modernism*, Cambridge: Cambridge University Press.
Lewis, W. (1927) *Time and Western Man*, London: Chatto & Windus.
—— (1937) *Blasting and Bombardiering*, London: Eyre & Spottiswoode.
Lidderdale, J. and Nicholson, M. (1970) *Dear Miss Weaver: Harriet Shaw Weaver 1876-1961*, London: Faber & Faber.
Lindberg, K.V. (1987) *Reading Pound Reading*, New York: Oxford University Press.
Lindstrom, N. (1981) 'Ezra Pound: creation and play in critical discourse', *Rocky Mountain Review of Language and Literature* 35, 4: 291-303.
Longenbach, J. (1986) 'The secret society of modernism: Pound, Yeats, Olivia Shakespear, and the Abbé de Monfauçon de Villars', in W. Gould (ed.) *Yeats Annual No. 4*, London: Macmillan, pp. 103-20.
—— (1987) *Modernist Poetics of History*, Princeton, NJ: Princeton University Press.

Lowell, A. (1955) *The Complete Poetical Works of Amy Lowell*, intro. L. Untermeyer, Boston: Houghton Mifflin.
McAlmon, R. (1970) *Being Geniuses Together, 1920–30*, rev. K. Boyle, London: Joseph.
McGuire, W. (1982) *Bollingen*, Princeton, NJ: Princeton University Press.
Mackail, J.W. (1896) *Latin Literature*, rev. edn, London: Murray.
MacLeish, A. (1983) *Letters of Archibald MacLeish*, ed. R.H. Winnick, Boston: Houghton Mifflin.
McLuhan, M. (1949) 'Pound's critical prose', in P. Russell (ed.) *Ezra Pound: A Collection of Essays*, London: Nevill, pp. 165–71.
M[airet], P. (1934) '[Review of] *ABC of Reading*', *NEW* 5, 9: 212–3.
Martin, T. (1986) *Marianne Moore: Subversive Modernist*, Austin, Tex.: University of Texas Press.
Marwil, J. (1983) 'Combative companions: Ezra Pound and Frederic Manning', *Helix* 13–14: 9–15.
—— (1988) *Frederic Manning: An Unfinished Life*, London: Angus & Robertson.
Menand, L. (1987) *Discovering Modernism*, New York: Oxford University Press.
Mencken, H.L. (1961) *Letters of H.L. Mencken*, selected by G.L. Forgue, New York: Knopf.
Meyers, J. (1984) 'New light on Iris Barry', *Paideuma* 13, 2: 285–9.
Middleton, C. (1965) 'Documents on Imagism from the papers of F.S. Flint', *Review* 15: 35–51.
Mizener, A. (1985) *The Saddest Story: A Biography of Ford Madox Ford*, New York: Carroll & Graf.
Monro, H. (1913) 'The Imagistes', *P&D* 1, 2: 127–8.
Monroe, H. (1938) *A Poet's Life*, New York: Macmillan.
Moore, M. (1928) 'Announcement', *Dial* 84, 1: 89–90.
Moulton, R.G. (1915) *The Modern Study of Literature*, Chicago: University of Chicago Press.
Norman, C. (1969) *Ezra Pound*, rev. edn, New York: Funk & Wagnalls.
O'Connor, W. V. and Stone, E. (1959) (eds) *A Casebook on Ezra Pound*, New York: Crowell.
Oderman, K. (1986) *Ezra Pound and the Erotic Medium*, Durham, NC: Duke University Press.
Orage, A.R. (1974) *Orage as Critic*, ed. W. Martin, London: Routledge & Kegan Paul.
Paideuma: A Journal Devoted to Ezra Pound Scholarship, Orono: University of Maine, 1 (1972)–.
Palmer, L.H. (1973) 'Matthew Arnold and Ezra Pound's *ABC of Reading*', *Paideuma* 2, 2: 193–8.
Pater, W. (1904) *Appreciations* [1889], London: Macmillan.
Patmore, B. (1968) *My Friends when Young*, ed. and intro. Derek Patmore, London: Heinemann.
Pearson, H. (1934) *The Smith of Smiths*, London: Hamish Hamilton.
Perloff, M. (1985) *The Dance of the Intellect: Studies in the Poetry of the Pound Tradition*, Cambridge: Cambridge University Press.
Pound, E. (1906) 'Raphaelite Latin', *BNM* 25, 1: 31–4.

—— (1909) 'The "Brunhild" of Frederic Manning', *BNM* 27, 8: 620–1.
—— (1913) 'Through alien eyes, III', *NA* 12, 13: 300–1.
—— (1913a) 'How I began', *T.P.'s Weekly* 21, 552: 707.
—— (1913b) 'Reviews', *NF* 1, 8: 149–50.
—— (1913c) 'The approach to Paris [V]', *NA* 13, 23: 662–4.
—— (1913d) 'Peals of iron', *Poetry* 3, 3: 111–3.
—— (1914) 'Preliminary announcement of the College of Arts', *Egoist* 1, 21: 413–14.
—— (1915) 'On "Near Perigord" ', *Poetry* 7, 3: 143–6.
—— (1916) 'A poet of the 'nineties', *Poetry* 7, 6: 313–7.
—— (1917) 'Editorial', *LR* 4, 1: 3–6.
—— (1918) 'The Yeats letters', *Poetry* 11, 4: 223–5.
—— (1918a) 'Chinese poetry [I]', *To-day* 3, 14: 54–7.
—— (1918b) 'Our contemporaries', *LR* 5, 3: 35–7.
—— (1918c) 'Nine Poems', *LR* 5, 7: 1–6.
—— (1919) 'Hellenist Series, VI', *Egoist* 6, 2: 24–6.
—— (1920) '[A review of] *Economic Democracy* [by Major C.H. Douglas]', *LR* 6, 11: 39–42.
—— (1920a) 'The island of Paris: a letter. September, 1920', *Dial* 69, 4: 406–11.
—— (1921) '[A review of] *Credit Power and Democracy*, by Maj. C.H. Douglas and A.R. Orage', *Contact* 4: 1.
—— (1921a) 'Historical survey', *LR* 8, 1: 39–42.
—— (1922) 'Paris letter. October, 1922', *Dial* 73, 5: 549–54.
—— (1923) 'On criticism in general', *Criterion* 1, 2: 143–56.
—— (1923a) 'Paris letter. February, 1923', *Dial* 74, 3: 273–80.
—— (1928) 'Data', *Exile* 4: 104–17.
—— (1930) 'Criterionism', *H&H* 4, 1: 113–16.
—— (1932) 'Readers and writers', *NEW* 1, 20: 483.
—— (1933) '"How to Read" ', *NEW* 2, 23: 551.
—— (1934) 'What price the muses now', *NEW* 5, 6: 131–2.
—— (1935) 'Leaving out economics (Gesell as reading matter)', *NEW* 6, 16: 331–3.
—— (1935a) 'Towards orthology', *NEW* 6, 26: 534.
—— (1935b) 'Private worlds', *NEW* 7, 3: 48–9.
—— (1936) 'Literary note', *NEW* 8, 19: 380.
—— (1936a) 'The return of the native [II]', *NEW* 8, 26: 510.
—— (1936b) 'Replying to Larrañaga. On stamp scrip', *NEW* 9, 16: 315–6.
—— (1939) 'Are universities valid?', *NEW* 14, 19: 281–2.
Pound Newsletter, Berkeley, Calif.: Department of English, University of California, nos. 1–10, January 1954–April 1956.
Pulik, R. (1977) 'Pound and "The Waste Land" ', *Unisa English Studies* 15, 2: 15–24.
Rabaté, J.-M. (1986) *Language, Sexuality and Ideology in Ezra Pound's* Cantos, Albany: State University of New York Press.
Raffel, B. (1984) 'A prose Proteus: Pound as a critic, literary and social', in *Ezra Pound: The Prime Minister of Poetry*, Hamden, Conn.: Archon Books, pp. 79–99.

—— (1985) *Possum and Ole Ez in the Public Eye*, Hamden, Conn.: Shoe String Press.
Reck, M. (1967) *Ezra Pound: A Close Up*, New York: McGraw-Hill.
Redman, T. (1987) 'Pound's Cavalcanti: an edition of the translations, notes, and essays', *Modern Philology* 84, 3: 340–3.
Rees, T. (1975) 'Ezra Pound and the modernisation of W.B. Yeats', *JML* 4, 3: 574–92.
Reid, B.L. (1968) *The Man from New York: John Quinn and His Friends*, New York: Oxford University Press.
Robinson, F.C. (1982) '"The might of the north": Pound's Anglo-Saxon studies and "The Seafarer" ', *Yale Review* 71, 2: 199–224.
Roessel, D. (1988) '"Near Perigord" and a Mycenaean trade war', *Paideuma* 17, 1: 105–7.
Rose, J. (1986) *The Edwardian Temperament*, Athens, Ohio: Ohio University Press.
Ross, R.H. (1967) *The Georgian Revolt*, London: Faber & Faber.
Russo, J.P. (1988) 'The tranquilized poem: the crisis of New Criticism', *Texas Studies in Literature and Language* 30, 2: 198–229.
Ruthven, K.K. (1969) *A Guide to Ezra Pound's Personae (1926)*, Berkeley, Calif.: University of California Press.
—— (1986) 'The disclosures of inscription: Ezra (Loomis) (Weston) Pound', *Aumla* 66: 159–78.
Said, E. (1985) 'How not to get gored', *London Review of Books* 7, 20: 19–20.
Schneidau, H.N. (1969) *Ezra Pound: The Image and the Real*, Baton Rouge, La.: Louisiana State University Press.
Shakespear, O. (1915) 'The poetry of D.H. Lawrence', *Egoist* 5, 11: 81.
Sieburth, R. (1978) *Instigations: Ezra Pound and Remy de Gourmont*, Cambridge, Mass.: Harvard University Press.
Smith, G. (1983) *The Waste Land*, London: Allen & Unwin.
Stein, G. (1946) *Selected Writings of Gertrude Stein*, ed. Carl Van Vechten, New York: Random House.
Stevens, W. (1967) *Letters of Wallace Stevens*, ed. H. Stevens, London: Faber & Faber.
Stock, N. (1965) (ed.) *Ezra Pound: Perspectives*, Westport, Conn.: Greenwood.
—— (1970) *The Life of Ezra Pound*, London: Routledge & Kegan Paul.
—— (1976) *Ezra Pound's Pennsylvania*, Toledo, Ohio: Friends of the University of Toledo Libraries.
Tate, A. (1932) 'Laundry bills', *Poetry* 41, 2: 107–11.
Taupin, R. (1985) *The Influence of French Symbolism on Modern American Poetry* [1929], trans. W. Pratt and A.R. Pratt, New York: AMS Press.
Torrey, E.F. (1984) *The Roots of Treason: Ezra Pound and the Secrets of St. Elizabeths*, London: Sidgwick & Jackson.
Tytell, J. (1987) *Ezra Pound: The Solitary Volcano*, London: Bloomsbury.
Untermeyer, L. (1919) *The New Era in American Poetry*, New York: Holt.
Wallace, E.M. (1983) 'Youthful days and costly hours', in D. Hoffman (ed.) *Ezra Pound & William Carlos Williams*, Philadelphia, Pa: University of Pennsylvania Press, pp. 14–58.

Bibliography

Wees, W.C. (1976) 'Pound's Vorticism: some new evidence and further comments', *Wisconsin Studies in Contemporary Literature* 7, 2: 211–16.
Weintraub, S. (1979) *The London Yankees*, New York: Harcourt Brace Jovanovich.
Weisstein, U. (1973) *Comparative Literature and Literary Theory*, trans. W. Riggan, Bloomington, Ind.: Indiana University Press.
Wellek, R. (1986) *English Criticism 1900–1950*, New Haven, Conn.: Yale University Press, pp. 152–69.
West, R.B. (1949) 'Ezra Pound and contemporary criticism', *Quarterly Review of Literature* 5, 2: 192–200.
Wilhelm, J.J. (1985) *The American Roots of Ezra Pound*, New York: Garland Press.
Williams, E. (1977) *Harriet Monroe and the Poetry Renaissance*, Urbana, Ill.: University of Illinois Press.
Williams, W.C. (1919) 'Prologue', *LR* 5, 11: 1–10.
―― (1951) *Autobiography*, New York: Random House.
―― (1957) *Selected Letters of William Carlos Williams*, ed. and intro. J.C. Thirlwall, New York: McDowell, Obolensky.
―― (1958) *I Wanted to Write a Poem*, ed. E. Heal, Boston: Beacon Press.
Winters, Y. (1931) 'The Symbolist influence', *H&H* 4, 4: 607–18.
Witemeyer, H. (1977) 'Walter Savage Landor and Ezra Pound', in G. Bornstein (ed.) *Romantic and Modern: Revaluations of Literary Tradition*, Pittsburgh, Pa.: University of Pittsburgh Press, pp. 147–63.
Wordsworth, W. (1926) *The Poems of Wordsworth*, ed. T. Hutchinson, London: Oxford University Press.
Yeats, W.B. (1950) *The Collected Poems*, London: Macmillan.
Young, T.D. (1980) 'The little houses against the great', *SeR* 88, 2: 320–30.
Zukofsky, L. (1932) (ed.) *An 'Objectivists' Anthology*, Le Beausset and New York: To, Publishers.

Index

Abercrombie, Lascelles 109
academic: appointments, Pound's 5, 28; critic, Pound as 1–39; education 1–39; *see also* qualifications; philology
academicism 3, 14–15, 16–17, 28, 31–2
Ackroyd, Peter (1980) 42
Adams, B.M.G.- (1923) 59
aestheticism 31, 118
aesthetic issues 115
aestheticist doctrine 27
Ahearn, Barry (1987) (*EP/LZ*) *see* Zukofsky
Aiken, Conrad 46, 83, 135, 162; (1963) 26, 58, 76, 90, 98
Aldington, Richard 37, 79, 89, 97–8, 99, 137; and Glenn Hughes 157, 158; and *Imagisme* 49, 50, 57, 67, 69, 70, 76, 157, 158, 160; (1912) 68; (1913) 135; (1925) 71; (1930) 159; (1958, 1965) 97; (1968) 48, 96
Alexander, Peter (1982) 148
Alford, John (1913) 65
Amdur, Alice S. (1936) 19
America 14, 147, 149
American: culture 75;

education/literary studies 1–37, 53, 156–7, 167; *see also* feminisation; Paris; poetry; poets
Anderson, Margaret 15, 19, 68, 73, 75, 76; (1930) 74
Anderson, Sherwood 81, 145
anti-Semitism 101, 152, 162, 163, 165, 169
anthology as critical genre 137–8
Apuleius 22
Aristotle 113
art 113, 118, 150, 151, 153; criticism 7, 114, 116, 153 *see also* 'Dias'
'Atheling, William' 7, 116, 144
Auchinclos, Louis (1984) 130
Auden, W.H. 148, 162, 163
'author-effects' and constructs 34
avant-garde movement 66, 83–4, 145, 156

Babbitt, Irving 156
banking history 147, 149, 152
Barnard, Mary 144; (1984) 92, 101–2, 103–4, 106, 158
Barry, Iris 23, 24, 31, 103–4, 114; (1923) 89; (1931) 133
Bateson, F.W. (1966) 123

180

Index

Baudelaire, Charles 113
Baumann, Walter (1967) 167
Bel Esprit scheme 93, 94
Bell, Ian F.A. (1981, 1982) 169
Belloc, Hilaire 54
Benstock, Shari (1987) 91, 145
Berryman, Jo Brantley (1983) 20
Binyon, Laurence 18, 47, 114, 128; (1938) 126
Blast 12, 44, 74, 75, 85, 98, 107; reputation 143; style 115; *see also* avant-garde; Lewis; Prothero; Vorticism; West, Rebecca
Blunt, Wilfred Scawen 48
Bodenheim, Maxwell 85, 87–8
Bollingen Prize for Poetry 161–4, 167, 168, 169, 170
Book News Monthly 43, 50
Born, Bertrans de 16–17
Bornstein, George (1985) 85, 101, 149
Bottome, Phyllis (1902, 1934, 1935, 1944) 124
Boyd, Ernest L. (1974) 5
Brancusi, Constantin 86
Brandt, H.C.G. 8–9
Bridges, Robert 38, 46, 129
Bridson, D.G. 148; (1961) 14, 30, 35
Brooke, Rupert 94
Brooke-Rose, Christine (1971) 121, 154, 167
Brooke Smith, William 47
Brooks, Cleanth (1951) 164–5
Brooks, David (1984) 15–16
Brooks, Van Wyck 65, 82
Brophy, Brigid *et al.* (1968) 31
Browning, Robert 121; (1840) 16, 136; (1855) 24
Bruno, Giordano (1582) 122
Burke, Carolyn (1987) 102
Bush, Ronald (1976) 128; (1983) 131
Bynner, Witter 33

Camoens, Luis de 23, 150
Campbell, Roy 148
Campion, Thomas (1602) 3
Cantos, The 16, 17, 20, 27, 63, 66, 74, 81, 100, 104, 141, 155; *1–16* 58–9; *8* 128; *15* 13; *17–30* 59; *18* 51; *29* 105, 118; *41* 59; *45, 46* 153; *53* 138; *74* 30, 36, 84; *77* 107, 146; *78* 59; *81, 82* 48; *113* 106; Annotated Index to 168; Concordance to 168; *Dial* rejection of 82; economy of language in 115; obscurity of 83; and *The Waste Land* 132; *see also* Baumann; Browning; Leavis; *logopoeia*
Carpenter, Humphrey (1988) 4, 32, 33, 35, 38, 39, 46, 51, 60, 102, 126, 129, 135, 140, 145, 146, 148, 167; on collaboration 65, 128; parodies 137; politics 117, 149, 154; social aspects: support 52, 90, 92, 100
Carswell, John (1978) 144
Cavalcanti, Guido 45, 154, 166
Cerebralist/Cerebralists 76
Chester, Carlos Tracy 43
Chesterton, G.K. 53
Chinese poems and plays 14
classics/classicism 11, 17, 23
Coleridge, Samuel Taylor 1, 4, 21, 26, 121, 155; (1798) 112
collaboration/interference 65, 126–32
'College of Arts' 28–9, 30, 32
Collins, John Churton 43, 63; (1891, 1902) 9
commercial aspects of authorship/criticism 61
Confucius/Confucian ethic 136, 138, 158
Conrad, Joseph 51, 94
conspiracy/persecution theory 12–13, 143, 145
constatation and presentation 117
Contact 75, 151
Cookson, William (1973) 168
Cory, Daniel (1968) 35
Cournos, John 29; (1935) 78
Cowley, Malcolm (1951) 36, 81, 92, 146
Coyle, Michael (1988) 27
Crabbe, George (1810) 110
Cravens, Margaret 28

Index

creativity 17–18, 21–2, 28, 29
Criterion 26, 31, 38, 62, 67, 93, 143, 146; political interest 150
critic 1, 4, 19, 84, 111; Pound as 5–6, 20–1, 23, 42, 81, 82–3, 85–7, 108–39; *see also* academic; avant-garde; poet-critic
critical: debate 169; education 53; essays 18; genres 136–8; prose 115; system 112; theory 111, 112, 170
criticism 5, 19, 34, 61, 64, 123, 135, 155; analytic 125–6; comparative 110; constructive 109–10; correspondence, through 126; Pound's 20, 24, 60–80, 124–5, 128–9, 161, 164–6; reasoned 138–9; spoken 127; subjective/objective 86–7; texts-in-themselves, using 137–8; *see also* art; creativity; dramatic; Leavis(ite); literary; music; social
culture/cultural criticism 75, 147, 149, 150
Cummings, E.E. 82, 134, 149; (1920) 61, 98; (1969) 100
Cunard, Nancy 58, 59, 152

Damon, S. Foster (1935) 61, 73, 106, 107
Daniel, Arnaut 16, 22, 45, 68, 85, 166
Daniel, Samuel (1603) 3
d'Annunzio, Gabriele 145
Dante 4, 166; *Inferno* 114, 152; *Purgatorio* 126, 128
Davie, Donald (1980) 44–5; (1984) 116
de Chasca, Edmund S. (1978) 58, 119
De Quincey, Thomas 4
de Rachewiltz, Mary (1971) 101
de Vega, Lope 4, 23
Dial, The 64, 74, 143; Award 81–2
'Dias, B.H.' 7, 27, 102, 116, 144
Dilligan, Robert *et al.* (1979) 168
Divoire, Fernand 68; (1912, 1924, 1928) 67

Dolmetsch, Arnold 29
Donne, John 115, 128
Doolittle, Hilda *see* H.D.
Douglas, Ann (1977) 75
Douglas, Major C.H. 14, 27; (1920) 13, 15; (1921) 151
Doyle, Charles (1989) 157
dramatic criticism 29, 143
Dryden, John 1
Duncan, Ronald (1968) 95
DuPlessis, Rachel Blau (1981) 102

Economic Democracy (Douglas, 1920) 13, 151
economics 19, 26, 27, 32, 124–5, 147, 149, 150–4, 155
economic theories 150, 151
editor *see* journals
Edwards, John (1953) 168; and Vasse, William (1957) 53, 168
Egoist 51, 56, 66, 74, 75, 77, 79, 84, 91; and Aldington 97; Frost review in 87; and *Imagisme* 57; Press 82; *see also* 'College of Arts'; *The Times*
Eliot, T.S. 32, 37–8, 58, 60, 73, 160; as critic 1, 21–2, 66, 149, 150, 161; as Pound's 'discovery' 47, 89, 148, 156; and finance 92, 93, 94, 154; language and style 3, 101, 115, 121, 134; –/Pound relationship 63, 64, 65–6, 99–100, 128, 129, 130–2, 138, 145, 146; and Pound's work 1, 26, 128–9, 130, 131, 132; and publishing world 93, 143, 148; *After Strange Gods* 3, 149, 163; *Four Quartets* 132; 'Gerontion' 129; *Literary Essays of Ezra Pound* (*LE*) 154, 168; 'The Love Song of J. Alfred Prufrock' 51; 'Metaphysical Poets, The' 37, 117; *Poems* 62, 66, 95; *Prufrock and Other Observations* 92, 131, 134, 144; *The Sacred Wood* 3, 66, 154, 155, 166; *Selected Essays* 76, 118; *The Use of Poetry and the Use of Criticism* 2, 3, 149; *The Waste Land* 66, 82, 94–5, 96, 99, 130–2;

Index

'Whispers of Immortality' 128; (1916) 22; (1917a) 132; (1918) 21, 22, 45: (1918a) 21; (1927) 150; (1928) 33; (1928a) 34; (1933) 2, 3, 149; (1946) 26, 83, 87, 91, 97, 98, 126, 130, 132; (1948) 14, 111; (1957) 21, 131; (1965) 61, 144; (1971) 90, 130, 131; (1988) 3, 29, 37, 46, 47, 63, 67, 75, 76, 92, 93, 129, 130, 135, 146; *see also* Bollingen Prize; *Catholic Anthology*; 'College of Arts'; *Criterion*; *Dial* Award; Leavis; modernist movement; poet-critic; Quinn; *vers libre*
Ellmann, Richard (1967) 127
England: literary criticism 53; *see also* social aspects
English Review 38, 43, 48, 49, 50, 83, 88, 106
essay(s): as critical genre 136; Pound's 27, 29–30, 115, 150
essentialist theory 33–4, 35
Evening Standard, London 61
experimentation/experimentalism 110, 112, 113
expressivist theory 33–4
Exile 74, 85, 148

Fascism 104, 117, 124, 149, 162, 163, 166, 169–70; and usury 152
Fairfax, James Griffith (1906, 1908) 50
feminism 75–9; in poetry 112, 118–19
Fenollosa, Ernest 14, 52; (1967) 114
fiction and *Imagisme* 125
Fitch, Noel Riley (1983), 105
Fitzgerald, Edward (1859) 136
Fitzgerald, Robert (1956) 62
Flaubert, Gustave 115, 117; (1881) 137
Flaubertian(s) 116, 117
Fletcher, John Gould 25, 26, 57–8, 78, 87, 119, 147, 157; (1937) 137; anti-Pound 100
Flint, F.S. 44, 62, 66, 76, 99; and *Imagisme* 67–9, 157, 160; (1909) 127; (1913) 71; (1932) 68
Flory, Wendy Stallard (1980) 102
Foerster, Norman (1928, 1929) 156
Fontenelle, Bernard le Bovier 84
Ford, Ford Madox (Hueffer) 21, 27, 35, 45, 49, 63, 96, 102, 106, 135; anecdotes 48; Belloc 54; *English Review* 43, 88; Flaubertians 116; language 129, 135; Lawrence 86; non-Imagist 157; and Pound 83, 86, 95, 99, 128; (1913) 119; (1914) 54; (1915) 12, 46; (1923) 59; (1930) 159; (1937) 38
formalism 165
Forster, E.M. (1949) 122–3
Foucault, Michel 33–4, 170
Fowler, Eva 51
free verse *see vers libre*
French, William (1983) 62
Frobenius, Leo 32, 151; (1928) 120
Frost, Robert 71, 85, 89–90, 106; anti-Pound 98, 100, 128; (1913) 87, 89; (1914) 87; (1964) 62, 98, 99
Frye, Northrop (1957) 34, 123
functionalist theory 113
Futurism 25, 160

Gallup, Donald (1963) 168; (1970) 38, 66, 96, 100, 131, 143; (1983) 59, 168
Galton, Arthur 52; (1885) 50
Gaudier-Brzeska, Henri 28, 29, 32, 86, 102, 107, 141; Pound sculpture 84, 103, 139; *see also* Pound (1916)
genius 1, 20, 38, 85–6
Georgian poetry/poets 45, 93, 94
German influence on American academic teaching 11, 12, 13, 23, 122, 146, 156
Germany, Nazi: and usury 152
Gesell, Silvio 14
Gilson, Etienne 15
Glebe 88
Goldring, Douglas 33, 88; (1932) 91; (1943) 99, 105

Index

Goodwin, K.L. (1967) 26
Gordon, Lyndall (1977) 132
Gosse, Edmund 109, 133
Gould, Warwick (1988) 56
Gourmont, Remy de 56, 120; (1902, 1903) 166; (1916) 64; (1922) 78
Graff, Gerald (1987) 8, 9
Graves, Robert (1955) 20
Greenbaum, Leonard (1966) 75
Grey, E.C. (1914) 76
Guggenheim Award/Foundation 65, 158

Hall, Donald (1960) 66
Hamilton College 4, 6, 7, 8, 16, 23, 47, 109, 150
Hanscombe, Gillian and Smyers, Virginia L. (1987) 77
Hardy, Thomas 35, 109, 129, 154
H.D. 50, 67, 70, 72–3, 88, 92, 97, 105, 107, 114, 156; as *Imagiste* 157, 158, 159, 160; (1912) 69; (1913) 72; (1980) 50, 72, 105; (1983) 124
Heap, Jane 75, 76; (1917) 158
Hemingway, Ernest 27, 75, 98, 145; (1923) 59; (1925) 96, 142; (1964) 125
Henderson, Archie (1984) 42, 81, 133
Hergenhan, Laurie (1984) 52
Hessler, L. Burtron 4, 139
Hewlett, Maurice 107
Hillyer, Robert 163–4
Homberger, Eric 162; (1972) 17, 19, 21, 27, 33, 43, 44, 61, 62, 65, 83, 95, 100, 113, 135, 143
Horace 18, 94, 111
Hound and Horn 74, 75, 88, 160
Hueffer *see* Ford Madox Ford
Hughes, Glenn 14, 157–9; (1931) 101, 158
Hulme, T.E. 42, 44, 45, 67, 68, 75, 87, 102; *Imagisme* 158, 161; (1909) 71
humanities 7–8, 9, 10
Huneker, James G. (1909) 79
Hunt, Violet 45, 48, 49, 77, 124

Hurwitz, Harold M. (1971–2) 125
Hutchins, Patricia (1965) 51; (1968) 35

ideology: politics and quality of work 169–70
Image: 'Doctrine' of the 71–2, 73
imagery 121
Imagisme/Imagistes 25, 35, 36, 50, 53, 61, 67–73, 96, 112, 118, 156; and Imagism 47, 73, 90–1, 106, 107, 114, 123, 157–9; aesthetic 113; -Cerebralists 76; and Frost 87; and Johnson 57; manifesto 126; Pound's domination 98; and Symbolism 118–19; and Taupin 158, 159, 160; *see also* Aldington; Hughes; language precision; Lowell; modernism; patronage; presentation; terminology
Impressionism 121, 160
innovation in writing 42, 112, 148
Italy 25, 145, 152

James, Henry 35, 55, 66, 85, 109, 134, 142, 150; (1886) 78
Janssens, G.A.M. (1968) 74, 75
Jeffares, A.N. (1949) 126
Johnson, Lionel 57
Johnson, Samuel 1
Jones, Peter (1972) 114, 127
journalism *see* language; literary
journals/magazines 73–80, 141, 143–5, 156, 165–6
Joyce, James 32, 45, 63, 73, 96; language 122; compared to Lawrence 87; as Pound's 'discovery' 89, 90, 91, 148; *Dubliners* 90; *Finnegans Wake* 122, 128; *A Portrait of the Artist as a Young Man* 80, 90; *Ulysses* 16, 81, 90, 128, 133, 134, 154; *see also* usury
judgement, literary 88–9

Kayman, Martin (1986) 70, 71, 72, 169
Keats, John 114, 118
Kenner, Hugh (1951) 19–20, 167,

168; (1953) 14; (1960) 65; (1971) 51, 84, 168; (1972) 168; (1975) 33; (1988) 131
King, Michael J. (1977) (*CEP*) 50, 71, 119, 144
knowledge 12–13, 24; -effects 34–5, 37–8
Koestenbaum, Wayne (1988) 132
Kojecký, Roger (1971) 150

Laforgue, Jules 51, 121, 122
Landor, Walter Savage (1824–9) 30, 50; (1853) 125, 126
Lane, Gary (1972) 168
Langbaum, Robert (1985) 131
language 33–4, 113–40, 154; archaisms 120; contemporary 129, 135; economy/precision 113–19, 140; journalistic 115
languages 5–7, 8–9, 11–12, 35–6
Larkin, Philip 20–1
Larson, Magali Sarfatti (1977) 10
Laughlin, James 92, 100, 103, 148, 149; (1940) 103; (1985) 32; (1986) 157
Lawrence, D.H. 33, 38, 45, 57, 87, 157; (1913, 1915) 86; (1917) 22; (1932) 98
Leavis, F.R. 31–2, 37, 75, 95, 117, 125; (1932) 12, 31, 32, 38, 165–6; (1936) 118; (1947) 166; (1948) 37; (1951) 165
'Leavisites' 87, 166
Le Comte de Gabalis: translation 55–6
lectures, Pound's 45; *see also* London Polytechnic
Leigh, John (1986) 47
Lesemann, Maurice (1927) 155
Levenson, Michael H. (1984) 79
Lewes, G.H. (1865) 9
Lewis, C. Day 148
Lewis, Wyndham 27, 28, 32, 42, 60, 75, 114; and Iris Barry 104; and Pound 64, 65, 86, 89, 98, 146; (1914) 56, 91, 102; (1915) 114; (1927) 64, 85; (1937) 65, 83, 91; *see also Blast*; 'College of Arts'; *Little Review*; Vorticism; women; War

Lidderdale, Jane and Nicholson, Mary (1970) 77, 79
Life and Letters 43
Lindberg-Seyersted, Brita (1982) (*EP/FMF*) 12, 21, 27, 63, 83, 113, 116, 124, 128, 142, 164
literary critic, Pound as 43–80, 146–50, 168–9
literary criticism 1–37, 54, 155; Pound's 18–19, 21, 26, 35, 42, 101, 108, 140, 155, 157; *see also* philology; social aspects; terminology; 'usurocriticism'
literary history 41, 48, 74, 118, 157
literary journalism 7, 140, 155
literary merit 41–2, 61; transcending time 110
literary motivation 96
literary theory 6, 19
literature 9–10, 22, 34, 115, 154; comparative 6
Little Review 3, 19, 56, 66, 68, 74, 75, 81, 88; and Pound 115, 135, 148, 156; and Wyndham Lewis 73; *see also* avant-garde; *Dial* Award; Douglas, Major; Quinn; patronage; terminology; *Ulysses*
logopoeia 121–2
London, Pound in 5, 7, 12, 14, 32, 39, 40, 102, 108, 141, 147, 168; and Amy Lowell 106; financial affairs 99; Polytechnic lectures 3, 23, 43–4; *see also* 'College of Arts'; literary critic
Longenbach, James (1987) 12
Longinus 4
Lowell, Amy 47, 57, 61, 105–8, 135; and *Imagisme*/Imagism 70, 90–1, 114, 118, 157, 158–9, 160; as *Symboliste* 160; (1915, 1916, 1917) 114, 159; (1917) 158; (1955) 33
Lowell, Robert 162, (1950) 163
Lowndes, Mrs Belloc 44
Loy, Mina 85, 121
Lyrical Ballads, The 21, 112, 155

McAlmon, Robert 145; (1970) 24, 60, 146

McDaniel, Walton Brooks (1927) 11
McEwan, Ian (1985) 72
McGuire, William (1982) 162, 164
Mackail, J.P. (1896) 140
MacLeish, Archibald 128; (1983) 27, 134
MacNeice, Louis 148
Mairet, Philip (1934) 28
Mallarmé, Stéphane 68
Manning, Frederic 52; (1907) 50; (1909) 51
Marsden, Dora 75, 76, 77, 78
Marsh, Edward 45, 94, 96; (1911–22) 45, 93
Martin, Taffy (1986) 82
Marwil, Jonathan (1988) 50, 51
'masculinity' in poetry 75, 89, 102, 112, 113, 118
Masterman, Charles 46
Masters, Edgar Lee 87; (1915) 110
Materer, Timothy (1985) (*EP/WL*) 27, 30, 91, 92, 102, 126, 134, 136, 140, 142, 146
Mathews, Elkin 49, 50, 63, 87, 145, 156
meaning, poetic 117, 165
Menand, Louis (1987) 10
Mencken, H.L. 120, 135; (1961) 59
mental hospital, Pound in 84, 126, 154, 176
metaphoricity 119
metric as basis of literary skill 111
Meyers, Jeffrey (1984) 104
Middleton, Christopher (1965) 67, 69, 127
Miller, Henry 86
Milton, John 31, 32, 48, 114, 125–7, 137, 166
Mizener, Arthur (1985) 46
modernism 42, 89, 100, 107, 114, 160–1, 169, 170
modernist movement 42, 95, 96, 100, 107, 156
modern writers/writing 90, 119; *see also* patronage
Mondolfo, Vittoria I. and Hurley, Margaret (1979) (*EP/I*) 150
monetary reform 149, 155

Monro, Harold 44, 67, 68, 88, 90, 96; (1913) 98
Monroe, Harriet 19, 38, 51, 54, 57, 58, 61, 68, 69, 70, 71, 86, 87, 110; and Pound 13, 139, 140; (1938) 26, 74; *see also Catholic Anthology*; *New Freewoman*; *Poetry*
Moore, Marianne 86, 148; (1921, 1928) 82
morphology 13, 29, 35
mot juste 115–16, 119, 121, 122, 125, 130, 152
Moulton, Richard Green (1915) 19
music 28–9, 59; criticism 7, 116, 134, 144; *see also* 'Atheling'

naming 136
Nation 46
New Age 2, 38, 44, 57, 94, 144, 151, 157
New Criticism 5, 161, 163–7, 169, 170
New English Weekly 44, 62
New Freewoman 25, 51, 74, 75, 77–9
New Humanism 156
New Statesman 66
Norman, Charles (1969) 24, 25, 104, 106, 167
North American Review 95, 129
novel, the: and Pound 35

occult 56, 71
O'Connor, William Van and Stone, Edward (1959) 68
Oderman, Kevin (1986) 106
Olson, Charles 101; *see also* Seelye
Orage, A.R. 28, 44, 62, 134, 138, 144, 151; (1917) 27; (1974) 38, 92
Others 88
Outlook 143

Paideuma 168
Paige, D.D. (1951) 154, 165, 167
Palgrave's *Golden Treasury* 144–5, 150
Paris, Pound in 40, 49, 81, 100, 105–6, 142, 145–6; American

expatriates in 145, 156; salons 145
Patmore, Brigit 49; (1968) 72
patronage 93–5; *see also* Cravens, Margaret; Quinn, John
Payne, William Morton (1895) 9
Pearson, Hesketh (1934) 38
pedagogy 24, 31, 36
Penniman, Josiah 2–4, 18; (1897, 1919) 2
Pennsylvania, University of 1–4, 5–6, 7, 10–11, 16–17, 23, 50, 99, 122, 124; teaching methods 3–4, 47; *see also* philology
personae, Pound's use of 34, 40, 165; versus personality 133
philology, humanistic 8, 14, 16–17, 19, 22, 34, 35, 156; German influence 9, 12, 13, 23
Plarr, Victor 48, 156
poem as critical genre 136–7
poet, Pound as, 42, 167
poet-critic(s) 1, 20–1, 81, 112, 154–5
poetic criteria, Pound's 110, 111–12
poetic theory 21, 34, 111
poetry: American renascence 157, 160, 161; Anglo-American 160; comparative 27, 110; and literary criticism 16, 35; modern 119; and politics: Pound's 24, 34, 35, 81, 82–3; taxonomy of 121–2; world 110; *see also* feminism; 'masculinity'; philology
Poetry 51, 57, 77, 93, 99, 127; and American renascence 157; and Pound 58, 74, 75, 78, 128, 129, 155, 156; reviews in 63, 86, 87; *see also* avant-garde; *Imagisme*; Monroe, Harriet; patronage; *sottisier*
Poetry and Drama 44, 62, 88, 98
Poetry Review 67, 68
Poetry Society of America 67, 163
poets: American 156; avant-garde 84; British (1890s) 47; female and Pound 101–8; male 99–101
politics 88, 101, 149–50, 154, 155, 166, 167, 168, 169–70; and literary texts 162, 163; Pound's belief in subversiveness of his own 142, 144
Pope, Alexander 66, 121; (1712) 111; (1714) 55, 129
Posnett, H.M. (1886) 6
Post-structuralism 154
Potter, Stephen (1937) 31
Pound, Ezra 22, 33–4, 35, 125; academic recognition, as subject for 14–15, 16–17, 19–20, 24, 29–30, 55–6, 167, 168; attitudes of literary world to 93, 95–101; background, literary 5–34; central concepts 113; contacts 41, 42, 43, 44–53, 54–60, 91, 93; 'death' 142; 'discoveries' 82, 83, 85–92, 95–7, 99–100, 149; early life 4, 43; financial affairs 92, 93; friendships 64–5; as innovator/inventor 42, 66; insanity plea 170; journalist, as literary 140; judgement, literary 33–8, 82, 83–4, 88–90; marriage 42, 56; memoirs/retrospection 157; own work, involvement in 101, 149; prose 140; revival of interest in 155–6; self-interest 97, 98–9; style 64, 123, 124, 133–5, 136, 140; tastes, literary 87; treason, tried for 32, 169–70; *ABC of Economics* 27–8; *ABC of Reading* (*ABCR*) 18, 26–7, 28, 30, 83, 115, 117, 119, 136; 'Abu Salammamm' 103; *Active Anthology* (*AA*) 148; *A Lume Spento* (*ALS*) 43, 47, 60, 118; 'Amities' 44; 'A Few Don'ts by an Imagiste' 25, 71, 127; 'Approach to Paris' 58; 'Black Slippers: Bellotti' 44; *Canzoni* 49; 'Canzon: The Yearly Slain' 50; *Cathay* 14, 49, 117; *Catholic Anthology* 46, 58, 87–8; *Certain Noble Plays of Japan* 52; 'Child's Guide to Knowledge' 25; *Des Imagistes* 57, 58, 88, 127, 135, 159; 'Encounter, The' 104; *Exultations* 43, 49; *Guide to Kulchur* (*GK*) 4, 11, 14,

Index

26, 27, 38, 109, 113, 114, 115, 120, 124, 134, 139, 142, 149, 151, 152; *Guido Cavalcanti: Rime* 15–16, 62; *Hesternae Rosae* 50; 'Histrion' 49; *Homage to Sextus Propertius* 15, 17, 19, 62, 121, 145; *How to Read* 12, 21, 26, 27, 31, 36, 37, 104, 123, 164, 165; *Hugh Selwyn Mauberley* 40–1, 55, 81, 88, 141, 145, 151, 165; 'Ikon' 76; *Indiscretions* 59, 157; *Instigations* 27, 29; 'Jodindranath Mawhwor's Occupation' 102–3; 'Lake Isle, The' 137; 'Langue d'Oc' 120, 129; 'L'Homme Moyen Sensuel' 6, 106; *Lustra* 49, 61, 104, 128; *Make It New* 85, 114, 134, 150; 'Moeurs Contemporaines' 48, 54, 129; 'Near Perigord' 16–17, 41; 'New Method in Scholarship' 2, 16, 68, 117; 'On Criticism in General' 31, 122–3; 'A Packet for Ezra Pound' 149; 'Papyrus' 113; *Passages from the Letters of John Butler Yeats* 52, 63; *Patria Mia and the Treatise on Harmony* (*PM*) 14, 28, 44, 53, 94, 103; *Pavannes and Divagations* (*PD*) 13, 25, 84, 103, 106, 113, 118, 155; *Pavannes and Divisions* 21; *Personae* 49; *Personae: The Collected Poems of Ezra Pound* (*P*) 2, 40, 48, 54, 68, 92, 103, 105, 106; *Pisan Cantos, The* 161, 162, 163, 167; *Poems 1918–21* 15; *Polite Essays* (*PE*) 116, 150; 'Portrait d'une Femme' 129, 141–2; 'Probable Music of *Beowulf*, The' 59; *Profile* 88; *Provença* 43; *Quia Pauper Amavi* 95; *Quinzaine for This Yule, A* 49; 'Revolt' 119; *Ripostes* 62, 68; 'Seafarer, The' 2; *Section: Rock-Drill* 20; *Selected Poems* 145; 'Serious Artist, The' 84; 'Sestina: Altaforte' 44, 49; 'Shop Girl' 104; *Sonnets and Ballate of Guido Cavalcanti* 17, 77; *Spirit of Romance, The* (*SR*) 3–4, 6, 7, 15, 22–3, 24, 36, 37, 49, 120, 134, 138, 140; *Ta Hio: The Great Learning* 27, 158; 'Tame Cat' 104; 'Tempora' 105; *Thrones: 96–109 de los Cantares* 66; *Treatise on Harmony* 25; *Umbra* 43, 49, 145; 'A Virginal' 106; 'Vorticism' 71; (1906) 10–11; (1912) 17, 62, 68, 77; (1913) 141; (1913a) 43, 46, 48, 111; (1913b) 109; (1913c) 117; (1913d) 147; (1915) 17, 49, 57, 63; (1916) 14, 34, 49, 63, 104, 107, 114, 132, 139, 140; (1917) 56, 61, 63; (1918) 63; (1918a) 117; (1918b) 134; (1918c) 16; (1919) 121, 144; (1920) 40, 43, 49, 81, 145, 151; (1920a) 156; (1921) 151; (1921a) 3; (1922) 146; (1923) 18, 31, 36, 66, 117, 121, 122–3, 129, 143; (1930) 160; (1932) 15, 53, 67; (1933) 28, 37, 148; (1934) 3, 30, 85, 114; (1935) 151; (1936) 125; (1936a) 3; (1936b) 134; (1938) 126, 139, 149; (1939) 14; (1966) 138; and Spann, Marcella (1964) (*CC*) 110; *see also Cantos*; critic; journalism; journals; King; knowledge; language; Lindberg-Seyersted, B.; London; Materer, T.; modernist movement; patronage; poetry; politics; primers; qualifications; Rapallo; Read; reviews; Scott; Seelye; sexuality; terminology; Venice; Yeats; Zukofsky

Pound, Dorothy 82, 92, 102; *see also* Shakespear

Pound, Homer 15, 41, 61

Pound, Omar and Litz, A. Walton (1985) (*EP/DS*) 11, 25, 45, 55, 69, 76, 111, 127, 135; and Spoo, Robert (1988) (*EP/MC*) 15, 28

'Poundian' effects 133–6

Poundians, British 168–9

Pound Newsletter 168

presentation and constatation 117, 118

primers, Pound's 27, 28, 36

professionalism 10

Index

Propertius 94, 120, 121, 122
Prothero, G.W. 143, 144, 145
Provençal 6, 7, 23, 24, 49, 50, 67, 120, 144
pseudonyms, use of 49, 74, 107, 155; *see also* 'Atheling'; 'Dias'
publishing: social aspects 54, 55, 58, 59; university 168; world of 41, 89, 92–3, 147

qualifications, Pound's academic 4, 14–15, 16–17, 29
Quarterly Review 143
Quinn, John 15, 32, 51, 52, 61, 76, 90; and Eliot/Pound 100, 129, 130, 131; and drama criticism 143; as Pound's patron 94–5; and Vorticism 116

Rabaté, Jean-Michel (1986) 117, 151
Raffel, Burton (1985) 39, 46, 135
Ransom, John Crowe 100; (1941) 5, 164
Rapallo, Pound in 27, 32, 49, 81, 95, 101, 146, 147
Read, Forrest (1987) (*EP/JJ*) 45, 79, 90, 91, 116, 128, 133
reader–writer response: knowledge-effects 34
reading 35, 36, 37, 152; close 161
Re, Arundel del 17
Reck, Michael (1967) 146, 149
Redmann, T. (1987) 15
Reid, B.L. (1968) 15, 32, 51, 52, 64, 76, 94, 131, 143, 144
religion 25, 153
reviewers/reviewing 37–8, 46, 110, 165
reviews 37, 38, 61–6, 151
rhetoric 132, 154
Rhys, Ernest 49
Richards, I.A. 37; (1929) 31
Rodker, John 88, 89, 142
Roessel, David (1988) 17
Romance languages 5, 6, 32, 122
Romanticism 20, 21, 34
Rome, Radio: talks 28, 139, 142, 149, 153, 169

Rose, Jonathan (1986) 114
Ross, Robert H. (1967) 93
Ruskin, John 20, 153
Russo, John Paul (1988) 165
Ruthven, K.K. (1969) 71, 121, 168; (1986) 122

Said, Edward (1985) 27
Sandburg, Carl 85, 87
Santayana, George 30, 32
Savoy 51
Schafer, R. Murray (1978) (*EP/M*) 59, 116, 155
Schelling, Felix 11, 12, 15, 17, 33, 96, 110, 122, 129
'scholarship' 2, 5, 12, 13, 16, 68; -poem genre 17
science and humanities 8–9
scientism 112
Scott, Thomas L. *et al.* (1988) (*EP/MCA*) 23, 63, 91, 102, 107, 115, 133, 135, 142, 155, 159; *see also* Anderson, Margaret
Scrutiny 18, 75, 138, 165, 166
Seelye, Catherine (1975) (*CO/EP*) 32, 92, 101, 134
sexuality, Pound's 101–8
Shakespear, Dorothy 25, 45, 50, 51–2, 55, 56, 69, 111, 127; *see also* Pound, Dorothy
Shakespear, Olivia 4, 51, 52, 73; (1914) 56
Shapiro, Karl 162
Shaw, George Bernard 53, 133
Shepard, William P. 6, 23; (1897) 7
Sieburth, Richard (1978) 121, 137
Sinclair, May 49, 62, 95, 143
Sitwell, Edith (1916) 58
Sitwell, Osbert 64
Smith, Grover (1983) 130
social aspects of literary world 52, 54, 55, 57–60, 93
Social Credit 13, 27, 151; journal 28, 44
social criticism 13
sottisier as critical genre 137
Spain, study in 4, 11
Spanish Civil War 152

Index

Spenser, Herbert (1896) 9–10
Stein, Gertrude 26, 105–6, 114, 145; (1946) 24
Stevens, Wallace 88, 92; (1967) 164
Stock, Noel 164; (1960) 16, 168; (1965) 158; (1970) 1, 4, 15, 16, 61, 109, 127, 142, 143; (1976) 15, 23, 41
subjectivity, theory of 33–4, 86
Swinburne, A.C. 48
Symbolisme 51, 57, 118–19, 126, 151, 159
Symons, Arthur (1899) 51
synaesthesia 119

Tacitus 140
Tagore, Rabindranath 71, 102, 133
Tate, Allen 161, 162, 163, 164; (1932) 164
Taupin, René 117, 157, 158; (1929) 159–60; (1985) 57, 160, 161
teacher, Pound as 24–8, 29
technique 111, 112–13
Tel Quel 154
Tennyson, Alfred Lord 31, 32, 129, 166
terminology 120–3
theory/theories *see* conspiracy; economic; essentialist; expressivist; Flaubertian; functionalist; literary; poetry; Vorticist
The Times 137; *Literary Supplement* 66
This Quarter 142
Thompson, Francis (1893) 53
timelessness; universality of poetic criteria 110, 111–12
Torrey, E. Fuller (1984) 104, 133, 155
tradition 23–4, 110
translations, 'creative' 17
Transatlantic Review 63
Tytell, John (1987) 4, 46, 54, 58, 85, 90, 102, 115, 125, 152

university, Pound's ideal 29, 30, 32
Untermeyer, Louis 6; (1919) 81, 161
'usurocriticism' 125, 153–4

usury/the arts/religion 152–4

Vasse, William and Edwards, John (1957) 168
Venice, Pound in 5, 29, 40, 43, 46
Verlaine, Paul 132
vers libre 23–4, 25, 68, 98, 99, 106, 115
virtù 111, 118
Vorticism/'vortex' 34, 65, 70, 116, 141, 156, 159
Vorticist: exhibition 141; photography 29; propaganda 144; theory 34

Wabash College 5, 24, 32
Waldock, A.J.A. (1947) 125
Wallace, Emily Mitchell (1983) 2, 33
War: 1914–18 28, 29, 92–3; Second World 30
Weaver, Harriet Shaw 51, 76, 77, 128
Wees, William C. (1976) 107
Weintraub, Stanley (1979) 87, 98, 100
Weisstein, Ulrich (1973) 6
Wellek, René (1986) 42
West, Rebecca 77–8, 102
Whistler, James McNeill 27, 114, 119, 142; (1892) 20
Whitman, Walt 61
Wilcox, Ella Wheeler 60–1
Wilde, Oscar (1894) 47; Wildeanism 133
Wilhelm, J.J. (1985) 15, 60
Williams, Ellen (1977) 58, 70, 71, 87, 88, 93, 126, 128, 135
Williams, William Carlos 4, 19, 26, 75, 79, 85, 101–2, 104, 142; in Pound's anthologies 87, 148; as doctor 92; journal 151; as non-Imagist 157; and Pound 64, 100; (1913) 63; (1919) 38; (1920) 64; (1923) 59; (1925) 82; (1948) 163; (1951) 60; (1957) 83, 127; (1958) 95
Winters, Yvor (1931) 160, 161
Witemeyer, Hugh (1977) 125

women, attitudes to 102–8
Woolf, Virginia 38–9, 46, 62; and Woolf, Leonard (1925) 58
Wordsworth, William 31, 87, 135, 155; (1798) 112; (1926) 21
writers 34, 82, 83, 85–9, 91, 110; typology of 122–3
writing 118, 119, 148, 149, 150, 151, 154, 169–70; style 123, 133–5, 140; technique 36, 111

Yeats (*née* Hyde-Lees), Georgie 52, 56
Yeats, J.B. 52, 63, 94, 141
Yeats, W.B. 44, 45, 47, 51, 96, 104, 146; as 'great critic' 4; and Joyce 57, 90; and Pound 4, 30, 46, 52, 55, 56, 99, 112, 126–7, 129, 141, 149; as reviewer 109; *Autobiographies* 49; 'Fallen Majesty' 126; 'The Lake Isle of Inisfree' 137; *Oxford Book of English Verse* 137; 'The Pedants' 22; 'The Two Kings' 127; *see also Catholic Anthology*; mystical philosophy; occult; rhetoric
Young, Thomas Daniel (1980) 164

Zinnes, Harriet (1980) (*EP/VA*) 12, 20, 23, 27, 53, 85, 86, 102, 114, 116, 133, 140, 144
Zukofsky, Louis (*EP/LZ*) 100, 112, 148, 158, 160, 161; (1932) 155

For Product Safety Concerns and Information please contact our EU representative GPSR@taylorandfrancis.com
Taylor & Francis Verlag GmbH, Kaufingerstraße 24, 80331 München, Germany